Uncle Cam

The story of William Cameron Townsend
founder of the *Wycliffe Bible Translators*
and the *Summer Institute of Linguistics*

James & Marti Hefley

Wycliffe Bible Translators
Huntington Beach, CA
92647

UNCLE CAM

Library of Congress catalog card number: 73-91556
Printed in the United States of America
ISBN 0-938978-03-9

Robert Burkett, Editor

ACKNOWLEDGMENTS

Our thanks to Cornell Capa for his photographs on
pages 213-220, 247-248, and the endpapers, and
for his work on all the pictures in the book.

OTHER BOOKS BY JAMES AND MARTI HEFLEY

God's Tribesman, The Rochunga Pudaite Story
By Their Blood, 20th Century Martyrs
Unstilled Voices
Are Textbooks Harming Your Children?

Contents

CONTENTS

PART III: NEW BEGINNINGS

Foreword

William Cameron Townsend, or "Uncle Cam" as many of us called him, was a pioneer in a new strategy involving the use of Bible translation to reach hidden peoples of the world for Jesus Christ. His burden was that all language groups should have the Word of God in their own "heart" language, so the Lord might speak directly to them.

Uncle Cam's strategy was simple. He began with the Cakchiquel language of Guatemala. He learned the spoken language, developed an alphabet, deciphered the grammar and translated the New Testament into it. He reached that previously unreached people with the Gospel in a 12-year period.

Next, Uncle Cam joined forces with Dr. L.L. Legters and began to train others to do what he had done so well in Guatemala. The Summer Institute of Linguistics was born as young men and women began translation work in Mexico. Today, the work has expanded to 728 languages representing 46 nations.

I regarded Uncle Cam, first of all, as my friend; then in the succession of the years as general director, founder of Wycliffe, and finally, as my "boss." He was a Christian gentleman who loved the common man, could fire up his staff to incredible feats, and always had a vision for every ethnic group in the world having the Bible in their own language.

A few days before his going home to be with Jesus Christ, Uncle Cam held my hand, looked up into my face with a twinkle in his eyes and whispered, "God is so good."

God was good to Uncle Cam, and all Uncle Cam ever wanted to do was to be obedient to his Lord. He was!

— John E. Kyle
Mission Director,
Inter-Varsity Christian Fellowship

Authors' Preface

Every century or so there arises a remarkable Christian innovator and servant of mankind. We believe William Cameron Townsend ("Uncle Cam" to thousands) is the man for this century. Thus we have spent years researching and writing his biography.

The idea of a biography was reluctantly accepted by Uncle Cam— and this only after a trip around the world when he decided that the publishing of his life story might speed the light of Scripture to the remaining Bibleless tribal and minority groups.

This book is not an official publication of the two organizations which he founded. However, leaders of the Wycliffe Bible Translators and the Summer Institute of Linguistics and other close friends and relatives cooperated and made available their recollections and judgments.

In writing *Uncle Cam* we worked principally from primary resource material: interviews with scores of individuals who have known Uncle Cam, some for almost three-quarters of a century; impressions of visits to fields where he worked in the service of foreign governments for Indians; voluminous personal correspondence and reports. Research involved twelve trips to Latin America, a summer's residence next-door to the Townsends in North Carolina, coast-to-coast interviews, even accompanying Uncle Cam for a visit with President Richard Nixon in the White House. The single-spaced typed index of the primary materials runs over 250 pages. The first draft of the manuscript was twice as long as the finished version.

No one can be completely objective in writing about someone they love and admire. However, we have tried to write responsibly and candidly. This effort was aided by the openness of Uncle Cam, his family, and close associates in interviews.

It is impractical, if not impossible, to name everyone who helped make this book possible. Contributors to research ranged from former presidents of Latin American countries to humble jungle Indians; from 1917 classmates of Uncle Cam at Occidental College to his twenty-year-old son, Billy. We thank all of those who helped.

The manuscript itself represents our combined efforts as a husband-and-wife team. Our picture associate was the distinguished photographer Cornell Capa. Mr. Capa, a long-time friend of Uncle Cam's, selected and edited the photographs, including some of his own, for the book. He is without peer in his field. We consider his professional aid a high honor.

Paula Kelly was our dependable, accurate secretary who transcribed hours of tapes and typed the final copy.

The life of William Cameron Townsend is significant for a wide audience. We hope that at least to some extent the telling adequately represents the man and his life.

JAMES and MARTI HEFLEY
Signal Mountain, Tennessee

Part I
BEGINNINGS

1. Poverty's Heritage

Sweating and itching, young Cam Townsend slogged across the jungle marsh. The pack of New Testaments and food rations rubbed his blistered back. Though covered with bites, he had learned it was much wiser not to scratch. His thin body ached for rest, but he knew that to sit beside the trail would only invite more bugs.

Cam daydreamed of plunging into the California surf, then coming home to climb between clean white sheets and awakening to the savory smell of a farm breakfast. He yearned to hear his deaf father reading the Bible at the breakfast table and thought how enjoyable life would be back at Occidental College finishing his fourth year as his mother had wanted him to. Even the army, where many of his classmates had gone, could not be as bad as this.

Suddenly the dark cloud that had been thickening overhead splintered with lightning and seconds later the usual afternoon downpour began. He broke to seek shelter under the spreading branches of a tree.

A half-hour later the storm stopped as abruptly as it had started, and Cam plodded on through a sea of mud, anticipating the smile of the Indian friend who was to meet him at the railroad station.

Actually, there was no question of returning home. He had committed himself to sell Bibles to farmers and villagers along the sparsely populated trails of Central America. "Go ye into all the world and preach the gospel" was the commission that burned in his bones. Neither heat, nor rain, nor chill of night, nor wild animals, nor hostile fanatics would hold him back. The Word of God must be planted. God would give the increase.

It was the year 1917, and the "apostle to the lost tribes" had launched his first enterprise. At the time he didn't dream that over

11

2,000 tribes existed without even alphabets. But as more awareness came, he would "by faith" cross the linguistic frontier of a baffling language and lay the pattern for thousands of future translators to follow. Cameron Townsend would become the most daring, innovative Christian leader of the twentieth century.

As is so often true of milestoners, he was never picked by any institution, denomination, or government agency as one most likely to succeed. His incipient greatness was hidden to most who knew him. Yet the evidences can be found in his own recollections and diaries and the memories of a few aging relatives and friends. The seeds of an audacious faith and discipline were there. But they were simply not recognized by most who knew him as a boy.

The Townsends came originally from England. Three brothers, Quakers, joined William Penn's seventeenth-century colony. But only one remained in Pennsylvania. By the mid-nineteenth century the Pennsylvania Townsends had become Presbyterians and were living about twenty miles east of Pittsburgh.

One of them, William, decided to enter the ministry and enrolled in a Pittsburgh seminary. While still a student, however, he died of pneumonia, leaving a two-year-old son Richard Cameron. Six months later his second son, William Hammond, was born. His widow then remarried and had three more children.

By the year 1876, William Hammond—Will—had grown to a wiry but sturdy five-foot-nine. He held a contract for hauling lumber to Pittsburgh for construction of a building to be used in the centennial celebration. But just before Will was to be paid, the major contractor ran away. Will was left with the bills in his name—and no funds to pay them.

The young man vowed to pay every cent even if it took the rest of his life. Then he said goodbye to his mother and stepfather and headed for the new state of Kansas, where he found work on a wheat farm. His long back-breaking days were brightened only by Sunday services at the local Presbyterian church and by visits to the Cormacks, a Presbyterian neighbor family that had migrated from eastern Tennessee. Mr. Cormack regaled him with tales about the hills and hollows of Tennessee, but Will was more interested in the oldest daughter. Molly, with the merry smile, straw-colored hair, and an infectious laugh, made Will feel that he could whip the world if she were beside him.

Molly and Will were married in 1884, the year Grover Cleveland was elected president. They rented a nearby farm and between dusts and droughts eked out a living. After daughters Oney and Ethel were born, Will wanted to move on in hopes of earning extra money to pay on the debt that nagged his conscience.

But life was little better in the Green Horn Range of Colorado. With two more mouths to feed, Lula and Mary, Will grew barely enough vegetables for the family table. Hearing talk of fortunes being made in California, he decided they should move again.

They arrived in California in 1893, the year of a great depression, and moved into an old farmhouse near Pasadena. With prices dropping and people returning east, Will still had trouble making ends meet. Bad fortune plagued him year after year. If he planted cabbages, they'd sell at an all-time low, while tomatoes were selling high. If he tried tomatoes, the bottom would drop out of that market. Then in the midst of their poverty, Molly gave birth to a stillborn son.

Will felt they could better themselves by moving again—this time to the desert Eastvale settlement east of Los Angeles. Here on July 9, 1896, in an old farmhouse that had only curtains for partitions, a healthy boy greeted the world with a yowl that could be heard above the wail of the hot Santa Ana winds that whipped against the house. They named him William for his father and grandfather and Cameron for his minister uncle.

For awhile the family was concerned that Cam might be spoiled or sissified, being brought up with four older sisters. That worry ended with the birth of Paul two years later. Little Paul dogged Cam's footsteps. Except for his having brown eyes and hair lighter than Cam's, the two boys looked very much alike. But in personality they were quite different. Paul was mechanically minded and enjoyed using his hands. Cam thought it more challenging to figure a new way to do things. Especially if he could talk Paul into doing the physical labor or deciding to do something the way Cam wanted it. On one occasion they had to choose between two puppies. Cam wanted the brown one and Paul the black, but Cam convinced Paul it was really the brown one he wanted. Another time after hearing a Sunday school lesson about Jacob shearing his sheep, Cam took his mother's sewing scissors and clipped off Paul's blond curls. Molly pulled a limb from the quince tree in the front yard and gave Cam a thrashing.

Cam was full of fun, sometimes at his younger brother's expense. There were irrigation ditches nearly every place they lived. Cam, agile and two years older, would jump the smaller ones and dare Paul to follow. Time after time, Paul fell in the water and was rewarded with a spanking when they got home. Eventually, though, Will and Molly discovered the real culprit and administered the proper medicine.

But Cam also had his serious moments. One incident seems a portent of his lifelong expectant faith. One night he rolled over in bed and squashed his pet bunny. The next day he and Paul held a funeral and buried the animal in a cracked mason jar under an umbrella tree. That evening Cam couldn't sleep for thinking of the bunny. Remembering from Sunday school that Jesus had raised Lazarus, Cam reasoned that a bunny would be much less trouble. So he prayed. Then he figured that if the bunny did come alive, it would soon die again without air. He climbed out of bed, lit a lantern, crept across the yard and exhumed the dead rabbit.

Poverty and ill fortune seemed to dog the family's footsteps. By this time Will had lost almost all his hearing. He attributed the cause to a rebounding plank that had bounced off his chin back in Colorado. A prize calf swallowed Cam's first store-bought necktie and choked to death. Produce from the tenant farm brought hardly enough income for the family to exist on.

But Will's stubborn, keep-trying, hard-work philosophy made an indelible impression on his children. "You never lose your vote when you stand for what is right," he would say as he continued to vote for the Prohibition Party. He was strict with the boys in the fields and expected instant obedience. "Finish one row before you start another," was a frequent admonition that stuck in Cam's mind. And if Cam did sloppy work, Will would insist, "Do it over until it becomes second nature to you."

Will's deep-seated honesty also left its mark on Cam. Because Will still felt obligated to pay the quarter-century-old Pennsylvania debt, he wrote letters back to Pennsylvania in an effort to locate the addresses of creditors. He even asked a lawyer to draw up a binding legal promissory note, but the lawyer talked him out of it.

When Will went on selling trips into Los Angeles, one of the children usually accompanied him. The first time Cam was allowed to go he felt very grownup and important. As they made periodic stops along cobblestoned Telegraph Road, Cam noticed that the merchants seldom looked at their fruit and vegetables before buying. When he asked a burly Italian grocer about it, he was told, "Your Papa, he say it's good, it's good. We call him the 'honest deaf man.'" The pride Cam felt has remained in his memory to this day.

Will had a very sensitive conscience. Once he traded a horse for a cow and then worried that he had taken advantage of the other man. He had no peace until he evened out the bargain with a precious five-dollar bill.

If Cam got his streak of stubbornness for hanging on to what he felt was right from Will, he received his cheerful disposition from Molly who tried to keep the house bright and happy. There were always flowers around, especially her favorite petunias or Will's sweet peas. She laughed and joked with the children. Sometimes this bothered deaf Will and he would frown and ask, "What's so funny? What are you laughing at?" By the time she had the joke written out, it never seemed quite as humorous.

However, neither Will nor Molly were the type to bemoan their troubles. They prayed for the needs of others, and under no circumstances tolerated disparaging criticism. If they were envious of more fortunate neighbors, the children never remembered it.

All his life Cam has been a man of one Book—the Bible. He recalls how every weekday morning before milking his father would read three chapters—five on Sunday. After breakfast came family devotions—Bible reading, a hymn, and prayers. Despite his deafness, Will loved to sing. When his voice cracked, the children were under strict orders from Molly not to laugh. He always ended his prayers with, "May the knowledge of the Lord cover the earth as the waters cover the sea."

At twelve Cam joined the Presbyterian church. Afterwards, Will took him out to the barn and questioned him concerning his beliefs. Cam wrote down his answers for his deaf father. Will was pleased and satisfied that his son had a firm personal faith in Christ as his Lord and Savior.

The summer Cam turned thirteen, Molly, Cam, and Paul took the train to visit relatives near Fresno. That was a big event for youngsters who had never been farther from home than Long Beach where the family went once a year to swim and watch the ships. While there the boys and their cousins went swimming in a canal. When the others dove in, Cam followed suit and discovered he was in over his head. Panic-stricken because he couldn't swim, he called for help, but went under twice before an older boy saved him from drowning.

The close call was a maturing experience. Cam applied himself more than ever in school the next year. In the spring he completed the eighth grade at the head of his class. But the following year produce prices took a sharp downturn, and it looked as if he might have to drop out of school to help with family finances. The two oldest girls were married by this time and the younger ones were engaged. The idea of Cam's interrupting his education was abhorrent to all of them, and Lula volunteered to postpone her marriage a year and continue her secretarial job to help pay for Cam's schooling. Her fiancé didn't understand the dedication in the close-knit family and broke their engagement.

After a time, Lula found a better job in Santa Ana and the family moved there for her convenience. On their first Sunday, Cam and Lula attended a Methodist church close by. Eugene Griset, Cam's bachelor Sunday school teacher, visited him the next week to invite him back to the class. When he kept visiting regularly, Cam decided his real interest was Lula.

During his sophomore year, Cam biked to the Santa Ana High School. His route passed a pasture where the young aviation enthusiast, Glenn Martin, was developing his first plane. Occasionally he stopped and peered at the plane, daydreaming of someday having the opportunity to fly.

In Cam's junior year both Lula and Mary married, and the rest of the Townsends moved to Clearwater. Cam got a job hauling fifteen schoolmates to school in a wagon for $70 a month, out of which he had to feed the team. He turned most of the profit over to his folks, leaving precious little for personal spending.

Despite the time spent in hauling his passengers, feeding and stabling the team, and regular chores, Cam was involved in many school activities. He edited the 1914 yearbook, took the lead in the senior play, served on the debating team, and with Bob Gillingham won the doubles championship in tennis.

He graduated with the highest average in the class, but being a transfer student he was ineligible to be valedictorian. However, his standing with his classmates was such that the class prophet predicted he would one day represent California in the U.S. Senate.

Above: Downey, California, in the first years of the century had dirt roads and "new-fangled" automobiles. *Below:* The Townsends lived in this house in Downey from 1902-1909.

Below: The Townsends lived in this house in Downey from 1902-1909.

The Townsends
in 1902. *L. to
r., back row:*
Ethel, Oney, Mary, Lula. Front row: Mollie, Paul, Cam, Will.

Above: Cam and Paul at 12 and 10. *Below:* Mary, Oney, Lula, and Ethel. Both pictures were made into postcards.

Above: Cam, with the flower in his buttonhole, was valedictorian of the class at his graduation from grammar school in Downey in 1910. *Below:* Cam and high school friends in Compton, in 1913.

Cam graduated from Compton High School in 1914.

"The greater need is where the greatest dark-
ness is."

2. Siempre Adelante!

Until his last year in high school, Cam had planned to be a teacher.
When he began thinking of entering the ministry, Will and Molly
were jubilant. His sisters and their husbands all said they would
help the aging parents financially while Cam got his education.

Since the ministerial scholarship from the Presbyterian church
wouldn't cover all his college expenses, Cam worked the summer
after graduation as a bellhop on the S.S. *President.* The big steam-
ship stopped at cities along the Pacific coast from San Diego to
Vancouver. Though Cam got seasick and was exposed to rough men
for the first time, the experience was invaluable.

World War I had already flared in Europe when he enrolled in
Occidental College, a Presbyterian liberal arts school in Los Angeles.
During his sophomore year Cam was drawn to the Student Volunteer Band, the local arm of the national Student Volunteer Movement. New joiners had to tell why they wanted to be members.
Though Cam belonged to the Debating Club, when his turn came
he found it hard to articulate his concern for foreign missions. He
could only say, "I'm not sure why I wish to belong."

His interest picked up, however, when John R. Mott, the leader
of the movement, came to the campus to speak. Cam sensed the
burden of the man and wondered if there might not be a place for
him overseas. He was further challenged by the life of Hudson
Taylor, founder of the fifty-year-old China Inland Mission. Taylor's
faith, pioneering, and adaptation to the Chinese culture appealed to
him. He felt that if God should lead him to become a missionary,
he would strive to be like this man.

But his Bible knowledge did not complement his budding interest in missions. Beyond what he had learned at home and in

23

church, he took only the Bible courses required by the college: a study in Genesis and Exodus, and New Testament Greek.

Once after Bible class, a fellow student asked, "Cameron, do you know how we're saved?"

"By the life of Christ, I guess," Cam replied lamely.

His classmate looked appalled. "No, by Christ's death! Haven't you studied the theology of the atonement?"

"Well, no," Cam said. "I guess maybe I should."

While managing to make good grades in college, he frankly questioned some teaching methods of the day. He thought memorization a poor method. "College men are too often unable to hold their own in the practical world," he wrote in a theme entitled "The Object of a College Education." "The reason is that the graduate is not capable of applying his learning to the problems of life. He has stored his brain with a great many facts and principles, but he is unable to use them."

A member of the Literary Club, he enjoyed writing essays on varied subjects which oddly enough seemed to forecast his later interests: "Eternal Life," "Many Paths to Mexico's Enchantments" (an armchair travelogue), "True Wisdom," "Language in the Embryo," and "Canvassing as a College Student's Vacation Work." He had had personal experience in the latter as an unsuccessful summer magazine salesman.

In one paper he weighed the relationship between genius and physique: "Success in any walk of life is as dependent upon the body as upon the inspiration. We may never become great but it is the duty of each one to bring to the highest degree of development those powers which God has endowed him with. To do this he must care for his body." Cam was then a skinny 130 pounds. Still he practiced what he preached by playing tennis, wrestling, and getting to bed every school night by ten.

Another lifelong interest surfaced early. His first poems were published in the student newspaper under the *nom de plume* of Eunice Bomsinger. One that illustrates some of the inner conflicts he was having at the time also shows a characteristic that has never left him.

> ### Limitation
> Oh hateful word
> That halts your aspiration,
> That downs your dreams
> And brands your schemes

As filmy speculation,
And says you shan't
Because you can't
In the face of limitation.

Deceptive word
That means procrastination;
That bids content
With every stint,
And pillows lowly station,
And says, "Just wait
Till time and fate
O'ercome your limitation."

. . . .

Yes! The challenge word
That dares against stagnation,
Brings out your stuff
And frightens bluff
With every consternation,
And calls for might
And bids you fight
To climb o'er limitation.

In 1916, Cam's junior year, a National Guard recruiter came to the Occidental campus. The war in Europe still seemed remote to most students. Woodrow Wilson was campaigning for a second term as "the president who kept the U.S. out of the war." When the recruiter told Cam and his best friend, Carroll Byram, of the engineering training available in the Guard, they joined, figuring that if war did come they would be drafted anyway.

That year Cam's parents rented a house near the campus for $6 per month and Cam moved in with them. Will planted barley, and Cam helped harvest it and the wild oats that grew on vacant campus land. Will and Molly kept hoping that Cam's interest in the ministry at home might return. But Cam's bent remained toward foreign missions. "The greater need is where the greatest darkness is," he wrote. "Our orders are to forget self and to give our lives in service for the Master."

In January 1917 Cam heard that the Bible House of Los Angeles wanted Bible salesmen for South America. Having taken Spanish in high school and college, he decided to apply to the Bible House with the idea of returning after a year to finish college. With the country still out of the war, he thought chances were good for resigning from the Guard.

The Bible House accepted his application and assigned him to Guatemala, a country he had not even known was in Central America. But when he told his parents, Molly was dismayed, fearing he might never return to complete college and attend seminary. When Congress declared war in April, Cam was sure he wouldn't be going south after all. Then a call came from R. D. Smith, director of the Bible House.

"Cam, there's a missionary from Guatemala in the area. I think you should go talk to Miss Stella Zimmerman about the country where you'll be going."

"It's no use," Cam replied. "My Guard unit will be shipping out to France shortly."

"Well, go see her anyway. You'll be coming back from war one day."

Cam agreed and asked his good friend Elbert Robinson to come along. "Robby," president of Occidental's YMCA and ten years older than Cam, was also an enthusiast for foreign missions. Miss Zimmerman, a tall angular blond about Robby's age, was glad to talk to them about Guatemala. After telling them about the rich history and great natural beauty of the little Idaho-shaped country that straddles Central America below Yucatan, and describing the spiritual needs of the people, she asked, "When will you fellows be going to help?"

Cam and Robby looked at each other rather sheepishly. "Well, you see," Robby replied, "Cameron here is a corporal in the National Guard. He'll be going to war before long. I may try to get into officer's training school."

"You cowards!" exclaimed Stella Zimmerman. "Going to war where a million other men will go and leaving us women to do the Lord's work alone! You are *needed* in Central America!"

Her visitors didn't like being called cowards. Robby blushed, cleared his throat, and said, "Well, Cam, let's go to Central America."

"Bu-but I'm in the Guard," Cam stammered. "I've never heard of an able-bodied soldier being discharged in time of war."

"We'll pray that you'll get out," Robby said.

"I'm willing, if that's what the Lord wants."

But Cam didn't leave it at that. He solicited the help of his history teacher, Professor Robert McClellan, who drafted a letter to the captain of Cam's Guard unit. Cam took it to the officer and waited at attention while he read it.

To Cam's surprise, the captain agreed to the discharge. "Go," he encouraged Cam. "You'll do a lot more good selling Bibles in Central America than you would shooting Germans in France."

At the same time Robby had accepted the challenge and had applied to R. D. Smith. He was quickly accepted. "I'm glad you'll be going," Smith said. "You can keep an eye on Cam. I'm not sure how he'll work out."

When Cam told his family, Will and Molly agreed it was a lot better than going to war. His sisters and brothers-in-law again pledged their support to the senior Townsends in Cam's absence, since Will's health was poor. Paul, then a college freshman, agreed to get a job the following year and help support them.

"But just as soon as you can, Cameron," Molly added, "you must come back and finish college and go to seminary."

The Bible House agreed to pay the two salesmen $30 a month each with a three-month advance to help on transportation. But they each had to raise an additional $150 for their passage. As soon as the school term was over, Cam and Robby headed north for summer work on a ranch.

In his first letter back to the "home folks," Cam reported that they had been "pitching hay and pulling weeds for the last three days," and would soon be "heading grain and planting corn. We're accomplishing a good bit with our Spanish. We memorize verses and catechism questions while we work."

Cam celebrated his twenty-first birthday that summer on the ranch. Then in mid-August the boys returned home to pack for Guatemala. Cam's old Guard unit, which included his closest college chum, Carroll Byram, had shipped out the previous month.

On Saturday, August 18, 1917, the Townsend family, with several friends and relatives, saw the two young men off at the Los Angeles train station. They were headed for San Francisco where they hoped to secure passage on a ship bound for Guatemala.

Cam penned his feelings in his log book: "Well, we're off. Left Los Angeles at five o'clock. . . . Had a wonderful send-off. I've got the greatest folks God ever blessed a fellow with. . . . May God help me to be as true as steel to them all. *Adelante*, now. *Siempre Adelante!* Eyes to the front! Forward march!"

"Lord, I'm a failure."

3. Failure

Cam and Robby arrived in San Francisco eager to set sail. But the first booking they could get was first-class passage on the S.S. *Peru*, which was due to sail in two weeks.

"First class" called for more money than they had, so they hired on with Wells Fargo and loaded crates at night for $15 a week to earn the extra. Living largely on poached eggs and milk, Cam complained in his diary that he "didn't like the waterfront a bit."

With the excited pair on board, the *Peru* slipped out of San Francisco Bay on September 15, 1917, Guatemala's Independence Day. Eighteen days after embarkation the ship anchored off Port San José, Guatemala, and Cam and Robby were swung over the deck in an iron basket to a waiting tugboat. Custom officials gave Cam's small suitcase and Robby's trunk hardly a glance.

On board a train chugging toward Guatemala City, an American engineer filled them in on the politics of this little tropical country. "You'll make out fine," he concluded, "if you remember to keep your mouths shut and your bowels open."

As the train rocked along the narrow gauge railway, Cam was enchanted by the scenery. Twin volcanoes, "Agua" (water) and "Fuego" (fire) coned upwards on one side while pristine Lake Amatitlán reflected fluffy white clouds on the other.

Near sunset the train crossed the lake and began climbing towards the mile-high elevation of the capital. When it jolted to a stop in the city, the boys donned their overcoats to ward off the chilly night air. To their great relief, Miss Zimmerman was there to meet them, along with another missionary and a national pastor.

The pastor called a carriage that took them across cobblestoned streets to a five-street intersection, then stopped beside a large brick

building. *Iglesia Cinco Calles* ("The Church at the Five Streets")
proclaimed a sign. Inside was an auditorium, offices of the Central
American Mission, and upstairs rear apartments.

The new arrivals were shown their room in the attic. Tired out
from the trip, Cam collapsed on the bed while Robby set to work
unpacking. Downstairs the "welcoming committee" briefly discussed
the new recruits. "Robinson will do fine," one predicted, "but that
skinny Townsend won't last two months."

After breakfast the next morning the young men called on Edward
Bishop, director of the Central American Mission work in Guatemala. Bishop had been asked by the director of the Bible House to
get them started.

"Our C.A.M., the Presbyterians, and two other missions have
divided the territory so we don't overlap in our work," he said in
his businesslike briefing. "As Bible salesmen you'll be working with
both groups. I'm sure you'll get full cooperation from everyone.

"I'll give you a little history of evangelical missions in this country. The first Bible salesman was thrown out by an autocratic Catholic government. But the great Liberal Revolution in 1871 under
General Barrios turned things around. He decreed freedom of worship and established public schools. Then he went to New York and
asked the Presbyterians for a Protestant missionary. The Presbyterian
board responded quickly and soon founded an evangelical chapel
and school where the president enrolled his own children.

"The C.A.M. came later to help evangelize the nation. We have
about forty missionaries in Guatemala and as many more in the
other four republics of Central America."

Bishop paused and looked at the two eager-eyed recruits. "As
Scripture salesmen you boys will sow the seed where there are no
evangelical congregations. It won't be easy. But you'll have our
prayers and God will help you."

After two weeks of getting acquainted with missionaries in the
capital, Bishop felt they needed to get out among the people.
"Come along to a Bible conference I'm holding for believers over
the mountain in the old capital of Antigua. You can start your
Bible selling there."

Bishop went ahead on horseback, leaving Cam and Robby to
take the stage. After the heavy rains, the road up the western mountain was in frightful condition. The driver kept lashing his four
mules unmercifully while cursing the president for spending public

funds on portraits of himself instead of repairing the roads. The old
coach creaked by more stalled oxcarts and burdened Indians than
Cam could count. Even the children carried loads of firewood. "It
looks as if the Indians are the beasts of burden down here," Cam
remarked soberly.

Once over the rim the driver whipped the mules into a dizzy
gallop, and the vehicle careened and bounced around hairpin turns.
They made Antigua before nightfall, where Mr. Bishop and other
workers welcomed them with a warm supper. Then after a freezing
night on army cots, they set out at 5:00 A.M. to explore the city.

Poking among the ruins of an old church, they left footprints in
the dust beside the bones of clergy that lay strewn around broken
crypts. At one place they saw ragged people kneeling and knocking
on a tomb, pleading to a long dead saint. They were overwhelmed
at the sight of pitifully poor Indians dropping coins into an in-
dulgence box.

The friendly caretaker at the old Capuchin monastery showed
them relics of the Inquisition. He pointed out one niche that formed
a strait jacket where heretics had been fastened while water dripped
on their heads until they either recanted or went mad. Further on
he stopped at an oven in which he claimed more serious offenders
had been roasted alive.

"For two hundred years Antigua was the capital of Central
America," he told them. "It was as grand as Lima or Mexico City.
But an earthquake in 1773 destroyed most of our city. Now Antigua
is only a market center for the valley and a hunting ground for relic
seeking.

"Look up there, *señores*," he said, as they entered the dark gloom
of the lizard-infested dungeon. "Those metal rings in the ceiling
were used to hang dissenters."

"Those black-robed friars were great representatives of God," Cam
commented cryptically.

The caretaker nodded in agreement. Then in a brighter tone, he
said, "Come, see what is now on these walls."

"Why, those are Bible verse cards from the Bible House in Los
Angeles!" said the astonished Robby. "How . . . ?"

"I put them there," their guide chuckled. "I am an evangelical.
The local priests don't appreciate them, but, ehhh!" he said with
hands turned up in assumed condescension.

The Bible conference was just beginning when they arrived at the church. Taking their seats, they watched the congregation. The few who could read and write were taking notes while the others listened reverently, straining to retain the precious words in their memories. When testimony time was announced, the response was immediate and enthusiastic.

A shoemaker turned evangelist rose, cleared his throat and declared, "Before I was a believer I was thrown in jail sixty-three times for drunkenness. Now I've been behind bars three times for preaching the gospel."

Other national workers told of similar experiences, including stonings and beatings by mobs. "It's just like the Acts of the Apostles," Cam whispered to his companion.

On the final day of the conference Edward Bishop urged everyone to go out and practice what they had learned. Cam felt his mentor's eyes looking right at him, and he shuddered at the idea of personal evangelization in Spanish. He had never even done it in English.

When the meeting ended he excused himself and hurried up a street alone. He didn't want anyone, not even Robby, to watch. Turning the corner he approached a man standing near the curb. Pursing his lips to speak, he could make no sound and he walked on past with a pounding heart. Twice more he tried, but could not summon the courage to speak. A block farther on he came upon a young man more his age. "Lord, help me," he prayed fervently.

Having read that a good opening question was, "Do you know the Lord Jesus?" Cam asked in halting Spanish, "¿Conoce Usted al Señor Jesús?" The Guatemalan's dark face showed puzzlement. "No, I'm a stranger in town myself," he replied in Spanish. "I don't know the fellow."

Cam hadn't realized that in Spanish señor may mean "Lord" or "Mr." and that Jesús is a common name in Latin American countries!

Feeling a total failure, Cam fled down the cobblestone street to his room. Dropping on his knees and burying his face in the bed, he cried, "Lord, I'm a failure."

4. Cakchiquel Challenge

When the conference ended Bishop assigned Cam and Robby their territories before he returned to Guatemala City. Cam's would be for now around the twin Indian towns of San Antonio Aguas Calientes and Santa Catarina, where there was a group of Cakchiquel Indian Christians. "I'll expect to see you both in the capital for our Thanksgiving conference," Bishop told them.

It was October 23 when they parted. Robby rode away on a horse purchased for $25.00, while Cam left on foot with Isidro Alarcón, the Guatemalan pastor of the Antigua congregation. Though he was still smarting from the failure of the previous day, he said nothing about it.

As they hiked along the dusty road that led across coffee plantations, Cam was full of questions.

How had the gospel come to the Indian towns?

"It's a most interesting story," Isidro replied. "Silverio Lopez, one of the few Cakchiquel Indians who could read and understand a little Spanish, bought a Bible in Guatemala City when he was working there. He found it hard to understand and put it away. Then when he came home one of his children died and another became ill. The witch doctor blamed the sicknesses on the spirits of dead ancestors and told Silverio to buy candles and put them before an image in an Antigua church. The cost of the candles and the witch doctor's fee put Silverio in heavy debt."

The light-skinned pastor pointed to the ground. "On this very road, *don Guillermo,** Silverio found a scrap of paper which read:

---

* Spanish for William. Cam went by his first name since Cameron is very close to the Spanish word for shrimp.

'My Father's house should be called a house of prayer, but you have made it a den of thieves.' When he got home he looked up the verse in the Bible and decided to stop paying the witch doctor. He went back to Antigua and bought medicine from the drugstore that cured his daughter's stomach. Then he looked me up and I told him how to believe. That was only six months ago. He has since led forty Indians to Christ."

Cam was curious about the burdened Indians they met all along the road. He noticed that the men wore dark blue togalike shirts tied at the waist with a sash over white trousers. The women wore handwoven blouses of ornate design with long wraparound skirts of handwoven cotton cloth. "You can tell the town a woman is from by the design of her blouse," Isidro pointed out. "That girl up ahead is from San Antonio. The Indians stubbornly hold on to their old ways and languages."

Cam sensed condescension in the tone of his companion's voice. He knew that the pastor was a *ladino*, that is, a mestizo or person of mixed Spanish and Indian heritage, who enjoyed higher status in society.

"Can an Indian become a *ladino?*" he asked Isidro.

The pastor shrugged. "If he can learn to talk and live like civilized people. Few do."

They were over a hill now and Cam could see below the two Indian towns tucked into a saucerlike depression with a small blue lake to the left. Behind Santa Catarina the slope climbed steeply toward the volcano Agua. Two other volcanoes, Acatenango and Fuego, rose south of San Antonio.

A barefoot Indian man met them at the foot of the hill. Isidro introduced Francisco Díaz, one of Silverio's converts. "We're happy that you are here, *don Guillermo*," the Indian said in Spanish. "You will eat and sleep in the chapel."

The pastor left Cam in a thatched hut with Francisco and some other believers. While struggling to get acquainted in Spanish, Cam took in the new surroundings. The thatched roof rested on a frame of rough logs and bamboo. Vertical cornstalks laced together with vines formed the walls. Chickens clucked across the bare earth floor and a smoky fire smoldered in the center. In a dark corner he spied a pile of thin blankets and mats.

He was finishing his supper of tortillas and soup spiced with eye-watering chili peppers, when the crowd began filling the hut. The men sat on benches while the women and children sat cross-legged on mats spread across the earthen floor.

Silverio, the first believer, lighted a paraffin candle, and they sang two hymns in stumbling Spanish. Then he motioned for Cam to come behind the table that served for a pulpit. Peering into the half-darkness alive with shapes and forms, Cam gave a short testimony of faith and quoted a few Bible verses he had memorized in Spanish.

The next morning, putting his first failure firmly behind him, the young foreigner boldly began a hut-to-hut campaign. He would walk through the opening in a cornstalk fence, present a tract to startled residents and quote John 3:16 with as much explanation as his limited Spanish permitted. Not until a scruffy dog bit him in one yard did he realize it was the Indian custom to call first from the gate.

Toward the end of the first week he entered a sort of beer garden and offered a tract to an Indian who was drinking liquor. "Sorry, señor, but I cannot read," the ragged man said. Cam smiled and walked away, but a few minutes later he heard the man's footsteps behind him. "Amigo, I have a friend who reads. If you will sell me a little book, por favor?"

Cam handed over a Gospel and invited the Indian whose name was Tiburcio, to the believers' Sunday services. To his great joy, Tiburcio came and at the end of Cam's sermon declared himself a believer. Cam's morale jumped 1,000 percent, for this was the first person he had helped find salvation.

When he had finished selling in the twin towns, Cam wanted to visit other Indian communities around Antigua until it was time to meet Robby and return to the capital. Francisco Díaz, the first to greet him on his arrival in San Antonio, wanted to be his escort. "But I must harvest my corn and coffee first," he told Cam. They agreed to meet early in December in a town south of Guatemala City and go on a two-weeks' campaign.

For the next two weeks Cam had a variety of guides and interpreters. From them he learned many of the Indians' traditions. One named Lucas told why Indian women were treated as servants by their husbands. "When God removed the rib from the first man's side, a little dog snatched it up and started to run away. God broke off the dog's tail, but the dog got away with the rib. So he had to make woman from the dog's tail."

When they visited a mountain town just after All Saints' Day, Lucas explained that food, cigars, and liquor had been placed on altars to satisfy the spirits of the dead who were supposed to return on the holy day. Further on, he pointed to a cross on the trail and said, "Someone died at this spot. The cross is to keep his spirit from wandering here forever."

Lucas also talked about the various Indian tribes. "Your friend is working Quiche territory," he commented, referring to Robby. "They speak a different language than we Cakchiquels, but both our tribes and the Tzutuhil people are descended from the great Mayans. The Spaniards made slaves of our forefathers. Those who tried to run away were tracked down with bloodhounds or hung as examples to others who might think of escaping. They even tried to force their religion on our ancestors, but it didn't work. The Indians continued to secretly worship the old gods. They still do today."

Cam was learning strategy, too. In the high valley of Chimaltenango he and his escort were surrounded by a town mob. "*Evangelistas!*" they shouted. "Stop the accursed Protestants!" Before the crowd could do any damage, soldiers came and escorted the two visitors to the town hall for their own protection. While there, Cam made friends with the town officials and won their cooperation. This taught him a lesson. In the future, he decided, he would contact local officials before starting to work a town.

Then it was time to meet Robby in Santiago and set out on the hot, dusty trail to Guatemala City. Taking turns walking and riding Robby's horse, they compared experiences. Both were eager to read the mail they hoped would be waiting for them in the capital. They weren't disappointed. But one of Cam's letters mentioned that his college friend Carroll Byram had been killed in France. Saddened, he remarked to Robby, "He could have been a big help down here. But we can't second-guess the Lord."

They soaked up Bible study and fellowship during the week-long conference of C.A.M. missionaries that began the day after their arrival, and they enjoyed Thanksgiving dinner with one of the Presbyterian missionary families. Then they separated again; while Robby stayed to work in the capital, Cam headed south to join his Indian friend Francisco.

They met in the town of Escuintla, and Francisco told Cam that Tiburcio, his first convert, was following the Lord faithfully. "The owner of the *finca* [big ranch] where he works has noticed the change in him and has made him a foreman! He is paying off his debts."

Cam was overjoyed at the news.

As they trudged across lowland plantations, Cam wondered why there were so many Indians working other men's fields in the lowlands.

"It's the *mozo* servant system," Francisco explained. "A man borrows a little for drinking. Then he borrows more and must work to pay it back. As he keeps drinking, the debt grows larger and the wages smaller. Soon he must mortgage himself to the lender and work on his *finca*. If he tries to leave, he is usually caught and taught a lesson at the whipping post. And he can be sold to another *finca* owner. The *mozos* you see here were purchased from *fincas* elsewhere."

Cam was amazed. "My father farms the land of others," he told Francisco. "He owes a debt. But he never had to sell himself into slavery."

By December 23 Cam and Frisco, as he now called the Indian, had worked around to a railroad station. Frisco wanted to be home for Christmas and Cam was due in Guatemala City. They planned to meet the next month in the capital and take off on another Bible selling trip.

Cam enjoyed Christmas with Robby and missionary friends. The food and camaraderie were cheering, but his mind was on the burdens of the Indians. "The Word of God will set them free," was his conclusion to the telling of Tiburcio's story. "We've got to get it out."

Christmas night, Cam and Robby were sleeping soundly at the Presbyterian school when an earthquake shook the building. The two salesmen jumped into their clothes and rushed out to help nurses and patients pouring from the Presbyterian hospital across the street.

Later in the day Cam walked across the stricken city to the plaza, where city officials had set up temporary headquarters, and gave each official a New Testament. Then with boldness, surprising even to himself, he suggested that the mayor immediately close the saloons to keep liquor from being sold in the streets. The mayor looked startled, but turned to a general and ordered them closed.

Aftershocks continued for the next three weeks, and Cam was kept busy distributing tracts and Gospels and doing relief work with the missionaries. "The opportunity for the spread of the gospel is tremendous now," he wrote his family on January 22. "I have bought Testaments for each of the president's cabinet with the money [sent by a Christian Endeavor group]. In presenting them, we will have an opportunity to give them the gospel."

With the aftershock of January 24, half the city had been destroyed. So when Frisco arrived from San Antonio, Cam was hesitant to leave with him until Edward Bishop assured him that relief agencies were getting things in hand.

Once again Cam set out with his Indian friend. For the next eleven months he would traverse a "thousand trails" in Guatemala, El Salvador, Honduras, and Nicaragua. Incredible hardships would toughen him. Spiritual experiences would deepen his conviction that the Bible was the Indian and peasant's best liberator. Comradeship and conversation with Frisco would draw him toward service with the Indians.

They ate whatever they could buy or was given to them, usually beans and tortillas, often sweetened with honey. Once they had spareribs for breakfast which Cam felt certain came from a starved-to-death cur. For overnight accommodations, any sheltered place would do, if one could be found, because drenching tropical rain-storms could leave them cold and shivering. Cam had a hammock which had been given to him by an American who was returning home. Frisco, without complaining, slept on the ground.

Dust, sometimes blinding, plagued them during the dry season. The jungle was so thick in some places they had to stay close together to keep in sight of each other. Both were deathly ill with the flu in the fall of 1918. Along the way Cam was given a pack mule to carry their books and literature, and later he purchased a riding mule which he named "Peregrina," or Pilgrim.

Cam had kept a regular diary until the earthquake. Now he made only occasional entries, some of which he inserted into letters for home. He complained of only one thing: Bugs!

I don't mind the heat like I do the insects. I am covered with bites all over. . . . The hang of it is that a fellow can't sit down anywhere along the road to rest or read without running into a nest of ants, mosquitoes, or something else.

He was so tormented with fleas at one place that he described his sufferings in a humorous blend of poetic Spanish and English.

> Hay pulgas en mis trousers,
> Millones en mis shoes,
> Habitando all mi underwear,
> Bailando twos por twos.
>
> Mi patria es California
> Y amo aun sus fleas
> Pero estas pesky pulgas
> De todas take the cheese.

Still he would write, "Frisco and I are having a great trip. The darkness is simply awful."

He was learning to use diplomacy. Arriving in a new settlement, he followed a consistent pattern of asking the mayor, plantation owner, or military commander for permission to sell in the town before attempting to visit any homes.

Although he was at times dismayed and disgusted by the Christo-paganism that pervaded the lowlands, Cam felt that harsh judgments would only close minds further. Instead he used the limited biblical knowledge the people did have as openers for proclaiming the gospel. For example, on "Holy Thursday" he and Frisco met a crowd of men carrying a long pine tree. "We're going to hang Judas in the plaza," one explained.

They followed the men into the small town and watched them lift a stuffed effigy up the trunk of the tree. Then they barged in on a group at a saloon and began telling why Christ died. After awhile, one of the men stopped and invited them to "come and tell my wife and mother this message." He led them three miles to his mother's farm where his wife and children lived in extreme poverty because of his drunkenness. That day his life was changed through faith in Christ.

Cam was determined to pass no one by. Along dirty alleys and narrow footpaths that served for streets they trudged until they had visited all the houses in view. In one town they could find no more huts until Cam spotted a brood of chickens scratching at the top of a hill. They followed the chickens and found another family.

During the long weeks and months, Cam's admiration for his Indian companion grew. As he watched the Indian preach and converse, he thought: "He certainly isn't lazy or dull-witted as some of the ladinos say Indians are. He's eager, industrious, and skillful in missionary work. What the Lord could do with a hundred like him! They could evangelize their people in their own language."

Around many a campfire Frisco described for Cam the plight of his people. "There are three kinds of oppressors who keep the Indians down. The witch doctors teach superstitions, telling the Indians that the sun is their father and the moon their grandmother, and that every hill and volcano has its spirit-owner who demands worship and sacrifices.

"The clergy try to impose the Spanish religion upon us. They only come when there are children to baptize or someone to marry or bury. Even then they use a language the people do not understand. And for all these services they expect to be well paid.

"And the saloon keepers. They are almost always *ladinos*. They sell liquor for religious festivals, marriage feasts, baptisms, and wakes for the dead. They cooperate with the *finca* owners who let the Indians drink on credit enough to keep them in the forced labor systems. My people have little hope."

"Aren't there any Indian schools?" Cam asked.

"Ha," Frisco exclaimed bitterly. "Who would teach us, when the *ladinos* say it is a disgrace to even talk to an Indian?"

"What about the evangelical missionaries?"

"They go to the Spanish-speakers. Not one evangelizes the Indian in his own tongue. *Don Guillermo*, why don't you come and be our missionary?"

"But I don't know Spanish well, much less Cakchiquel," Cam protested.

"We'll teach you," Frisco promised.

In the silence that followed, Cam mulled over the challenge. If he learned Frisco's unwritten language, he could then translate the Bible into it. But with no special training, how could he ever do it? The task seemed monumental, even impossible.

Perhaps he could still do something. "You know, Frisco, that I only get thirty dollars a month salary, but I also can keep half of anything I sell over five dollars per month. I could give that half toward starting an Indian school in San Antonio."

"Would you, *don Guillermo*?" the Indian said excitedly. "All of us will help."

"Well, I'll pray and you pray. We'll see."

A few days later Cam wrote his parents that he wanted to stay on in Central America awhile longer. It was a hard letter to write because he knew how much they—especially his mother—wanted him to finish college and go on to seminary.

He was delighted to receive an understanding reply.

May God direct you, Son, in everything you do. When you do God's will, you do mine, for I don't want you to do anything but His. I want you to live for that end for which He created you—to honor and glorify God, and I am glad you are doing so. Here is a dollar. Papa.

They were in El Salvador on November 12 when Cam overheard an Indian woman say that the war was over. It was a time of sober reflection. Carroll was dead and he was alive. There had to be a purpose in that. And he had to fulfill that purpose.

The middle of the next month they reached the railroad town of Moran south of Guatemala City. From here Frisco would take the cart road to San Antonio and Cam would go to the capital to rest, for he was still weak from his bout with the flu and covered with red welts from insect bites.

"We'll be looking for you to come and start the Indian school," Frisco said in parting.

"I'll be there," Cam promised.

"Each language must have its own pattern."

5. A New Bride and a New Language

Robby was not there to welcome Cam back to Guatemala City. He had been called home for induction into the army shortly before the end of the war. The other missionaries welcomed Cam as a seasoned worker, but he found himself missing his friend.

One evening at dinner with the William Allisons, Presbyterian missionaries, Cam was seated by Elvira Malmstrom, a first-term missionary from Chicago. Though four years Cam's senior, she was younger than the other missionaries. She listened eagerly to stories about his travels and laughed at his jokes and amusing incidents. Cam decided she was much too vivacious to fit the old-maid missionary stereotype, and he felt strongly attracted to her. Adept in social graces, she spoke Spanish like a cultured Guatemalan.

She was excited about his plans to start a school for Cakchiquel Indian children. Though she taught a class of girls in the capital, she had made mission trips into the country and thought the Indians "charming," but in great need of the gospel.

Cam felt himself more and more drawn to her. He kept finding excuses to be with her during the Christmas holidays and confided to her his hope of learning the unwritten Cakchiquel language and translating the New Testament. To do that he would have to resign from the Bible House and work independently until affiliating with a mission. "I've saved $100 from sales commissions and contributions from my folks at home," he said confidently. "Mr. Bishop has promised a cow and calf to help get the school started. Other missionaries have pledged money. When I need more, the Lord will send it." Elvira smiled and made him feel that she shared his vision.

He would have enjoyed staying longer in Guatemala City, but duty came first and he rode off on his mule, Pilgrim, toward San

41

Antonio. He got only as far as Antigua, however, when he became
deathly ill with malaria. By February, however, he was eagerly awaiting a visit by a C.A.M. couple, Mr. and Mrs. A. B. Treichler along
with Elvira. When they arrived he proudly escorted them to San
Antonio and Santa Catarina, with Elvira riding Pilgrim along the
shady road. The sickness had not dulled his enthusiasm, and he
talked eagerly of the Bible and education as complementary keys
to the uplifting of the Cakchiquels.

"The Lord will help us break down the barriers, and the Cakchiquels will be examples to their Indian brothers in other tribes," he
predicted. "They'll become full citizens of the Republic."

The believers turned out in force to greet them. None was hap-
pier than Frisco. "When will you start the school, *don Guillermo?*"
he wanted to know. "I've told everybody."

"Just as soon as possible," Cam assured him.

Certain now that Elvira felt as he did about the Indians, he
proposed on Valentine's Day. She waited a few days, then just
before leaving said yes. Cam saw her acceptance as another indication of God's approval of his work with the Indians.

When the engagement was announced, the Presbyterians wanted
Cam and Elvira to join their mission. Although Elvira was not
officially a member, they felt that she, along with Cam, was fully
qualified. They would ask their board to accept them on the basis
of experience, since neither had the required education. However,
the Presbyterian area did not take in the Cakchiquels.

Cam wanted to keep an open mind, so he rode three days across
the mountains into Presbyterian territory where Quiche Indians
lived. "I felt as if I were in a foreign country," he reported back to
Elvira. "I feel stronger than ever that my place is with Frisco among
the Cakchiquels."

Back in Cakchiquel country, Cam wasted no time in starting
the school. Frisco helped him arrange housing for boarding students
from other villages. A chief loaned a room in his house for classes.
One of the few literate Cakchiquel believers who could teach in both
Spanish and Cakchiquel accepted employment as a teacher. Cam
felt he should be paid ten dollars a month, equal to plantation
wages for a free man.

Since the school was primarily for the children of believers, and
Cam knew their parents couldn't afford to pay tuition out of local
wages of five to thirty-five cents a day, outside support was neces-

sary. But Cam was becoming known in Antigua. The governor had him teach the Bible twice a week to his children. Then the straw boss on a plantation gave a sizable donation. After deliberation, Cam made a radical departure from usual mission policy and asked some of the merchants to contribute. "The whole area will benefit from Indian education," he told them. "They'll get better jobs, earn more money, and become better citizens."

And so in March 1919, Cameron Townsend opened what is believed to be the first local *Indian* mission school in Central America, and possibly in all of South America. The school had less than twenty-five students.

In inaugurating this milestone in Indian education, Cam was further ahead of his time than anyone realized. Educators in the Americas would long be (and many still are) shackled to the melting pot philosophy of offering schooling to minority linguistic groups in the language of the majority.

But schooling wasn't the whole answer. Convinced that the Cakchiquels must have Scripture in their own language, Cam began building a notebook of Cakchiquel expressions. The Indians responded with amazed delight, for he was the first outsider ever to attempt this task.

He took time out only for the wedding, set for July 9. Cam wanted to be married on his birthday as his father had on his. Having put all his money into the Cakchiquel school, he was grateful for the help of friends. A. B. Treichler of the C.A.M. gave him a $2.50 gold piece which a jeweler hollowed into a wedding band for Elvira. The visiting president of the C.A.M. board of directors, Luther Rees, paid for his wedding suit. Others provided an array of palms, ferns, and flowers to decorate the Presbyterian church. Elvira's white bridal gown was made by a Guatemalan Bible woman, one of the best dressmakers in the capital.

Paul Burgess, a Presbyterian missionary, officiated, and Elvira's brother Carl, who had come to represent their family, was Cam's best man. Elvira's Sunday school class of girls sang and a small reception followed.

The couple spent their wedding night in a missionary's home in the capital. The next morning Carl joined them on the bouncy stage for Antigua.

After a week of meetings in Antigua the three embarked on an eighty-five-mile evangelistic safari into the mountains. Elvira rode

Pilgrim, while Cam and Carl walked, and an Indian porter carried bedding and Elvira's portable organ. They stopped at villages to hold services and pass out Gospels and tracts. Such a "honeymoon" was not unusual for missionaries in those days, for their calling came before everything else. Also, Cam wanted to let his bride's minister brother have a taste of Indian work before he went home.

The Townsends had joined the Central American Mission a month before the wedding, even though the missionaries weren't enthusiastic about Cam's Cakchiquel language study, and Edward Bishop warned them they would have to look to God for funds. "Our mission has no central treasury for support," he said. "We all live by faith."

At first they lived in Antigua and traveled back and forth to San Antonio, but their financial situation was uncertain and erratic. And even with a buggy they found the ten-mile ride from San Antonio and back time-consuming. With $70 from Elvira's home church—Moody Church—in Chicago, they built a one-room cornstalk and log house next to the school in San Antonio, then added a kitchen with $25 given by a visiting American agriculturist.

Cam and Elvira were both hard workers. Besides writing dozens of letters to supporters each month, Elvira played the portable organ for all the services, and taught singing, organ, and sewing. She also called on sick people a good bit. In the housework she was assisted by Tomasa, the twelve-year-old Indian daughter of Cam's first convert.

Cam kept busy developing and encouraging Indian workers. He started a "school of the prophets" for Cakchiquel Christians that involved both classroom teaching and practical training. He believed that a strong cadre of Indian evangelists and pastors was essential for spiritual increase and growth. A missionary, he felt, could never do enough on his own, and the believers he won could easily become too dependent on him.

Frisco, Cam's old trail partner, was the star worker, and Cam was counting on him to become the spiritual leader of the Cakchiquels. Then he fell ill with malaria, and never recovered. His death was a serious blow to Cam. Not only had they been close, but in a unique way Frisco had been his teacher. He was more concerned than ever to train the Cakchiquel believers.

With Frisco gone, Cam had to do more counseling and exhorting. When one worker came to resign because of criticism, Cam's re-

Cam and Elvira were married on his birthday—July 9, 1919—in Antigua, Guatemala.

By 1922-23 Cam and Elvira had built a home for needy Indian children in San Antonio where the children could live while attending the Indian school. Here the Townsends pose in Guatamalan Indian dress.

sponse was, "Very well, let's kneel in prayer and you can tell the Lord you wish to quit." The shamefaced Indian gulped. "No, I, I don't want to quit the Lord."

All this time Cam had kept building his word and phrase lists, and working on pronunciations. The differences of some words were almost impossible to detect. There were four different "k" sounds that were especially hard to distinguish. One was something like an English "k"; one sounded like a deep cough; one wasn't right unless it came out with a kind of pop; the hardest of all was sort of a choking sound. The last two were further differentiated by the way the Adam's apple moved—whether up or down!

There was one list of words that all had the same vowel "e" but that ended with one of the "k" sounds. He had to master these sounds if he was going to be able to hear and say the difference between "black," "flea," "red," "stingy," "their chicken," and "our chicken."

He further discovered that the Cakchiquels had their own numerical system. "One person" meant twenty, "two people" meant forty, and so on. When he learned that this was because one person has ten fingers and ten toes, it made sense. He always felt a surge of satisfaction upon finding new evidence of Indian smartness. The Cakchiquels weren't stupid. You just needed to understand them and their language.

Given enough time, he knew he could learn the words and their pronunciations. But the countless verb forms seemed to defy explanation.

One day in Antigua Cam met an American archaeologist who was looking for old manuscripts. Cam invited Dr. Gates home for the night and the two sat up late discussing the Cakchiquel language. "I'm trying to analyze the grammar, but this language doesn't work the way you'd expect. It puzzles me," Cam confessed.

The archaeologist smiled knowingly. "Young man, I suspect you've been trying to force Cakchiquel into the Latin mold. Dr. Sapir, the University of Chicago linguist, stresses the importance of a truly descriptive approach."

Cam pondered that statement. Then his frown slowly turned into a smile. "Of course," he said. "Each language must have its own pattern!"

"Exactly. Try to get the Cakchiquel viewpoint. You'll find a regular and logical development of the language."

This advice turned the would-be linguist in the right direction. He badgered language helpers with questions. He listened. They patiently repeated words and phrases over and over and over. He wrote and wrote. The pages of notes piled up. And slowly the pieces of the puzzle began fitting together.

It soon became clear that Cakchiquel was built by attaching prefixes and suffixes to word roots—just as a simple English word like "point" can become "disappointed." In time he discovered that one verb could be conjugated into a possible 100,000 forms in contrast to five possibilities with some English verbs, not counting compound forms. A single Cakchiquel verb could indicate time, number of subjects, number of objects, location of the doer(s), several aspects of action, and many other ideas.

As Cam became more fluent in Cakchiquel, he realized that in San Antonio the Indians had adopted many Spanish words. So he and Elvira began spending more time in the highland town of Patzun where purer Cakchiquel was spoken. Patzun had a strong evangelical congregation—thanks to Indian evangelists. But life was cheaper here among the unbelievers than in San Antonio. A dog sold for ten pesos, a cat for five, but a young girl could be bought from her father for four pesos (then about 12¼¢ U.S.). The Townsends were upset to find Indian girls of ten to fifteen often serving as common-law wives and looking old at twenty.

It was terribly hard not to start a campaign for eradicating social vices. They did what they could to help, but they felt only the gospel could work permanent changes. And for the gospel to take effect, Scripture must be translated into the Indian tongue.

With the help of an Indian from the neighboring town of Comalapa, Cam began translating the Gospel of Mark, using the Cakchiquel expressions he felt were closest to the Greek. He realized his grasp of the language was far from perfect after only a year of study, but he was sure that even this "temporary" Mark would be a blessing to the Cakchiquels.

After he had translated four chapters, Elvira typed them up, and Cam took the manuscript to a printer in Antigua. He found the printer in the office of the mayor. When the mayor discovered what the American wanted printed, he became quite upset. "We're trying to get rid of the Indian languages. We want everybody to speak Spanish!"

The printer nodded in agreement. "But you see, your honor,"

Cam suggested diplomatically, "we have the Indian language on one page and the Spanish on the other. This way they can learn to read first in their own language and then make an easy shift to Spanish."

The printer brightened. "Oh, well, I guess we could print that." The mayor agreed and the job was done cheaper than Cam had expected.

The first printing of Scripture in their own language created great excitement among the Cakchiquel Christians. "God talks our language," was their reaction. Copies of the translation sold rapidly. The Cakchiquel preachers carried it as a badge of status whether they could read or not. Adults began begging for a reading class.

In November of 1920 a historic diplomatic congress was held in Antigua to discuss the possible union of all Central American countries. After a special mass was announced in honor of the delegates, a Guatemalan lady asked the Townsends, "Why couldn't you hold a Protestant service in their honor?"

Cam thought this a great idea. He and Elvira sent written invitations to the delegates, mentioning that Indian believers would participate in the service.

That Friday afternoon the evangelical chapel was filled. A group of Indians from San Antonio sang special hymns and Cam concluded with a short gospel message. He was preparing to dismiss the group when a distinguished Guatemalan congressman asked for the floor. "It's marvelous what the Bible has done for these Indians, a people that the conquerors saw only as beasts of burden," he declared. Then the brother of the president of Honduras jumped up and voiced his delight, and the secretary of the Congress expressed his approval.

The enthusiasm of the delegates gave Cam a vision of what such quasi-official ceremonies could do in advancing the liberation of minority groups from spiritual darkness.

Shortly after the Congress, Robby returned from the States with his bride Genevieve. The two buddies were excited at being together again, so much so that the Robinsons decided to stay over for the Cakchiquel Bible Conference scheduled for January 1921.

The invited speaker, a former missionary to the Comanches in Oklahoma, had been highly recommended by a missionary friend of Cam and Elvira's. Leonard Livingston Legters was loud, colorfully outspoken, and sometimes given to exaggeration. But Cam saw that he was a go-getter. He would preach in English, Cam would translate into Spanish, and an Indian would translate from Spanish into Cakchiquel. (Cam later learned to do both Spanish and Indian himself.)

Legters delighted the Indians by acting out key points in his messages. "When you enter a new life," he would declare, "close the door behind you," and he would stride to the door of the chapel and slam it behind him. In speaking he was not at all like Cam who rarely raised his voice.

Cam and Robby were both pleased with the results of the conference. Sixty Indians, including an influential chief, surrendered their lives to the Lord's service. They agreed to make the conference an annual affair for the Cakchiquels. Then Robby and Genevieve left for the mission station they were to occupy at the Cakchiquel lake town of Panajachel.

Legters, however, wanted to preach to more Indians. So he, Cam and Elvira, and a Cakchiquel worker made a mule trip through the western mountains. Then he visited other Indian areas without the Townsends. However, all the translating so cramped Legter's style that he too became an advocate of translating the New Testament into the language of the local people.

Cam saw in Legters a valuable ally for promoting the Indian work in the United States, and invited him to return the next year. Back in the U.S., Legters demonstrated his enthusiasm. He became the first field representative for the newly founded Pioneer Mission Agency, created to forward funds to worthy missions, and he bombarded every audience that would listen with the spiritual need of the Cakchiquels. Some of his letters were printed in the widely read *Sunday School Times*. When copies reached Guatemala, a missionary pointed out to Cam exaggerations such as "I have seen the fires of a *thousand* villages." Cam smiled and said, "Forget the exaggerations. He has a marvelous vision."

6. Sorrow and Loss

While the Cakchiquel work was going very well, the same could not be said about Cam's home life. Cam discovered very early in his marriage that his wife had two personalities. One was sweet and charming, especially with visitors. The other Elvira would explode in uncontrollable bouts of temper, seemingly without provocation. She would scream and scold, completely losing control of herself. Then after the emotional tirade had run its course, her sensitive conscience would move her to confess her failings with great remorse.

One such outburst occurred when she was riding with Cam and Legters near San Antonio. She suddenly reined in her mule and began screaming, "Call the police! Call the police!" for no apparent reason. After helping Cam calm her, Legters was very sympathetic and understanding, yet definite in saying, "Elvira must have rest, Cam. She can't keep up this pace."

As a result, Cam felt Elvira should go to Chicago for some relaxation and spend time with her aging parents. Later he would join her in California at his parents' home. It would be his first visit home after four years on the field.

Cam wrote his parents about these plans. "Standing on her feet so much is awfully hard on her hernia and it is getting worse," he said. "She keeps up as bravely as can be and turns out more work than I do but we realize something must be done." He did not mention her emotional problems.

Robby agreed to oversee the school and a training conference for pastors in Cam's absence. After a long train trip across Mexico, during which he saw the Lord provide for him when he ran out of money, Cam arrived in California where Elvira was waiting for him at his parents' home.

The pleasant Elvira charmed the whole family. Then her other personality showed up. Cam's folks were very understanding. Always one to look on the positive side, Molly said, "Elvira has so many wonderful qualities. This is a sickness. Can't you get her to a psychiatrist?" They did and he advised her to get back to work among the Cakchiquels.

It was at this time that Cam moved his church membership to the independent Church of the Open Door in Los Angeles. It was a strong Bible-teaching church with an active interest in missions. And when the missionary committee invited him to tell about the Indians in Guatemala, he eagerly accepted.

In the audience were young Dr. Charles Ainslie and his wife. As Presbyterian mission volunteers, they had been trying to decide between going to Alaska or to Guatemala. After hearing Cam, they settled on Guatemala.

Cam's brother Paul and his new bride Laura also expressed interest in missionary work, and Cam encouraged them to come to Guatemala under the C.A.M. They made no promise, except to pray.

Cam took time to look up some old friends and teachers. Mrs. Louise Heim, a former Sunday school teacher, remembered him well. "When you were about four years old you used to lead my blind father around Santa Fe Springs," she reminded him. "And now you're leading Indians to Christ."

He shared with her his dreams for the Cakchiquels. "We want a new school, and children's home, a clinic, a light plant."

"But, Cameron," she said, "you aren't with a denomination. Who will pay for all that?"

"We believe the Lord will provide some way."

Before he left for Guatemala, Mrs. Heim gave him a check for $3,000. "That's for the new enterprises," she said. Cam was overwhelmed at this unexpected gift, the largest he had ever received. Later, his old Sunday school teacher followed up with $4,000 more.

He met Charles Fuller, the president of the Orange Growers Association and teacher of a large Bible class. The Fuller family pledged to support two Cakchiquel preachers. Through Charles Fuller's father, he met the Joe Woodsuns. They donated a manual multilith printing press for Cam to take back.

A letter came from Robby reporting that the four-week training conference had succeeded beyond all expectations. Robby wanted to start a permanent Indian Bible Institute at Panajachel.

All Cam could say was, "The Lord is so good. Look how He is honoring our faith."

In February 1922, the couple returned to Guatemala. With Robby now responsible for training the Indian preachers, Cam had more time to concentrate on mastering the Indian language and doing some translation work.

After spending nearly six months grinding away at that task, a welcome invitation came from Robby to come to Panajachel on beautiful Lake Atitlan. "Lady Genevieve is going to visit a plantation for a week or ten days," he wrote, "so how about spending that time with me in concentrated language, Bible study, prayer, and conference relating to the Lord's work in our fields?"

The two friends met at the village of Guatalon on Thursday, June 23. They evangelized villages along the way to the lake, arriving at the Robinsons' lakeside home about noon the next day. Robby told Cam about the dramatic recovery of a woman he had treated for gangrene poisoning. "The doctor had given her up, and the family had even prepared a crypt for her. But I stayed with her, soaking her swollen foot in warm water all night long, and God intervened."

The two ate dinner, took a nap and then Robby suggested a swim. Cavorting through the water Cam felt the cares of the world slipping off his shoulders. He was swimming on his back, headed back to shore, when he noticed Robby suddenly throw up his hands, shake his head, and slide under. Fearful, Cam started toward his friend. By the time he reached the spot, Robby was going under for the third time. Cam grabbed him, but Robby pulled him under about nine feet. As Cam struggled to the surface, Robby's arms suddenly went limp and he fell away. Cam swam to shore where he called for help.

Upon finally recovering the body, they tried artificial respiration for nearly two hours. A vacationing judge came to assist. He looked at Robby's purplish face and shook his head. "Cerebral hemorrhage," he said grimly. "There's no hope."

While the rest sat in stunned silence, Cam opened his Spanish Bible and read from the eleventh chapter of John. Then he sent telegrams to Genevieve and the Treichlers of the C.A.M.

It was Sunday morning before word reached Genevieve. The young widow rode eighteen miles on muleback to catch a boat across the lake.

The funeral was held Monday morning with a short service in the lakeshore home and a public service in the school. Robby was so well loved in the town that the mayor declared a day of mourning and the town orator gave a eulogy. Trinidad Bac, the Indian pastor, preached the sermon. "Robinson's coming marked a new day for Indians," he declared. "He gave us the Good News and helped us turn from superstition and fear to love and the true God." Then raising his voice, the Cakchiquel preacher shouted, "You say our friend Robinson is dead. That's not true! He is alive. He lives right now in heaven with God."

At the cemetery near the lakeshore, Cam saw his best friend placed in the crypt which had been prepared for the woman whose life he had saved a few days before. Then a stone was pushed in place behind the coffin with the inscription,

W. E. Robinson
Bearer of Good News

It was one of the saddest times of Cam's life. Frisco was dead, and now Robby. They had been his strongest allies in the Indian work.

"I believe in grace. God's grace."

7. Cam's Theology

"Panajachel is a splendid center for training Indian preachers," Cam wrote in the C.A.M. *Bulletin*. The town lay in the heart of Indian country, surrounded by Cakchiquel villages. It was near the main east-west road and on the lake, so it was accessible by land and water. He asked readers to pray that God would send someone to fulfill Robby's dream of a training school, since he had the translation to do.

The need for leadership at the San Antonio station was solved with the arrival of Paul and Laura Townsend. Cam's younger brother didn't have Cam's ear for language, but he had skilled hands. He became not only the preacher but also the carpenter, mechanic, plumber, electrician, and agriculturist.

By this time the boarding school at San Antonio had grown to an enrollment of around one hundred, and three single lady missionaries worked with the students. But Cam saw the need for further expansion. He wanted San Antonio to be a model for Indian work elsewhere: a strong group of believers, a well-equipped school, vocational training facilities, a clinic, an orphanage, and cooperative enterprises for building the Indian economy—all were needed. He felt the Indians had to gain self-sufficiency if they were ever to rise above the centuries of degradation and oppression.

Money given by Cam's former Sunday school teacher enabled Paul and a team of Indian carpenters to build a clinic. When the buildings were completed, the C.A.M. assigned a new missionary nurse to San Antonio. "Doc" Ainslie, whom Cam had recruited in Los Angeles, was now in charge of the Presbyterian Hospital in Guatemala City, and he began making trips into Indian country to treat the most serious ailments.

Cam next put Paul to work building a home for needy Indian children. The twenty or more children Cam and Elvira were helping in various Indian homes needed a dormitory. Two of these were very special to them. Elena Trejo was a Quiche Indian girl who had been brought to them by a missionary. Joe Chicol was a Cakchiquel from Comalapa. Although Cam and Elvira had considered it, they decided not to adopt these two formally. They wanted to be free to love and help all the Indian children. Also they still hoped to have children of their own.

Cam was very pleased when A. E. Forbes, a coffee manufacturer in St. Louis, read about the work in the *Christian Herald* and sent money for a turbine and coffee sheller. He helped the Indians form a coffee cooperative. By bringing their coffee to the sheller and shelling their own beans, they increased profits immensely. And the Forbes Company bought all they produced. The cooperative was another milestone for Cam and may have been the first of its type for Indians in Latin America.

Soon after the 1922–23 year-end conference, a new C.A.M. recruit appeared in San Antonio. Archer Anderson, a graduate of the Philadelphia School of the Bible, had read Cam's article in the C.A.M. *Bulletin* asking for help in establishing a Bible institute for Indians. "What's been done about it so far?" he asked.

Cam looked amazed. "Well, we've been praying about it. I guess God has sent you."

Cam took Anderson to Panajachel and the two of them started renovating the building Robby had purchased for the Bible school. Six weeks later the Robinson Bible Institute opened its first session with students from the three surrounding tribes. Elvira taught music. Cam gave chapel talks and some lessons and interpreted for Anderson, who was the Bible teacher. After classes Cam worked on his translation while Anderson and about fifteen students erected the first dormitory building from plans Robinson had sketched before his death.

Cam insisted on a balanced regimen of study and practical work. Each Saturday students and faculty took off on foot and by launch for villages in the area. By Monday noon they were back with stories of ministering to spiritual need.

Cam saw that every student was given some menial task to perform, besides his work on the building project. One fellow was assigned to feed the hogs they would later butcher for meat. When he didn't clean the pen thoroughly, Cam showed him how it should be done, all the while delivering a lesson about doing a task correctly.

Visiting missionaries were continually amazed at Cam's common-sense adeptness in dealing with difficult situations at the Panachel station and on itinerant trips. On one such trip Cam and a new Presbyterian worker met five *ladino* drunks, who insisted that the two Americans have a drink with them. "No thanks," said Cam.

A short while later the gang overtook them on the road and one of the drunks whirled his mount in front of Cam's and thrust a pistol into his face. A second slid off his horse and jabbed his machete against Cam's stomach while demanding Cam take a drink or else. "But aren't we friends?" Cam asked. "Yes," the pistol-wielder replied, "but you must prove your friendship by drinking with us."

"If you came to my house and I offered you something you didn't like, what would you do?" Cam asked.

The man rolled his eyes and finally said, "I'd pretend to take it, then when you weren't looking I'd throw it away."

"Well in that case, give me the flask," Cam said. He poured himself a palm-full, shouted jovially, "To your health!" and turned his hand over. The new missionary, who had not understood much of the conversation, followed suit and the appeased drunks rode away.

Cam could handle situations like this, but Elvira remained a problem. Since returning from California her health had improved, but not her emotional instability. She would have been content with a more conventional work among *ladinos*, but Cam was determined to stick with the Indians. His adaptation to the Indian culture irritated her. Things that were important to her didn't bother him in the least. Like the broken windowpane in their cornstalk house in San Antonio. She had begged him for weeks to take the frame into Antigua and have a new pane inserted. One day he finally got around to it, though the day seemed to him wasted on the trip. They were returning in Paul's Model T when Cam slowed to pick up an Indian. "Go on, Cam," Elvira urged, "we're in a hurry." Cam ignored her and stopped anyway. The Indian climbed into the back seat and sat down smack in the middle of the new glass.

She was happy when Cam decided to make Panajachel their new headquarters. The C.A.M. home the Robinsons had lived in was a larger, frame house, and faced the beautiful lake away from the main town. There was more room for entertaining official visitors and it was surrounded by a lawn and flowering trees and shrubs, providing an atmosphere that helped reduce her outbursts.

Still Cam never knew when she would fly into a rage. One day she suddenly turned on him and began kicking him—hard. To avoid more violence he went down the trail that led to the next town. Finally in a secluded spot he found a log and sat down.

While he was sitting there, feeling very sorry for himself, an Indian came along and noticed Cam's feet sticking into the trail. Cam forced a smile and mustered his Cakchiquel to greet him.

As they exchanged greetings, Cam's sense of duty wrestled with his despair. Finally he asked, "Have you heard God's Word?" The Indian had not. Cam began explaining the Good News, rather mechanically at first, then warming as he continued. After awhile he became so engrossed in giving the message that the pain inflicted by Elvira vanished. He returned home with joy in his heart.

Despite Elvira's outbursts, which continued throughout her lifetime, Cam loved his wife. He was very patient with her and always remembered her on every appropriate occasion with a bit of sentimental verse or doggerel, if not with a gift. On one anniversary he wrote her a three-verse poem of which this is the first verse:

> Nineteen, nineteen, on the ninth of July
> By the Jefe Politico we were married, you and I.
> You remember, I'm sure,
> How so love-sick we were.
> How our lives were united
> And our promises plighted
> On that glorious day
> Not so far, far away.
> Nineteen, nineteen, on the ninth of July.

The school work was encouraging, though, and Anderson was a gem. He quickly learned Spanish, freeing Cam from interpreting for him. Cam still had administrative and teaching chores and field trips, for the school was growing, and surrounding Indian congregations were increasing in size and number. He struggled to find time for translation.

It would have been easier had all of his fellow missionaries believed in what he was doing. Many of them felt the Indian work was divisive and would only drive a deeper wedge between *ladino* and Indian believers. Some were irritated by Cam's practice of socializing with the Indians and thought it unseemly to bring Indians into their homes. They saw no future in translating Scripture into the Indian languages. Cam, however, continued to believe that the Indian Christians must develop on their own with only limited financial help and guidance from missionaries and *ladino* leaders.

The displeasure of colleagues developed into formidable opposition. Cam was notified that the issue of translation would be debated at the next general council meeting in Chicago, so when Dr. Lewis Sperry Chafer, the executive secretary of the Central American Mission, arrived from the home office in Dallas, Cam was anxious to make his views understood. Despite a broken foot from a motorcycle accident, he drove Chafer around to various mission points.

As they jolted along the bumpy roads in the Model T, Cam explained his reasons for trying to reach the Indians within their own culture. "If the work was integrated," he told Chafer, "the *ladinos* would continue to dominate and discriminate against the Indians as they have always done. When the Indians attain education and economic freedom, then they can meet the *ladinos* as equals. But to do this they must have a training school and Scripture in their own language."

Chafer agreed that education was important and confided that he was starting a new seminary in Dallas that would counteract the liberalism in some denominational schools. "What's your theological background?" he asked Cam.

"Well, I didn't finish college and never went to Bible school," Cam admitted. "Maybe I'll finish my education sometime. But here I seldom see a book on theology or church history. I spend my devotional time studying the Bible and Scofield's notes. And I keep trying to find more time to translate the Bible into Cakchiquel."

Chafer was surprised that Cam was a missionary and hadn't had theological training. But he conceded that one could learn a lot from Scofield. He asked if Cam had met the famous Bible teacher, who had founded the C.A.M.

"Well, no," Cam replied. "But I have worn his pants! Got them from a missionary barrel. They were twice too big for me and didn't fit my needs. Not any more than the Spanish Scriptures fit the needs of the Indians."

Chafer chuckled at Cam's ability to keep getting back to the Indians and steered the conversation back to theology. Did Cam

agree with Scofield that the Sermon on the Mount was meant for
the dispensation of the Kingdom?

"Well, you'd know more about that than I," Cam replied. "I must
confess that at times I do try to apply the principles Jesus taught
there in my daily life. I remember one time I was selling Spanish
New Testaments in San Juan Sacatepequez when a fanatical Indian
pulled a Testament from my hand. The crowd began throwing
sticks and stones and trying to club me, so I ran to ask the mayor
for protection. After I told him what had happened he put the
main troublemaker in jail.

"But I knew I hadn't acted in love, so I went back and begged the
mayor to release him. After he had been freed I explained to the
grateful Indian, the mayor, and the big crowd that had gathered
that I only wanted to tell people about God's love.

"The Indian listened and then meekly admitted to the crowd
he had been wrong to fight against us and advised them to listen. I
then had an attentive audience as I delivered a gospel message."

"What are your views on election?" Chafer persisted.

"Oh, I believe in election all right," said Cam. "I also believe in
my responsibility to tell the Good News to every person possible.
One time two of the Cakchiquel preachers and I went to a Quiche
community. Each time we would approach a group of huts where a
clan lived, everybody would hide. But at one place a woman stayed
out to tend the ants she was toasting in a big skillet over a campfire.
I pulled out a coin and politely asked if she would sell me some.

"She called inside for a bowl which she filled with the Quiche
delicacy. The Cakchiquels frowned. 'We've never eaten ants,' they
told me. 'Well, I haven't either, but we're going to eat some now,'
I said. 'It'll be worth it if it encourages them to listen to the gospel.'

"And you know, it worked. While we were munching on the ants
the Indians began to emerge from their hiding places. They were so
impressed at outsiders eating ants that they lost their fear and
listened to the gospel as long as we kept eating. So one of us would
preach while the other two ate. The people received a steady sermon
as long as the ants lasted."

Chafer laughed and asked Cam if, indeed, he held any strong
doctrinal positions.

"Well, I guess Mr. Bishop—he's sort of my 'missionary daddy'—
influenced me to be strong on fundamentals and on grace. I believe
in grace. God's grace. And I want to share it with the Indians."

The discussions went on day after day as they toured Guatemala and El Salvador. When the tour was completed, Chafer told Cam that he was convinced that the Indians needed Scripture in their own language. "When the question comes up for a vote at the council, I'll be on your side," he promised. Then before leaving he invited Cam to speak at the seminary he was planning to start.

During the weeks that followed, Cam was more convinced than ever that he should attend the 1925 council meeting in Chicago. "There's too much at stake for them to stop the translation now."

Cam and Elvira first went to California for a few weeks with his family, then went on to the council meeting at Moody Church in Chicago. There the C.A.M. directors received Cam cordially and asked to hear his side of the controversy. After he spoke, they had a short discussion and recessed for lunch.

Cam and R. D. Smith walked along North Avenue on their way to a restaurant. The man who had first sent him to Guatemala urged Cam to retract his stand on translation and serve as a general missionary. Cam, who rarely became ruffled, suddenly boiled in anger at the thought of having to leave translation work. "Whether you like it or not, Mr. Smith," he said sharply, "the Cakchiquel New Testament will be translated."

That afternoon they voted. Louis Sperry Chafer and Luther Drees, the man who had bought Cam's wedding suit, stood with the majority of six in Cam's favor. Smith and one other member remained in opposition to the Cakchiquel translation.

Cam and Elvira returned to Guatemala rejoicing over the victory. Paul and Laura were happy when they heard the outcome, but they had made a decision of their own to transfer to the Presbyterian Mission. Paul was now teaching at the Presbyterians' Industrial College in the capital.

Without his dependable brother around, Cam had to shoulder all the responsibilities at San Antonio, in addition to the work at the Robinson Institute. In the year following the council meeting, Cam managed to spend only two weeks on what he considered his main work—translation. Searching his soul, he recalled the sharp remark he had made to R. D. Smith back in Chicago. He felt convicted that he had spoken in the wrong attitude.

"Please forgive my anger," he wrote Smith. Then with all the pride drained from him he added, "I've found that unless the Lord undertakes, I will never finish the Cakchiquel translation."

"The airplane could be the solution . . ."

8. The Lost Sheep

The next year language work started going better. The days seemed to hold more hours. "I've learned a lesson," Cam told Elvira. "It isn't *my* work, but the Lord's. I pray I'll never again be filled with false pride about what *I* am doing."

The first achievement was the Cakchiquel grammar. Only forty-nine pages, it was for 1926 a significant contribution to linguistics. Comparative linguistics, the study of the relation of languages to each other, had been developed over a century before in Germany. But descriptive linguistics, which describes the grammar of a language from its own point of view, was then in its infancy and there were very few reference works or texts available on the subject because of the paucity of field research. Though Cam was not a scholar, he had lived among the Indians and tenaciously applied what he had learned to the study of the language. His grammar was another demonstration that so-called primitive languages had developed their own complex patterns.

Cam mailed a copy of his grammar to Edward Sapir at the University of Chicago. Sapir called the work "an adequate analysis of the (Cakchiquel) grammatical system."

With Elvira typing and Cakchiquel language helpers checking, Cam began spending seven and eight hours a day on translation. "We feel like hurrying," he wrote home, "but then we realize that the work must be done well, and so we plod on."

The Cakchiquel preacher Trinidad Bac was Cam's most helpful critic. If a meaning wasn't clear to Bac, he didn't hesitate to say so or to suggest an alternative. He knew the colorful Cakchiquel idioms better than anyone Cam had found and would explain them in vivid detail. For example, he told Cam that the expression for "neighbor," when broken down, meant, "your companion in cootie cracking." A *good* neighbor, Bac explained, is one "who will pick your cooties without pulling your hair."

Cam found the work fascinating, but prefixes and suffixes didn't make for exciting reports to mail home. Supporters preferred thrilling stories of evangelizing on the trail. Then too, Cam and Elvira had influenced many of their backers to contribute to the varied ministries at San Antonio and the training of Indian preachers at Panajachel. So they weren't surprised when personal support took a down turn.

When Cam mentioned this in a letter home, Molly became disturbed. She felt "most Christians want to identify with some denomination. . . . How much you could accomplish if you had the Presbyterian Board back of you. There is nothing wrong with receiving guaranteed, regular support." Will disagreed. "Some of us . . . are depending more on money and wealthy organizations than we are on God. . . . Nothing is too hard for Him if we will only commit and trust all to Him."

Having been influenced earlier by pioneer missionary Hudson Taylor, Cam agreed with his father. He and Elvira saved by making fewer trips. When they did get to the capital, however, Cam refreshed his interest in the outside world by reading the Spanish newspapers. In the fall of '26 he was intrigued by an announcement that five U.S. Navy planes on a goodwill flight around South America were due to land in Guatemala City. Though Lindbergh would not make his famous solo flight until the next year, interest in aviation was rising. And Cam had been thinking about how airplanes might help missionaries reach tribes in remote areas.

Cam was at the airport when the navy planes landed and managed to meet the commander, Major Herbert Dargue, and tell him about the Cakchiquel work and his idea for using planes in Amazonia. "How much do you think an aviation program for a jungle area might cost?" he asked the flier.

Dargue liked Cam and what he was doing. "I really can't give you an intelligent answer," he said. "But I'll get together some facts and figures and mail you a report."

Cam pushed the idea of missionary aviation to the back of his mind and returned to translation. But the idea surfaced from time to time, especially some months later when Legters arrived for the annual Cakchiquel Bible conference, and told Cam about his second missionary trip into Amazonia with his seventeen-year-old son, David Brainerd. "Look at the map," he told Cam. "The Amazon basin covers two and a half million square miles. There must be Indian tribes all over the area."

"How many missionaries are in there?" Cam asked.

"Precious few," Legters replied. "Amazonia is a missionary graveyard. If disease doesn't get them, hostile Indians will. Arthur Tylee and his wife are trying to reach Indians in the Xingu area. He told me that twice he has felt cold steel at his throat. They're so far from civilization that they could be killed and the world not know about it for months. Why it once took Arthur three weeks to travel forty-two miles!"

"A plane could make that in three or four minutes," Cam responded, and told him about Major Dargue and the idea of a jungle aviation program.

"You have something here, Cam. Keep thinking while I'm home recruiting pioneers."

When Legters left, Cam pitched into the translation work with renewed vigor. As he worked he kept thinking of all the unknown tribes without even an alphabet. From what Legters had said, he guessed there must be about 500 in Latin America alone. He prayed Dargue wouldn't forget to send the report. Then he could make a presentation to C.A.M. leaders. But first the Cakchiquel translation had to be completed.

By June he was able to report in the C.A.M. *Bulletin* that the first draft of all the New Testament except Revelation was done. It was five years since the portions of Mark and three since John had been printed in Cakchiquel.

But then the bottom fell out. A generating plant was given to the San Antonio station, and with Paul gone Cam had to set it up. The rest of the year was one long series of complications. The big ditch from the turbine to the river seemed to cave in every day or so. Cam finally had to build a conduit of cement and stone to carry off the water. Everything was a crisis. Everything took time, precious time. And when he did get a day free for translation, his helpers would be off planting corn or harvesting coffee. Always something.

The frustrations continued on into the spring of 1928. Finally he reached the end of his patience and announced to Elvira one day, "We're leaving. We're going to California to get away from all the interruptions so we can finish the translation. We'll take a couple of language helpers along. If we stay here it will take years." Arrangements were made for fifteen-year-old Joe Chicol and for Trinidad Bac to accompany them as language informants, and in the fall they arrived in southern California. Away from tribal distractions, Cam and Elvira, Joe and Trinidad translated and revised and typed —checked and double-checked, changed and improved. Cam wondered why they hadn't thought of this before. It was a must, he decided, for the translator at some point in his work to find an interruption-free haven away from the tribe to facilitate study and tedious labor.

By the spring of 1929 Trinidad felt he should return to his family, so Cam and Joe continued alone. Finally, on October 15, 1929, ten years from the time Cam began working on the language, Elvira typed all but the last two words in Revelation.

Before sending the manuscript off to the American Bible Society in New York, they held a dedication service in the First Presbyterian Church of Santa Ana. Cam phoned the news around, and a large crowd of friends, relatives, and supporters gathered for the event. Dr. P. W. Philpott, Cam's pastor at the Church of the Open Door, spoke and Robert McAuley, a Presbyterian minister and friend from college days, presided. Cam recalled the ten years of work in a short, emotion-filled address. Through the difficulties, God had been faithful. After acknowledging the help of the Cakchiquel informants, Cam said, "I'd like Daddy and Mother to come forward now and write in the last two words."

Molly nudged Will, who had not heard a word, and they stepped forward from their front pew. Beaming with pride, Molly wrote the Cakchiquel word for "you." Then Will took the pen and laboriously scrawled "Amen."

Cam then gave an impassioned plea. "Over one thousand years after the New Testament was written it was translated into English. Nearly two thousand years have elapsed until now it is given to the two hundred thousand Cakchiquels. How much time will you let go by before the other 500 or more languages in Latin America have the gospel?"

They mailed the manuscript the next morning. Then Cam rested —briefly. In the six months before the proofs would be ready to check he wanted to stir up interest in the airplane project.

Major Dargue had not forgotten his promise, and had sent an outline of what he felt was needed at a jungle outpost: three "flying boats" with pilots; mechanics, radio operators, and medical personnel; a hangar equipped with repair facilities, spare parts, and extra fuel; and insurance. He had estimated the first three years' operational cost at $134,000.

Cam talked the idea up around southern California. Most who heard him were pessimistic and some were incredulous that it could ever be done. With the stock market crash of October 29, 1929, the nation plunged into the Great Depression, and not enough money was being given to support missionaries on the fields. Something as experimental and extravagant as aviation seemed unlikely to attract support.

But as Cam talked and wrote letters, he had the satisfaction of receiving encouragement from a few far-sighted persons. Dr. Howard A. Kelly, the famous Baltimore surgeon, endorsed the proposed plan. "This," he predicted, "will open up a new era in missions." Harry Ironside, Elvira's pastor at the Moody Church, was convinced and declared, "Surely the unevangelized Indians should be reached in the shortest possible time." And, naturally, Legters added his voice. "If the wild jungle tribes of Latin America are to be reached for Christ in this generation," he wrote, "this is the only way it can be done. Why, I've recruited forty volunteers this past year, but they have all been siphoned off into Spanish or Portuguese missions. We need those planes!"

By this time Cam and Elvira were in Chicago where they had rented a small apartment while waiting for the proofs. Here a well-known missionary brought Cam down to earth with a lecture about his responsibilities to the Cakchiquels. "Now that you've finished the New Testament, your work is just beginning," he said. "You know their language and their ways. They believe in you. Go back and train more preachers."

Cam had hoped the Indian pastors would be able to assume full leadership when the New Testament was available to them. But how could he be sure? He did know the language better than any other outsider. Would he be deserting them by moving on to another tribe?

Wrestling over the direction to take, Cam finally did something very unusual for him. Shutting his eyes, he closed his Bible, then opened it and put a finger on a verse. It read: "What man amongst you, having a hundred sheep, if he lose one of them, doth not leave the ninety and nine in the wilderness and go after that which is lost, until he find it?" (Luke 15:4). "Well, Lord," Cam prayed, "that settles it. Unless you definitely lead me down a different path, by closing doors and putting obstacles in my way, then I'm going to the one percent."

Cam translated his vision into a poem he titled "Other Sheep." Elvira matched it to a tune and sang it at a missionary rally at Moody Church.

> Out where lost sheep are wandering,
> Far from the Shepherd's fold,
> Perishing there in dark despair,
> Since they have ne'er been told
> That there is One Who loved them
> So that He bore their sin,
> Out in the night won't you go with Him
> There some lost souls to win?
>
> Africa, Russia, Asia,
> Romanist lands as well,
> Latin America's Indian tribes
> Waiting for you to tell
> How the dear Lord would save them
> Who then will gladly go?
> Numberless thousands depend on you
> For the Good News you know.

A few days later Elvira spoke to the Missionary Union at the Moody Church about Cam's plans for Amazonia, and mentioned the plane project. Lynn Van Sickle, a recent graduate of the Moody Bible Institute, told her afterwards, "I must talk to your husband. I've felt planes were the answer for some time."

Cam and Van Sickle soon discovered they both had had the idea of using planes about the same time. "How much experience have you had?" Cam asked.

"I can get one up and down. That's about all."

"I think you should apply for membership with the C.A.M.," Cam advised him. "Then maybe we can get them to underwrite our project." Van Sickle agreed to do this.

By now the proofs had come and Cam and Elvira were laboriously checking them, always conscious that one misplaced letter could change the whole meaning of a sentence. Letter by letter, word by word, page by page they checked and rechecked day after day, week after week, month after weary month. The knowledge that no one else would be able to spot a mistake spurred them to strive for perfection.

They were almost finished when they received the news that Arthur Tylee, his baby daughter, a missionary nurse, and three friendly Indians had been killed by savage Indians in Brazil. Mrs. Tylee was left for dead, but was recovering in a hospital.

After a long silence in which he had to blink back the tears, Cam said, "Maybe now people will realize the need for airplanes in situations like that."

The news gave Cam a stronger urgency than ever. He felt they should go back to Guatemala and hold literacy campaigns while the book was being paged and bound, then prepare to pioneer again.

With $300 that had come in, the Townsends planned to buy a car to drive to Guatemala. Then they heard about Mr. and Mrs. Frank Bundy, recent Moody graduates who wanted to go to Guatemala under C.A.M. but had no funds to get there. Without hesitating, Cam and Elvira gave the Bundys the $300 for the trip. "The Lord will provide a car for us some other way," Cam said.

Then they took the last of their money and bought train tickets to Denver where Cam had speaking engagements. While there they heard from Legters, offering them a Whippett car that had been given to him by a Denver friend. Thankful again for this provision, the Townsends drove on across the Rockies for a few final days with his family.

Cam's nephew Ronald White was home from college when they arrived. Cam challenged him to take time off to help in the Cakchiquel literacy programs. "The Lord has given me a new system to teach reading," Cam said. "You'll have fun trying it out. I call it the psycho-phonemic method. The alphabet I've used is phonemic—each letter stands for only one sound. Then, instead of throwing the whole alphabet at them at once, I form words with just four or five letters. That way they can be reading a few words the first day. This really encourages them and gives them confidence that they can learn. Each day I add a few more letters, and make words using all that they have learned to that point. Adults can learn to read in a month or less."

Ronald was properly impressed and eager to go. When their visit was over Cam and Elvira, with Ronald, headed for Dallas where Cam was to link up with Van Sickle and present the airplane project to the C.A.M.

"The key to Indian education is the mother tongue."

9. Cakchiquel Triumph!

The C.A.M. leaders in Dallas remembered Cam well from the disagreement over Bible translation five years earlier. This time Cam spoke fervently about the unreached tribes in the Amazon basin and related some of Legters's adventures. Catholics were already utilizing airplanes in three missionary fields. "With an aviation base we can sustain Bible translators and keep them healthy and working."

Someone asked about the cost. When Cam mentioned the major's figure, there was a general look of horror. Their conclusion was that the mission had neither the people nor the money to go into Amazonia. "We are the *Central American* Mission," they said. "There are other groups working down there."

"But they aren't reaching many Indians," Cam protested.

When Cam saw that they would not change C.A.M. policy, he asked permission to try a plane project in northern Guatemala. "The jungles and rivers there are like Amazonia," he pointed out.

Though skeptical, the council gave the go ahead on the condition that Cam raise the money.

The optimistic Cam wrote his sister Ethel, "The council okayed the airplane crusade." Then he found a Christian broadcaster with an early morning program in Dallas who agreed to let him present the plane project to listeners. A single dollar bill was all that came in the mail. Undismayed, Cam told Van Sickle to "come on anyway. You've been accepted as a member and the Lord will work something out. We'll just have to keep praying."

Cam, Elvira, Van Sickle, and Cam's nephew, Ronald, arrived in Guatemala City on December 23, 1930, where they spent Christmas with Paul and Laura Townsend and other friends. Paul was still teaching at the Presbyterian Industrial College in the capital.

Leaving Van Sickle behind for orientation with other missionaries after Christmas, Cam, Elvira, and Ronald took the stage to San Antonio where serious problems were awaiting them.

The clinic and boarding school were still operating, but some of the Indians had broken with the C.A.M. The congregation had been agitated by anti-American propagandists and was making life uncomfortable for the missionary staff. They welcomed Cam, however, as a beloved brother. The old men poured out their grievances to him as they couldn't to the Spanish-speaking missionaries. He sympathized with them, but encouraged them to cooperate with the mission. "You can do better working with them than against them," he advised. Because of their great admiration for Cam they took his advice.

Another concern was the education of Elena Trejo, their beloved Quiche girl. The Townsends felt she should go to the States. They were grateful when Will and Molly gladly invited the young Indian girl to stay with them while she was learning English.

For the four months before they would receive the printed New Testaments, the Townsends planned literacy campaigns, all of which were very successful. At the same time Cam was at work on the plane project. He had heard stories about the wild Lacandon Indians that were supposed to live in the jungled Peten region of northern Guatemala. Thinking this might be a good place to start, he and Van Sickle took a commercial flight to an airport near the Peten jungle. It was Cam's first flight and it didn't exactly inspire great confidence in the future of aviation. The tri-motor plane lost one motor as it climbed over a steep ridge. When a second motor conked out they had to land in a cow pasture where the pilot made emergency repairs so they could return to Guatemala City.

Van Sickle and a Nazarene missionary then decided to explore the Peten territory by trail. Cam asked them to look for a training camp site for future Bible translators, who shouldn't be sent green into the jungle. He would have gone himself, but he felt he couldn't spare that much time away from the Cakchiquels. After crisscrossing the territory by horseback, dugout canoe, and on foot, the two explorers finally located one Spanish-speaking Indian who claimed to be Lacandon. While still in Peten territory, Van Sickle came down with malaria and dysentery and had to return to the States.

By this time the Cakchiquel New Testaments were overdue from the Bible Society. Cam drove into Guatemala City and persuaded a postal clerk to let him look in the archives. There were all eighteen copies of the advance shipment. He took one of the beautifully bound volumes and rubbed it to make sure it was real. He had special plans for these first copies—a dedication ceremony with the president of Guatemala.

The arrangements took some time to make, but at 4:30 P.M., May 19, 1931, President Jorge Ubico received them into his office. After exchanging greetings, Trinidad Bac, the Cakchiquel preacher, handed the president a leather-bound inscribed copy of the Book. Cam made a brief presentation speech about what the Bible had already done for Guatemala. Then after R. R. Gregory explained the part played by the Bible Society, Bac gave a personal testimony.

"I congratulate you and thank you, for this is a forward step for our country," the president answered. He then suggested that Cam translate the New Testament into another Guatemalan Indian language.

The formalities over, Cam asked the president to pose with the group for a picture. Although the president was known to be reticent about having his picture taken, he agreed. The photo was published with a front-page story about the Cakchiquel New Testament in the newspaper the following day.

From the capital, Cam and his friends went to Patzun for a dedication ceremony in Cakchiquel territory. When Mr. Gregory presented Trinidad with a copy, the Indians repeatedly shouted, "*Matiox chire Dios!*" (thanks to God). Various Cakchiquel preachers read from the new Book. Although a hard shower dampened the congregation in the leaky tent, they sang "Showers of Blessings" and continued on into the evening. The last Cakchiquel to speak declared, "This Book marks an epoch for us. Each year we should celebrate the twentieth of May as the day upon which we received God's Word in our own language!"

After the Patzun celebration, Cam and Gregory left for an eleven-day trip on mule back visiting sections of the Cakchiquel field. Cam talked earnestly about future goals. "There must be an intensive literacy campaign. The masses of Cakchiquels must be taught to read and write, with new literates teaching others. And the other tribes of Guatemala must receive the Scriptures in their native tongues. Freed from superstition, vice, and ignorance they can journey together to a new day of freedom and prosperity. "God will send young men and women to the north and to the south with a burning desire to plant His Word in every language. I tell you, Gregory, the tribes of South America will have the Bible. And North America, Africa, and Asia also."

For the moment Cam seemed to have forgotten the airplane project, he was so occupied with the literacy campaigns. But his brother Paul hadn't. He wrote in the Presbyterian newsletter, "We want an airplane. We want a good plane. We're going to get it and you may be the one to help. There is surely some Christian oil man who would give us a plane."

Cam was still thinking of reaching Amazonia, though. One evening at Panajachel he theorized to Frank Bundy that a specially constructed steamboat could carry people and cargo up the Amazon. "It could be taken apart and carried over areas where portage was necessary."

Bundy chuckled and shook his head. "It would never work, Cam. It just isn't practical."

Cam was turning other ideas over in his mind, when one afternoon he noticed a stranger with a camera in Panajachel. When he introduced himself, the stranger said he was Moisés Sáenz. Cam had heard of the educator from Mexico and his statesman brother General Aarón Sáenz. Dr. Moisés Sáenz had studied the Indian problem extensively in his own country and had come to see what was happening in Guatemala.

They talked education for awhile and Cam told him about the work he was doing. "My parents were pillars in the Presbyterian church," Dr. Sáenz said. "We had missionaries in our home all the time."

Cam invited Dr. Sáenz to stay overnight and the next morning showed him around the Robinson Institute, which now had fifty-three students, and explained his *modus operandi*. "The key to Indian education is the mother tongue, the language of the soul. Help them learn to read their language and become proud of it and their heritage. Give them the Bible to set them free from vice and superstition. Have Indians teach Indians and allow them to stand on their own feet. Once they have dignity, spiritual freedom, and self-assurance, they can move into the Spanish-speaking world as equals with the *ladinos*."

The Mexican educator was impressed. "Why not transfer your

efforts to my country?" he suggested. "You would find a favorable climate of social reform. Our revolutionary leaders will help you." Several weeks later Cam received a letter that repeated the invitation. He filed it away for future reference.

While at the lake Cam heard that his mother, who now had cancer, was growing weaker. His sisters, who were taking care of her, were also concerned about their father, who devotedly stayed by her side, cooked her breakfast each morning, read to her, and did what little he could to comfort her.

Cam wished he had the time and money to go home, but since he didn't he wrote her that he believed she would be healed. He also sent her a long poem that began:

> Mother dear:
>> How I long that you were here;
>> That I might look into your eyes
>> And see
>> The love that time defies,
>> My mother's love
>> For me.

Shortly before Christmas of 1931 a resolution came from the C.A.M. committee in Dallas that was disappointing to Cam. While expressing "deep appreciation of the monumental work done in translating the New Testament into the Cakchiquel language," and "recognizing" Cam's "gift and vision for pioneer work," the committee recommended that he "exercise this gift in occasional exploration into unoccupied fields, at the same time continuing his directive leadership in the Cakchiquel work . . . at least until adequate leadership is raised up to continue the work."

The committee cited as reasons: (1) Cam and Elvira were "the only missionaries with a working knowledge of Cakchiquel"; (2) as translators they were "best fitted for bringing adequate returns on the large investment of time and money made by themselves and the American Bible Society"; (3) the "abundant fruitage of their past labors" was evidence of "the divine blessing upon their ministry" [among the Cakchiquels].

Cam took "adequate leadership" to apply to missionaries. "What they mean is missionary bosses," was his reaction to Elvira. "They should let the Cakchiquels themselves take over. They have enough well-trained leaders, and more being turned out every year.

They have the New Testament. Why do they need American overseers?

"And they want me to do 'occasional exploration into unoccupied fields.' How can I do that, when five hundred tribes in Latin America await God's Word?"

In Patzun a few weeks later Cam received the news of his mother's death. He had believed that God was going to heal his mother—but no. He had taken her. The cloudy afternoon became dark, until suddenly he became aware of a golden glimmer. Looking up he saw that the setting sun had set the upper clouds aglow. The break in the darkness rekindled his spirit and enabled him to say, "Praise God, my wonderful mother's up there now—her pain and suffering are gone forever."

Despite the discouragement over the executive committee's resolution and the blow of his mother's death, Cam completed the month-long literacy campaign at Patzun with a big ceremony presided over by town officials. Then they drove to Guatemala City, where Dr. Ainslie diagnosed Cam's cough as T.B. and ordered him to go to the warm climate of the lowlands. "The rest will do you both good," he said.

After five months of recuperation Cam and Elvira returned to Guatemala City to pack up and leave for good. "Our ministry to the Cakchiquels is finished," he announced to their missionary friends. "We believe the Lord is leading us to pioneer again."

They were saying goodbye to friends when they heard an encouraging story. A Cakchiquel Indian was sent by his town to complain to the president about the Protestant workers bothering them about a new religion. The president asked him if he could read. "Yes," he answered, so he was handed a copy of the Cakchiquel New Testament. After reading a few lines, he looked up in amazement. "This is wonderful! God speaks our language! Where can I get a copy of this book?"

"From the people you were complaining about," the president replied. The spokesman returned home, bought the book in his own language, and became a believer. "Now he goes everywhere," Cam was told, "telling people that the president evangelized him."

"You're right. They [the Indians] have had too much religion. But they have never had the Bible in their own tongue . . ."

10. Chain of Providence

When Cam and Elvira had left California less than two years before, it had been with a feeling of triumph. The Cakchiquel New Testament was completed and they were going to present it to the tribe. Cam was full of ideas for evangelizing the jungles of Latin America by plane. Now, they were back home, tired, discouraged and sick.

Not only did Cam have T.B., though he didn't have to stay in a sanitarium, but Elvira was discovered to have a serious heart condition. The doctor ordered complete rest in bed for her—no housework or any other kind of work, and as little emotional stress as possible.

This meant Cam had to do all of the housework. He was so eager to get at the task of reaching Bibleless tribes, and instead he was up to his elbows in dishwater. One day, however, when he was reading Colossians 1, he came to the eleventh verse, and his frustration calmed. With the assurance that God would strengthen him "unto all patience and longsuffering with joyfulness," he could wait.

Meanwhile, he started a fifteen-minute weekday radio program on KVOE, Santa Ana. While the dreary pall of mid-depression hung over the land, Cam called for prayer and workers to reach the lost tribes.

The arrival of L. L. Legters and his new bride was a tonic to both Cam and Elvira in February 1933. Edna Legters was petite and demure, a very feminine complement to her boisterous husband. She had been a college professor before meeting Legters at a "Deeper Life" Keswick Conference in New Jersey.

Legters recalled a visit he had made to Mexico. "Why not start

75

closer by instead of South America?" he suggested to the Townsends. "There are at least fifty Mexican Indian tribes without the
Bible, and some are large. I'm told there are three hundred thousand Mayans in Yucatan alone. Tell you what; you go, and I'll help
raise support."

Cam was agreeable to Mexico, but he wanted a broader strategy.
"It isn't enough for Elvira and me to go to only one tribe. We
need to start a summer training school where young pioneers from
all missions can come and rough it and learn how to reduce a
language to writing and translate the Scriptures. Only three or four
universities in the country now offer much in the way of descriptive
linguistics and their courses are spread out over four years. That
makes it difficult for the average missionary candidate to take
them."

This seemed logical, so they decided to go to Mexico the following fall or winter and seek permission from the Mexican government to bring in translators. The next summer (1934) they would
start the training camp for recruits.

After the Legters left Cam began compiling notes for the training school. Under "methods of reaching Indians," he wrote:

The methods used in the cities won't work. They don't serve the
needs of the Indians. Counting in a city is different from counting
in a village. . . .
We should utilize the experiences of the Indian. His information
isn't organized in his mind. Study the situation in which he lives.
Endorse the good traits. Exhort against the bad ones. Don't try to
teach things that are outside the realm of the Indian's daily living.
Develop your own system rather than follow others.

Cam wrote old friend Karl D. Hummel, secretary of the C.A.M.
in Dallas, that they were "pulling up stakes for good" in Guatemala
and would be launching Bible translation in Mexico. Hummel replied that he "hoped they would not have to start another mission,"
adding that the "multiplicity of independent missions in recent
years is making it hard on all concerned."

In his next letter Cam forwarded money to the C.A.M. which
he and Elvira had received for Guatemala. He inquired about support for C.A.M. missionaries working in Cakchiquel territory, suggesting a replacement for himself. Neither Cam nor the C.A.M.
secretary mentioned resignation.

Meanwhile Legters was barnstorming across the country. The second week in August he arrived at the Keswick Bible Conference in New Jersey where he and missionary James Dale from Mexico were the main speakers. Dale gave a bleak report about conditions in Mexico. "Antiforeign and antireligious feelings remain high fifteen years after the Mexican Revolution that broke up the big plantations. Rebellion against the feudalistic Catholic hierarchy in Mexico has caused a backlash of feeling against all religion. All religious schools have been taken over by the government and all church properties have been placed under government control.

"New foreign missionaries are not being allowed in, and those already there are working under severe restrictions. Perhaps saddest of all is that it is very difficult to work among the Indians, who have the greatest need."

Dale then challenged the group to pray. The result was that Thursday, August 10, became a day of prayer. The Legters prayed all night in the auditorium, and after Director Addison Raws announced that the leaders would be fasting for the day, none of the group went to the dining hall for dinner. Even the waitresses spent the dinner hour in prayer.

So sure were the people at Keswick that God had heard their prayers that they felt Legters and Townsend should go immediately to Mexico and ask authorities for permission to send in Bible translators. (They did not then know that a group at the original Keswick conference in Keswick, England, had been praying for Mexico's Indians at about the same time!) A woman at the conference gave the Legters a car. Others gave money for gasoline and oil. Legters wrote to Cam suggesting they meet in Dallas early in November. Although Cam had no funds, he agreed to come, wondering as he did so how the Lord would work it out. For awhile it looked as though John Brown, the evangelist educator from Arkansas, would pay the Townsends' way to Texas to produce some Spanish programs for a broadcast to Mexico. But that fell through.

Cam still knew that God would take them to Texas. When the time came for them to leave California, they still had no money for train tickets. Nevertheless, they made the rounds of the relatives, saying goodbye. At Oney's house, Lula handed them a letter from a "friend" in San Diego. It contained $200. "Half for Cakchiquel work and half for 'pin money' for your trip"! The "pin money" bought their train tickets for Dallas.

In Dallas Cam found Karl Hummel preparing to leave for several days in the Wichita Falls area. "Come along with me," he invited Cam. Since the Legters had not yet arrived, Cam accepted.

In Wichita Falls a civic club invited Cam to speak on the Indians of Mexico. Just before the meeting an Episcopalian rector phoned Cam. "I saw the announcement in the papers that you are to speak. I can't come, but I've traveled in Mexico and am interested in the ancient Aztec religion. Could you come to my house?"

After Cam agreed, Hummel mildly reprimanded him. "Why didn't you make him come here, Cam?"

"I just thought it would be more courteous to go there."

At the rector's home Cam listened attentively to a long discourse on the Aztec religion. Then the rector scribbled on a card: "This will introduce you to the Episcopalian dean of Mexico City. He can put you in touch with some influential people."

Back in Dallas, Cam and Elvira discussed with Karl Hummel their future relationship to the C.A.M. Elvira was opposed to resigning, and Cam saw a possibility of returning later to the Cakchiquels for a year of literacy work. Hummel suggested they let matters stand until they returned from Mexico.

When the Legters arrived, it was agreed that Elvira, who still had a heart problem, should go on to Chicago to be with her family while the three others went on to Mexico. But when they reached the Rio Grande on Armistice Day, 1933, the Mexican immigration officials refused them entry. As they sat in the waiting room at the customs station through the noon hour, they wondered how God was going to break this roadblock. Over and over Legters hummed the chorus of his theme song:

> *Faith, mighty faith the promise sees,*
> *And looks to God alone.*
> *Laughs at impossibilities*
> *And shouts, "It shall be done!"*

With a sudden flash of memory, Cam began digging in his battered briefcase, finally extracting the letter written by Dr. Moisés Sáenz, the Mexican educator who had visited him in Guatemala. "Come to Mexico," Dr. Sáenz had written, "and do for our Indians what you have done in Guatemala."

The officials read the letter closely. They knew of Moisés Sáenz, the "father" of Mexico's high school system. His brother Aarón was Head (Mayor) of the Federal District (Mexico City) and an important political figure. Obviously the letter could not be ignored. For instruction, the border officials called Mexico City. The director of immigration said that the foreigners could enter with the stipulation that if Legters should preach or Townsend try to study Indian languages they would be fined and expelled immediately.

That evening at a hotel in Monterrey, Cam and the Legters' turned to the Scriptures for encouragement. The outlook was not bright. The reading for November 11 in the devotional guide, *Daily Light*, changed their gloom to joy. It included, along with other reassuring verses, Exodus 23:20: "Behold, I send an Angel before thee, to keep thee in the way, and to bring thee into the place which I have prepared."

"Well, amen!" Legters shouted, slapping his knee. "Amen!"

"Praise the Lord!" was Cam's quiet but equally fervent response.

At Tamazunchale the next day, they met the James Dale family who had returned to Mexico before them. Their news was not good. Dale's son Johnny said he had spent hundreds of dollars and still couldn't get a resident visa for Mexico. "And I was born here!"

In Mexico City, the more missionaries they talked to, the darker their chances seemed. They waited days in government offices, trying to find someone high up who would listen to them. Cam's advocate, Dr. Sáenz, was lecturing at the University of Chicago. With him out of the country Cam had no official friend to help.

But Cam continued to feel confident. "The Lord has brought us this far and He will carry us on," he assured his companions. Legters, however, became impatient at spending so much time sitting around in anterooms, unable to preach. In desperation he announced, "You can stay here and sit it out, Cam. Edna and I are going back to the States next week to renew our Bible conference ministry."

Then Cam pulled out the card of introduction to the Episcopalian dean of Mexico City which he had been given back in Wichita Falls. Maybe this man could help.

After the service the next Sunday at the Episcopalian cathedral, he presented the card to the dean, who invited him to a dinner on Tuesday night. An English ethnologist Bernard Bevans, who had been studying Indians, would be there.

Cam accepted gratefully, and at the dinner managed to sit by

Bevans, who quickly became interested in what Cam wanted to do. "You simply must meet some of my friends who can help you," he said. "I know—I'll give a little luncheon at the Lady Baltimore Dining Room and invite these people. Especially Dr. Frank Tannenbaum. He's from Columbia University and is well liked by Mexican educators."

After he arrived at the luncheon, Cam learned that Tannenbaum had written a book on the economic effects of the Mexican Revolution. While the others were chatting, he discreetly dashed to a nearby bookstore, bought a copy of *Peace by Revolution*, and rushed back to the luncheon. In his disarming manner, he asked Tannenbaum to autograph the book. To Cam's delight Tannenbaum also scribbled an endorsement of Cam's work in Guatemala. "I'm giving you a note of introduction to the director of rural education, Rafael Ramírez," he said. "He can take care of your problems, but right now he's away in the north visiting schools."

"Where can I locate him?" Cam asked eagerly.

"He'll be in Monterrey on the 23rd."

Cam and the Legters were waiting when Ramírez arrived in Monterrey. The prominent educator frowned when they introduced themselves. "You're the men who want to translate the Bible for the Indians. We certainly can't have that. The Indians have too much religion as it is."

Cam smiled. "You're right. They *have* had too much religion. But they have never had the Bible in their own tongue to teach them morality and good citizenship."

Ramírez was momentarily flustered. "I don't know about that," he admitted. "But you can't bring in translators for the Indians. And if you did, we wouldn't allow the Bibles to be distributed."

Then he noticed the book under Cam's arm. "You have Tannenbaum's book I see. He's a good man. Understands our Revolution. Most people in the States don't."

When Cam showed him Tannenbaum's endorsement of the work among the Cakchiquels, his attitude changed. "Tannenbaum's word is good enough for me. I think I'll invite you to study our rural education system, but not the Indian languages. You can visit areas where Indians live and see what we are doing. Maybe you can write some articles."

Ramírez wrote out the authorization and the door to Mexico opened another inch.

Equipped with the permit, Cam set out on a six-week tour of rural government schools in Indian areas of the states of Chiapas, Campeche, and Yucatan. He interviewed teachers and students, making extensive notes, and also compiling word lists from several languages for comparative purposes. He observed that the breaking up of big estates, transferring all education to the government, and establishing of new schools in once neglected villages, had vastly improved rural society. He sensed a strong reaction to feudalistic Catholicism, especially in Campeche where there was an official propaganda attack against all religion.

His notebooks were filling fast when an urgent message caught up with him that Elvira was gravely ill and wasn't expected to live long. He immediately boarded a north-bound train.

*"We will enter Mexico as linguists rather than
as missionaries."*

11. Rolling Back the Waters

At the border Cam left the Mexican train and took a bus to Sulphur Springs in the northwest corner of Arkansas, where his brother Paul was the new director of the John Brown Academy. Then he borrowed Paul's car and with his nephew Fleet White at the wheel drove to Chicago.

He found Elvira improved, but the doctor gave her only a year to live. Feeling that the warmer climate would be better for her, Cam made a bed in the car, and drove back to Sulphur Springs. There he accepted Paul and Laura's invitation to stay with them. But when Elvira suffered another attack, Dr. George Bast, a naturopath, and his wife, requested that they move into their fourteen-room house. "I can keep a close eye on her here," Dr. Bast told Cam, "and you can be freed to do more work."

Cam reviewed his notes from the interrupted tour of Mexican rural schools and began writing to inform Americans of the progress in Mexico. He cited examples of how the Mexican Revolution had transformed rural education, and gave statistics showing that Federal rural schools had increased from 309 in 1922 to 7,504 in 1933.

The articles were printed in the *Dallas News* and *School and Society Magazine*. After receiving copies of the published articles from Cam, Rafael Ramírez wrote, "They were written with the deep sympathy which characterizes you."

Ramírez's response made Cam feel that the door to Mexico had opened a little further. He wrote their financial supporters of their intentions to serve Indian tribes of other lands, and requested that gifts be channeled to C.A.M.'s work in Guatemala rather than to them. "We will enter Mexico as linguists rather than as missionaries," he told them. "The Indian languages must be learned and the New Testament translated into them. It matters not to us whether we be classified as missionaries or ditchdiggers if we be given a chance to labor toward that end."

He also shared plans with five Christian leaders. Four cheered him on: Lewis Sperry Chafer, president of the new Dallas Theological Seminary; Charles Fuller, director of the "Old-Fashioned Revival Hour" broadcast; Harry Ironside, pastor of Moody Church in Chicago; and Will Nyman, a retired businessman in California. The fifth, a prominent evangelical Bible teacher, replied, "I cannot back missionaries going into a country under another label."

Nyman was then head of the missionary committee at the Church of the Open Door where Cam held membership. "Have the church transfer our support to a regular missionary," Cam told him. "We are looking to the Lord to raise up individuals to back us. Then if officials ask how I get my living, I can refer them to individuals rather than to a church."

All along Cam had been thinking and planning for the first training camp, although the economic outlook in the spring of 1934 couldn't have been more discouraging. Some Christian schools had closed. Many congregations had lost their church buildings through mortgage foreclosures. He and Legters lacked a campus, a student body, and faculty. Their intended field had closed its doors to missionaries. Cam's wife was a semi-invalid. But they had a vision!

When Loren Jones, a revival song leader for John Brown, offered the barn on his farm near Sulphur Springs, they had a campus. And when Cam worked up a one-page outline of subjects with possible faculty, they had a catalog. The "Catalog" announced:

SUMMER TRAINING CAMP FOR PROSPECTIVE BIBLE TRANSLATORS

June 7–September 7, 1934

PLACE: Happy Valley Farm, Sulphur Springs, Arkansas

TEACHERS AND SUBJECTS TO BE COVERED AS TIME PERMITS:

L. L. Legters	Indian Distribution and Tribal History
	Indian Customs and Psychology
	Indian Evangelization and Spiritual Development
	How to Get Guidance
	How to Work with Others
J. M. Chicol	Spanish

Indian Orthography and Pronunciation
Indian Superstitions, Vices and Religions

W. C. Townsend   Economic and Cultural Status of the Indians
Governmental Programs Regarding the Indians
Indian Translation—Field Problems
Indian Philology
Why and How of Reading Campaigns

Paul Townsend   The Indian Workers' Practical Living Problems

An added footnote mentioned that the school hoped also to secure Frank C. Pinkerton, M.D., for courses on "keeping well in the tropics," first aid, and Indian archaeology; and Dr. E. L. McCreery, a returned missionary from Africa and teacher at the Bible Institute of Los Angeles (BIOLA),. for a short course in phonetics.

In search of students Cam sent an announcement to Dallas Seminary. Richmond McKinney promised to come.

Then he went to Columbia Bible College in South Carolina where Legters had recommended him to Dr. Robert McQuilkin, the president. Here he persuaded one student, Ed Sywulka, to drive back with him.

The week before the training camp was to begin, Cam was walking through the park in Sulphur Springs when he noticed a man fidgeting on a bench. In conversation he discovered that Amos Baker was a widower and was in town waiting for his children to finish classes at a local boarding school. "I work for an oil company," he told Cam. "What's your line?"

Cam was off and running. When he stopped talking about the training camp and the goal of Bible translation for all tribes, the oil man squinted into the sun and remarked sourly, "What a crazy thing to do."

Instead of replying defensively, Cam resumed talking as if his new acquaintance had just given him a pat on the back. Finally he said, "We need your help."

"I'm all tied up," Baker replied lamely.

"Oh, you can make time for the Lord. Come on out and see what we're doing."

"Well, you see, I'm not even a Christian."

Cam switched gears and began evangelizing the visitor, who remained unmoved. "Tell you what," Cam concluded, "I'm going to pray for you until you accept the Lord."

A few days after this encounter, a vacant farmhouse on nearby Breezy Point was offered for $5 a month. It wasn't much, but it beat using Jones's barn. When school opened, the faculty outnumbered the students. Besides Richmond McKinney and Ed Sywulka there was only Joe Chicol who had been studying at John Brown University. And since the Cakchiquel teacher merely sat in on classes he did not teach, Cam could count him only as a half student.

"What shall we name our new school?" Cam asked. Several names were suggested, but they chose Camp Wycliffe after John Wycliffe, the translator of the first English Bible.

Cam and Legters, who stayed only two weeks, both insisted that the students train by living like pioneers. They sat on nail kegs furnished by local hardware merchant Tom Haywood, and slept on hard lumber softened only by a spread of cut grass. They prepared their own meals from local farm products. Water came from a pump in the yard.

Finances were lean. A few dollars trickled in from Cam's relatives and the Nyman family in California. Moody Church continued sending a small allowance to Elvira. Students and faculty picked up small offerings by speaking at nearby churches. Despite grumbling stomachs, they prayed, studied, and hung on to the vision. Their theme song was Legter's favorite, "Faith, Mighty Faith."

As the three-months' school session drew to a close, Cam realized the boys needed more phonetics. Dr. McCreery had been unable to come from California to teach, so Cam sent the students to him. They stayed with the Will Nyman family in Glendale, a suburb of Los Angeles.

The year following the first session of Camp Wycliffe was spent battling illness and just waiting. A landslide kept them from getting to Mexico City and Elvira's heart condition forced them to return to Dallas. While they waited, Cam launched a new effort to acquaint Americans with the needs of Latin American Indians. He wrote a short pulpy novel about the spiritual and economic struggles of an impoverished Cakchiquel Indian. *Tolo, the Volcano's Son,* was more fact than fiction. With a few facts changed and names disguised, the people and events were straight from the Townsends' experiences. *Revelation* (now *Eternity*) magazine published it in serial form.

In the spring of 1935 the Townsends returned to the Ozarks

where the Bast family again welcomed them into their home. Cam wrote many letters promoting the second session of Camp Wycliffe, and prayed for patience. In his eagerness to get workers to the field, time seemed to crawl. Colossians 1:11 was again his verse for those days. Everything seemed to call for "patience," including Elvira's illness and emotional upsets.

Reports from Guatemala were discouraging. The New Testament he had toiled so long to translate was not being pushed. After missionaries wrote reminding him about the year he had promised to give to Cakchiquel literacy, he and Elvira began making plans to return to Guatemala after the second Camp Wycliffe.

A few days before camp began a shiny automobile stopped in front of the Basts' home. A long-legged man with a big smile emerged. "Amos Baker!" Cam exclaimed.

"I had to let you know your prayers were answered," Amos said. "I've accepted the Lord. Now I'm so glad to be a Christian I want to tell everybody about it. And I'm ready to help with your training camp in any way I can."

"Well, amen!" Cam responded. "This is the best news I've had in weeks."

The student body for the second camp session more than doubled. Besides Joe Chicol, who taught again, Richmond McKinney returned. Max Lathrop, Bill Sedat, Kenneth Pike, and Legters's son Brainerd were new recruits. Young Legters, Lathrop, and McKinney were seminary students. Bill Sedat was from the National Bible Institute in New York. Pike was a graduate of Gordon College. Brainy, but thin and nervous, he had been rejected twice on the grounds of potential health problems by the China Inland Mission.

The students were moved by Townsend's tremendous interest in their potential. Cam insisted that the students elect their own officers, manage their own affairs, make their own rules about day-to-day living. "When you're in a tribe and on your own, you won't have anybody to turn to except the Lord." This year also the group had to live frugally. Amos Baker sometimes got them donations of groceries from local churches. Will Townsend, Cam's father, was the camp cook.

Legters was there again for two weeks and lectured on anthropology, missionary policies, and the victorious life. And Dr. McCreery came for ten days to teach phonetics. Joe Chicol taught Indian customs. But Cam was the main teacher, showing how the

Cakchiquel language worked with a little chart in which he could slide different stems, prefixes, and suffixes to make up 100,000 possible forms for a single verb. The students also tried to analyze the dozen or so American Indian languages sketched in a handbook published by the Bureau of American Ethnology.

Amateur night was initiated as a regular event in the calendar of Camp Wycliffe. Cam was the lively master of ceremonies for hilarious games. On such social occasions, Cam would say, "If you don't have a sense of humor, you shouldn't be a missionary."

Everyone kept an ear tuned to Mexico, which remained closed to newly assigned religious workers. The new president, Lázaro Cárdenas, reportedly had several very antireligious officials in his cabinet.

Late in June Dr. McCreery called for a day of prayer that Mexico would welcome Bible translators at least. Students and faculty knelt around the nail kegs and implored God for a miracle. When they arose at noon, joints and muscles ached. But the discomfort was forgotten upon hearing through a radio news broadcast that President Cárdenas had dismissed his cabinet, including the fanatical atheists. "Praise the Lord," Cam exclaimed, for he felt that the reformist president would now have more liberty to utilize Christian linguists in his program of helping poor peasants.

Cam was anxious to go to Mexico immediately after the second session ended. But there was the promise of a year of literacy work in Guatemala. He had already secured the necessary visas when a letter came from Guatemala. Elvira's brother Carl wrote, not as a relative, but as a representative of the C.A.M. missionaries. "We want you Cam," he said, "but not Elvira. We feel she would be more of a hindrance than a help."

Cam was upset. "If you can't take Elvira, then I won't be coming either," he replied.

The way now seemed clear to stay in Mexico after escorting the first corps of workers there. To help care for Elvira, whose heart condition remained uncertain, Cam's niece Evelyn Griset had offered to spend a year with them.

Cam had already made arrangements by mail with Rafael Ramírez and other officials in Mexico City to bring some of his students into the country for linguistic research. Pike, Lathrop, Brainerd Legters, and McKinney planned on staying only three weeks and could get by with tourist visas. But Cam, Elvira, and Evelyn were under a different classification and were supposed to have $60 each for every month they planned to stay in the country. Not until they got to Dallas did they even have money to travel on. There they received a $90 check from Moody Church. On the strength of that they started toward the border in an old Buick pulling a cumbersome housetrailer. The students had preceded them in another old car.

At the border, while the chief inspector thumbed through the papers, Cam talked at full speed about his work and his plans. The official stamped the papers and waved them across the border without asking about money.

The Townsends and Evelyn caught up with the students near Monterrey, and the caravan made good time on the road to Mexico City except for a near catastrophe when the Buick nearly skidded over a precipice. A crane operator helped them pull the car back to the road and across the bad spot.

When they reached Villa de Guadalupe, on the northern edge of Mexico City, Cam stopped to check his trailer taillights before plunging in the madcap city traffic. Their destination was Coyoacan on the opposite side of the city. Suddenly two motorcycles roared to a stop behind him. Policemen! One smiled and said in excellent English, "Last year I visited Los Angeles, California, and was treated royally by the chief of police. Please allow us to escort you through the traffic."

With their sirens blaring, the motorcycles parted the traffic before them. "It's just like the Lord rolling back the waters of the Red Sea," Cam chuckled in delight. "I wish some of the skeptics could see us now!"

"Let's run our own affairs from the field."

12. The Summer Institute of Linguistics

When Cam read in the next morning's newspaper that the Seventh Inter-American Scientific Congress was about to convene in the Palace of Fine Arts, he hurried all the students down to the national theater. There he spotted Rafael Ramírez and embraced him heartily with a Mexican *abrazo*. Ramírez responded cordially and introduced him to three other influential Mexicans who were concerned about Indians: Genaro Vasquez, Secretary of Labor; Dr. Silva y Aceves, founder and director of the Mexican Institute of Linguistic Investigations; and Professor Javier Uranga, secretary of the Indian division of the Congress. Presenting the young Americans as "linguistic investigators," Cam led them to seats for the opening session.

During the days that followed, Cam mingled with delegates from many countries, mentioning at every turn the praiseworthy results of the Mexican Revolution he had seen on his survey trip the previous year. He patiently answered questions about what his group hoped to do in Mexico. "We want to help by carrying out a thorough investigation of the Indian languages. In doing this, we want to serve our fellow-man in any way possible. I disagree with scientists who use people as laboratory specimens in their research but do nothing for their welfare. We wish to have a small part in the great work of your government in bringing Indian peoples into the social and economic life of the nation."

Cam told some of the leaders of their intent to translate the Bible. "We will not propagate any sectarianism," he assured them, "but we will translate the Book of goodwill and brotherly love for the Indians."

The highlight of the Congress came when President Lázaro Cárdenas made an appearance. Even before the reformist leader was

89

introduced, Cam recognized him from newspaper pictures—a man
with a short bushy mustache and dark hair curling slightly over a
high receding forehead. Cam whispered to his companions, "They
call him the 'Peasant's President.' He shocked Mexican aristocracy
by moving from the presidential palace into a middle-class home."

When the students' three weeks were up, Brainerd Legters and
Max Lathrop went home to get married, and Richmond McKinney
returned to school. Ken Pike, however, arranged to stay on in
Mexico and traveled south to the mountainous state of Oaxaca,
where he began work in a Mixteco village. Cam, Elvira, and Evelyn
set out with the Buick and trailer for the sixty-mile trip to Tetelcingo, the town which people had told them was the most backward
Aztec settlement in the state of Morelos.

As Cam maneuvered the car and trailer along a cobblestoned
street, dark eyes peered from every doorway. By the time they
reached the dusty plaza, a mob of ragged Aztec children were warily
circling around them. Cam stepped out onto the running board of
the old car and asked for the mayor. A short swarthy Indian with
a serious, square face came forward. He wore huaraches, the open
peasant sandals, a baggy white muslin suit, and a black sarape bearing a red and orange Aztec design. He was one of the very few citizens of the town who spoke Spanish fluently.

Cam showed Mayor Martín Méndez his papers from the Ministry
of Education and announced that he had come to learn the Aztec
language and help the villagers in practical ways.

"How do you greet one another in your language?" Cam asked
while Mayor Méndez was still trying to absorb what he had heard.

"Shimopanotli," he replied automatically.

"Shimopanotli," Cam echoed, writing the word in his notebook.
A grin spread across the mayor's face. Cam asked him for more
words, repeating each and writing it down. "Your language is very
beautiful," Cam said with a disarming smile.

When the mayor welcomed them cordially and invited them to
live in the town, Cam pulled the trailer into the shade of a tree
beside the public fountain in the center of the plaza. Nearby was
the village hall and the school. On the opposite side was a Catholic
church with an old tower. Above the door of the church Cam
noticed a painted cross, with a sun on its left and a moon on the
right. The ancient symbols of Aztec worship had been syncretized
with Catholicism.

With the first mail they received in Tetelcingo was a check from Moody Church for $70. Cam felt it was oddly providential since Moody Church had sent the same amount when they were building the cornstalk house in Guatemala. He used the money to buy rough timber and bamboo for building a shed around two sides of the trailer. The narrow L-shaped lean-to became kitchen, dining room, reception room, and Evelyn's bedroom. He covered the bamboo walls with cheesecloth to ward off the insects.

Cam's experience with Cakchiquel made learning Aztec easier, since both languages were agglutinative, having constant root stems but with numerous prefixes and suffixes forming the various verbal forms and nominal derivatives.

As he had with the Cakchiquels in Guatemala, Cam became thoroughly involved with the life of the Mexican Aztecs. He felt that to learn the language of the people and to gain their complete trust, he must as far as possible become one of them. He took advantage of every opportunity to make this desire known.

One morning, for example, he asked a peddler for a sample of her wares. She replied in Aztec, "Help yourself." He popped into his mouth worms which had been wrapped in cactus skin to keep them alive. The peddler smiled at his apparent enjoyment and asked if he wanted to buy a supply. He also ate tadpoles, fried or raw in a salad Aztec style. Elvira and Evelyn declined.

Elvira spent a great deal of time in bed, and did not become intimately involved with the people. But she kept their business affairs in order, wrote many letters to their friends at home, and was a charming hostess to the many visitors that stopped by. Cam was always inviting officials to Tetelcingo.

Cam and the mayor of Tetelcingo became fast friends. Don Martín had served in the Mexican army before becoming mayor of the one thousand citizens of Tetelcingo, and Cam soon learned that he had moral problems and carried a pistol because of his enemies.

As their friendship grew, the mayor asked to borrow the little Book Cam frequently read to him. He began reading the New Testament to hangers-on at the municipal building. Some days he read for three hours at a time.

A few weeks later he told Cam, "Professor, something has happened to me. I can't lie or get drunk as I used to. I've quit beating my woman. This Book stops me."

Shortly after this he asked to buy three New Testaments from

Cam. "I'm sending one to each of my chief enemies with a letter saying that this Book has helped me to forgive them and that I hope they will read it and forgive me too."

When he explained that he had put away his gun also, Cam exclaimed, "*Don* Martín, you have been spiritually reborn. Now you must help your fellow Aztecs find this same new birth."

Cam planted other seeds too. First he got villagers to carry manure, bat dung, and ash heaps to the plaza to replenish the soil that had been scraped off to make adobe. Then he had *don* Martín hold a citizens' meeting to find what the town needed. Cam took careful notes and then made a trip into Mexico City to see his government friends. He returned with vegetable seeds.

A few days later Cam went back to Mexico City where Professor Ramírez made a donation of fruit trees. With regular irrigation and the tropical climate, the plaza became a horticulturist's delight. Visitors could follow flower-scented paths around vegetable beds. There was a rich harvest of lettuce, radishes, celery, and beets. Beginning with the mayor, the cautious Aztecs broadened their diet beyond tortillas, chilies, and beans.

Evelyn and Elvira started sewing classes for the women while Cam set off again for Mexico City to report to the officials the results of the garden. He left a giant head of lettuce in some of the offices he visited, making it easy to tell what had happened. In each conversation he was careful to give due credit to the government policies which were raising the standards of village life. He told how the Indians now had land to till. The school had more teachers and a cooperative store started. The saloon had been closed. A basketball court had been built to provide recreation. Water had been piped from a spring to the plaza.

The officials were pleased and listened appreciatively as Cam presented a list of additional village needs: a doctor to make a medical survey and treat the poor free of charge; printing of a bilingual Aztec-Spanish primer which he was preparing for literacy classes; a loan to the cooperative store so its inventory could be increased; a swimming pool; 500 trees to plant along the streets, including orange trees; more school supplies; cows for a community dairy; lumber for outhouses, and pipes to extend the municipal water system. The officials became enthusiastic and agreed to help.

Genaro Vásquez donated an old truck which Cam taught the Indians to drive. Then they went to work on the street that connected the town with the highway. Each Indian was responsible for repairing a section of road, and Cam took his turn with the others. When Professor Flores Zamora, the new director of rural education, visited Tetelcingo, Elvira served a delicious lunch and Cam showed him around and talked about future plans. The Indians were going to whitewash their homes inside and out, a pottery industry was in the works, and there was a campaign to eradicate hills of "sacred" cutter ants. Zamora was so impressed with these and other changes that he readily agreed to help as much as he could.

Early in December of 1935, Cam, Elvira, and Evelyn drove to Mexico City for a time of rest, and Cam had a chance to tell Ambassador Josephus Daniels about the work at Tetelcingo. Daniels suggested Cam write a report that he could take back to Washington, showing something favorable about the changes in Mexico.

Cam's four-page report explained his goals in Mexico and the developments at Tetelcingo. "Our contacts with Mexican officialdom have inspired us with confidence," he concluded. "I doubt if there is a country in the world where more interest would be shown in helping a backward town. . . . We consider it an unusual privilege to participate even in a small way in one of the greatest surges forward recorded by any people."

Because he wanted to be open and aboveboard with Mexican officials, Cam gave a copy of the report to his friend Genaro Vásquez, the secretary of labor. Vásquez had it translated into Spanish and took it to the president.

The Townsends hadn't been back in Tetelcingo long when on Saturday, January 21, 1936, a chorus of dogs began barking. Dressed in his working clothes, Cam peered around the trailer to see what was causing the commotion. Four or five men were walking away from two shiny black limousines toward the schoolhouse. He recognized the stride of the man in front—President Cárdenas!

Feeling he should not take time to change, Cam hurried through the crowd to where Cárdenas was talking with the teachers. When the president turned toward him, Cam followed the Latin American custom of the inferior extending his hand first.

"*Buenos días, Señor Presidente,*" Cam said respectfully.

"*Buenos días, Señor* Townsend," replied the ruler who had rankled foreign businessmen with his socialistic efforts to elevate peasant life.

Cam was amazed that the president knew his name. But Cárdenas knew much more, having read the report.

"*Señor Presidente,*" Cam continued, conscious of his soiled clothing, "I am glad you are a friend of peasants, for you have found me one today. Will you come to our trailer home and inspect the work we are trying to do?"

Cárdenas looked across at the trailer beside the green garden, and nodded. "After I finish my visit to the school and talk to the people. Wait for me."

By this time a large crowd had gathered in the school. Even the normally shy women were there in their blue costumes and long black braids. Cárdenas spoke to the crowd briefly, then asked, "Are there any special needs you wish to bring to my attention?" He listened to the Indians' petitions for half an hour. Then he accompanied Cam across the plaza toward the trailer.

He appreciated Cam's report to Ambassador Daniels, the president said, and the articles about the rural school system Cam had written. He was glad for the publication of the primers and for the reading classes Cam had started for both adults and children. The government intended to stop all restriction of religion and would not interfere again if the church stayed out of politics.

As they walked through the garden, Cam presented his hope of bringing young people to Mexico to translate the Bible into Indian languages. Cárdenas shaded his eyes against the hot sun and squinted at the rows of vegetables. "Will they help the Indians in the practical way you are doing?" he asked.

"Certainly, *Señor Presidente*," Cam declared. "We only want to follow the example of our Master who came not to be served, but to serve and to give His life for others."

"This is just what my country needs," was Cárdenas's response. "Bring all you can get."

Cam sent an enthusiastic report of Cárdenas's visit to Ken Pike who was struggling with the knotty Mixtec tonal language across the mountains. And when Max Lathrop returned to Mexico with his bride, they went to work with the Tarascans in President Cárdenas's beautiful home state of Michoacan. Cárdenas paid special attention to the Lathrops and sent commendations to Cam.

As June approached, Cam wondered how many new students would come to the third Camp Wycliffe. Two of Evelyn Griset's UCLA classmates, Eugene Nida and Florence Hansen, had written for information. Ken Pike's nurse sister Eunice had also inquired. Altogether, fourteen regular students and four part-timers turned up for the opening of camp in Sulphur Springs. The faculty was the same with one change. Cam invited Pike to teach phonetics. When Legters arrived and saw the boyish instructor before a class, he called Cam aside. "Don't you think he lacks maturity?"

Cam replied, "I believe he has exceptional possibilities. If he doesn't make it, we won't use him next year."

Legters conceded on Pike, but was very reluctant when Cam proudly announced that the two single girls, Florence Hansen and Eunice Pike, intended to work in a tribe. "Think of the criticism we'd get for sending two young girls into an Indian tribe where not even male missionaries have ever gone."

Cam pleaded their case until Legters said, "Oh, all right. Go ahead, Townsend, and do what you think best. But I don't like it."

When the training camp was over, Evelyn Griset returned to UCLA, and Ethel Mae Squires, another of Cam's nieces, came to be Elvira's nurse and helper for the coming year. Trailed by a second carload of linguistic investigators, including the brilliant Gene Nida, a Phi Beta Kappa graduate, and the two single girls, they headed for the border, again on the faith that God would supply the money.

In Mexico City a check caught up with them. A mining engineer and his wife in El Paso had heard Legters speak and sent $1,500. This would keep the entire group going for at least two months.

The group now needed an office larger than Cam's briefcase. H. T. Marroquin, the American Bible Society secretary, came to the rescue and offered to share his own small facilities for their growing correspondence and records.

Then a letter from Legters presented a new problem. He was having trouble with the Pioneer Mission Agency. "The board says we can't continue forwarding funds to workers on the fields who have no organization," he wrote. "You must organize a committee."

His disagreement with the Central American Mission over the Cakchiquel translation and the advance into other tribes had influenced Cam against forming a Stateside organization. He did not like the idea of placing the fledgling group under a board of home supporters who might not understand what they would be doing. The channeling of support through the Pioneer Mission Agency had left them free to develop their own policies, and he wanted this to continue. If Legters and the P.M.A. wanted a field committee, they could form the committee among themselves.

Cam called his group together. He pulled a few letterheads from his briefcase and passed them around. "When Bill Sedat went to

Guatemala after the second training camp, immigration required that he have a document from some academic institution sponsoring him. I had this printed up with the name Summer Institute of Linguistics. What do you think?"

There were differences of opinion. Some preferred International Institute of Linguistics, a name Legters had previously suggested. "The advantage of a name like Summer Institute is that it doesn't sound too pretentious," Cam explained. "A suspicious country wouldn't consider it a threat. And we do train during the summer. We could have a lawyer draw up a constitution here in Mexico and the Pioneer Mission Agency can continue forwarding money to us."

The seminary men argued that this was highly unusual. Missionary groups usually organized in the homeland and operated under a board of directors in the States. "Do we want well-meaning people at home who lack knowledge telling us what to do?" Cam asked. "Let's run our own affairs from the field under the Lord's leading."

When they finally agreed, Cam suggested that the group be democratic and meet annually for business conferences. Between times, an elected executive committee of three or four members would function. This committee would have authority over the director who would be elected periodically by the conference.

It was obvious that Cam would be elected director, but his proposal that he be under the executive committee surprised them. This was something new in the history of missions—a founder-director telling a crew of young green members, some unhappy with past decisions, to take charge. But Cam believed it was dangerous for one man to have control. It meant he would have to use persuasion and charisma in attempting to put across his policies.

Ken Pike, Brainerd Legters, Eugene Nida, and Max Lathrop formed the constitutional committee and worked with a lawyer in drawing up the document. When executed and signed in the fall of 1936, it marked the first time in history that an organization had been formed for the primary purpose of reducing languages to writing and translating the Bible for minority groups.

The third Camp Wycliffe almost tripled in size over the previous summer. *From l. to r., top row:* Joe Chicol, Gene Nida, Ken Pike, Walter Miller, Robert Smallwood, Jacob Johnson. *Middle:* Eunice Pike, Ethel Squire, Elvira, Cam, John Twentyman, Isabel Twentyman, Grace Armstrong, Florence Hansen. *Bottom:* Joe McCullough, Rowland Davis, Landis Christiansen, Wilfred Morris.

During the first years of Camp Wycliffe in Arkansas, equipment was scarce. One lack was solved by a gift of old nail kegs.

Above: Elvira, Evelyn Griset (later Pike), and Cam stand in front of the Buick and trailer which took them to Mexico and the town of Tetelcingo, Morelos, in 1935. *Below:* In 1937 Cam visited the place in Morelos where Zapata, one of the revolutionary leaders, was shot and killed in 1919. Zapata was an Indian and the Indians had responded to his leadership and agrarian program.

*"He [President Cárdenas] is helping us because
we're helping Mexico in practical service to the
Indians."*

13. Cam's Social Service

"Who permitted your workers to enter Mexico?" a veteran missionary asked Cam.

"President Cárdenas. He is helping us because we're helping
Mexico in practical service to the Indians."

"How are you listed on the immigration forms?"

"Linguistic investigators."

"You're in the country under false pretenses," the missionary
complained.

"The government knows that we will translate the Bible."

"Perhaps so. But you're doing other things besides linguistic work.
You're deceiving your home supporters."

Cam did not press the matter. A few weeks later the critic left
for the States to warn churches about the "fakery" and "dishonesty"
of Cameron Townsend.

A different criticism came from a Presbyterian missionary friend
of Cam's. "Captain" Norman Taylor disapproved of Eunice Pike
and Florence Hansen going to live in a Mazateco village. "I've been
through there," he told Cam, "and heard there is a lot of killing.
Please don't let them go."

Cam respected Taylor, but when he mentioned the warning to
the girls, they looked at him in surprise. "Why, don't you believe
God can take care of us?"

Set back, Cam replied, "If you put it that way, go ahead."

But before any of the translators could leave for their tribes, an
official messenger came from the president saying he wished to
welcome them back to Mexico with a banquet in Chapultepec
Palace. The presidential limousine would call for them.

They assembled for the nine-course meal in the large chandeliered salon where visiting heads of state were entertained. Cam and Elvira sat on either side of the president at his request. Two key officials sat nearby. As the hungry translators ate ravenously, Cam spoke of their motivation and aims to Cárdenas. "Each of us wants to follow Jesus Christ by serving the Indians in practical ways, assisting your government in its program of bettering the masses. We have found, too, that it helps to translate God's moral and spiritual revelation into the Indian language."

The president was attentive. "My government will help you in every way possible," he promised. "But have these young people enough money for living expenses?"

"Well, two have their support pledged by friends in the States."

"In that case," the president resolved, "I will assign rural school-teachers' salaries to the other eight."

Cam was overwhelmed. Here was the man some thought to be anti-Christian offering government support for the needy trans-lators. "*Gracias, Señor Presidente, gracias.* They will try to be worthy of your government's confidence."

The following day the Townsends and the young ladies went by invitation to visit *Señora* Cárdenas. When Elvira inquired about Amalia Cárdenas's young son, the First Lady said she would send him to the Townsends' apartment the next day.

Buoyed by the backing of President and Mrs. Cárdenas, the linguists scattered to their chosen tribes. Brainerd and Elva Legters went to the large Maya tribe of Yucatan. Richmond McKinney selected the needy Otomis in the dry Mesquital Valley north of Mexico City. Walter and Vera Miller took the large Mixe tribe in Oaxaca. The scholarly Gene Nida rode a bus to the cold Sierra Madre Mountains of the north where fleet-footed Tarahumaras lived in shanties and caves. Cam personally took Landis Christiansen into the rugged mountains of Puebla where Totonacs grew corn on land so steep they sometimes had to tie themselves to trees or boulders to keep from falling out of their fields. And Ken Pike escorted his sister Eunice and her partner Florence Hansen to their mountain Mazatec village in Oaxaca. Then after helping them rent an Indian house and learn their first Mazatec words, he walked to a country depot and caught a train into his Mixtec area.

As he waited at a remote stop for his luggage to arrive, Pike watched a line of Indians carrying big bags of grain to warehouses. Remembering Cam's emphasis on service, he walked over and shouldered a hundred-pound bag. He made it only to the railroad track where the steel cleats on his boots caused him to slip and break his leg. The Indians put him on the next train to a hospital.

He had vowed to "come back with four Gospels in Mixtec or bust." Now he was laid up for no telling how long. Suddenly he remembered the paper on phonetics Cam had suggested he write "to demonstrate that we are really linguists." While in traction he started on the manuscript.

When he was permitted to leave the hospital, Cam brought him to Tetelcingo where he finished the 125-page manuscript which Cam mailed to Dr. Edward Sapir. When a complimentary reply came from the distinguished linguist, Cam suggested that Pike go to the University of Michigan the following summer and take the special linguistic course. At Camp Wycliffe he had seen Pike's scholarly potential. He knew that the group had to have teachers to train future translators and set the scientific pace while also providing a witness to the academic world. Pike was his trusted lieutenant and it was hard to send him off. But future advance had to take precedence over present needs.

In Tetelcingo, President Cárdenas was fulfilling all the promises he had made to the villagers. In addition a new industrial school and an elaborate farm irrigation system were built. To some of his critics who disapproved of lavishing so much aid on little Tetelcingo, Cárdenas wrote:

When there are folks like this American couple living in a village with the know-how and enthusiasm to help personally in the improvement projects, that's where the government can put forth special effort with more assurance of adequate returns on its investment.

On one of his frequent trips into the capital, Cam suggested that the Summer Institute of Linguistics [SIL] and the Mexican Institute of Linguistics cooperate in a week's seminar on Indian languages in January 1937. Dr. Silva y Aceves liked the proposal and had Cam summon the translators from their tribes.

The Mexican scholars were pleased at what the American linguists had learned in so short a time. The minister of education awarded Cam the title "Honorary Rural School Teacher of Mexico." Silva y Aceves invited Cam to teach a class on linguistics at the

National University. Cam accepted and twice a week he commuted to the university to teach the class of three students until it was time to leave for the fourth Camp Wycliffe.

Before leaving for the 1937 session, Cam went to say goodbye to the president. He found Cárdenas deeply disturbed about the petroleum industry. "The oil workers are on strike," he told Cam, "but the companies are mainly owned by U.S., British, and Dutch interests, and they refuse to submit to our courts. Gasoline is hard to get. Mexico City's bus lines are partially paralyzed. I'm trying to get the workers back to work by promising a thorough government study of the foreign-owned oil business. But the greatest problem of Mexico, as elsewhere, is the human heart."

"Christ can change the heart," Cam declared.

Cárdenas raised his eyebrows. "What about your religious capitalists in the United States who exploit the poor?"

"We must distinguish between a hypocritical profession and a true faith that changes the heart," Cam pleaded. "Look at Christ as your example. He 'being rich, became poor that we through his poverty might be made rich.' "

Cárdenas seemed moved. "Perhaps my government can cooperate with the evangelical missionaries if they are willing to help people in practical ways as your group is doing."

Cam had been disappointed by the attitude of some missionaries, but he felt confident that the majority would help the government if they knew the president felt this way.

"When I return in the fall I will get them together," Cam promised. "I'm sure, *Señor Presidente*, they will join hands."

This summer classes were held at the wooded Baptist Assembly grounds near Siloam Springs. Two of the fifteen newcomers were Otis and Mary Leal, who had been recruited by L. L. Legters. Otis was a recent graduate of Westminster Theological Seminary.

The students were not sure how they should address Cam. *Doña*, the Spanish equivalent for "Madam," was used for Elvira. Legters was always "Mr." or "Reverend." But Cam was not ordained and looked too young to be called "Mr." When she was introduced to him, Mary Leal had asked, "Are you the son of the famous missionary?" When the question of address was put to Cam, he chuckled and said, "Well, my nieces Evelyn and Ethel Mae called me 'uncle' in Mexico." And so he became "Uncle Cam."

Gene Nida, who had had to return to the States because of

illness, had recovered sufficiently to teach morphology—the study of form and structure of a language. Pike taught phonetics part of the summer. He had spent time with Dr. Sapir to discuss the Mixtec puzzle of tone. The only difference in many words was a higher or lower pitch on a syllable. Sapir thought that pitch, or tone, in language was centered in "relationships, and that the pitch of each word should be compared with the pitch of others." This idea helped Pike develop a formula for analyzing tone languages that made linguistic history. Through Sapir, Pike met University of Michigan linguist Charles Fries, who arranged a scholarship for Pike's study the following summer.

Support was low for the group even with the small salaries coming from the Mexican government. Attacks by critics may have caused some prospective donors to close their purses. There were frequent editorials in U.S. newspapers lambasting the Mexican president for following a "socialistic" policy, and Cam found himself criticized when he tried to defend Cárdenas and his programs.

However, their friends from Sulphur Springs continued to help. The biggest boost came from newly married Amos Baker who stopped, learned of the need, and promised Cam, "I'll borrow money to keep your new kids from going hungry in Mexico."

Returning to Mexico City, the SIL linguists held their annual business conference, then dispersed to their tribes. Remembering the president's desire to work with the evangelical missionaries, Cam and Elvira stayed on in the capital to try to foster some co-operation. Cam drafted a letter which Cárdenas approved:

Missionaries of Mexico:
You missionaries will be surprised to receive this letter, because some of you do not even know me and I, in turn, am but poorly acquainted with the work you are doing. Nevertheless, I am not unacquainted with the religious, social, economic and even political problems of this great nation, for I have made a careful study of them during the past four years. I must confess that I have fallen in love with the country and her aspirations and am doing my bit to help in the crusade of reform headed up by President Cárdenas. . . .
It seems to me that the movement needs now more than anything else a spiritual force which can bring about a rapid regeneration of men. . . . Apart from the personal example of the President himself, which is indeed exercising a tremendous moralizing influence, there is little in the revolutionary movement which serves to develop

in the people a spirit of self-sacrifice, absolute honesty, and an ability
for cooperating with one another in a democratic fashion. . . .

To this end I invite you to attend or to be represented at a meeting for an exchange of impressions which will be held at . . . [the
Bible Society office], January 3rd, at 10 o'clock in the morning.

I should make it plain from the beginning that I shall not be able
to serve you in this matter further than to help get the project
started and to present it to the President, since my linguistic work
and writing would prevent it.

In these moments of such great importance in the history of
Mexico we evangelical believers should remember what the Bible
says: "Pure religion and undefiled before God and the Father is this,
to visit the fatherless and widows in their affliction, and to keep himself unspotted from the world."

Affectionately your fellow believer,
(signed) W. C. Townsend

On a separate page Cam presented his "Suggestions for an
Evangelical Project." These included such things as a center to help
drug addicts, alcoholics, and prostitutes; bringing in experts in irrigation, reforestation, small industries, etc.; opening clinics and cen-
ters for Bible teaching; the sale of some mission buildings to the
government and the investment of at least half the sale price in
some social service; teaching peasants principles of practical morality
and citizenship, with help from the Bible.

Only a few of the missionaries then in Mexico turned up at the
meeting. The Presbyterians showed some interest, but most of the
independents saw little possibility of working with the government.

Not having been involved in issues that were then dividing U.S.
Protestants, Cam could not understand why so many missionaries
felt as they did. The Stateside controversy over the "social gospel"
had made some feel that spiritual work should not include social
service. The traditional separation of church and state in the U.S.
made others unwilling to cooperate with the government. A third
factor was separatism. Many felt that accepting help and/or cooperating with the Cárdenas regime would mean compromise and
dilution of the gospel.

By coming to the field as a green college student, Cam had missed
being influenced by the ecclesiastical and theological controversies
of the times. With a mindset shaped primarily by the Bible, he
had no qualms about stepping across social and political boundaries
to accomplish the goal of Bible translation.

*"I'm willing to go to Washington and New York
and plead Mexico's case."*

14. "Good Neighbor" Policies

Early in February 1938 President and Mrs. Cárdenas joined the
Townsends for lunch in Tetelcingo. Elvira had fixed a simple but
delicious meal and had served it in her gracious style. After the
meal the men carried folding chairs to the shade behind the trailer
and talked about Mexico's problems with the foreign oil companies.

"The companies are getting more belligerent each day and the
workers who returned to their jobs at my request are getting rest-
less," Cárdenas told Cam.

Cam nodded his sympathy. He recognized the workers' plight:
low pay, rampant disease in some oil fields, and lack of safety pre-
cautions, while the oil companies kept extracting high profits from
the nation's soil. He knew that the foreign companies had obtained
most of their leases during the prerevolutionary Díaz regime, when
outside interests were buying their way in through bribes.

"If I could only reach the stockholders of these companies," Cárdenas sighed, "instead of their high-salaried agents who refuse to
concede the justice of our demands. But I can't. If the companies
keep up their defiance, Mexico will have to meet the issue squarely."

After awhile Cam turned the conversation to the Bible. He tried
to explain how prayer could help with burdens of life.

Cárdenas listened with interest. Then he promised to let the
Bible and other books of high moral value come into the country
free of duty.

He gave a fountain pen inscribed with his name in gold letters
to Cam. "With this I have signed my documents and decrees for
the past three-and-a-half years. More land has been given to peasants
with it than any pen in Mexican history. I want you to have it."

Cam was deeply moved. "I will treasure it as a gift from a dear
friend and a great man," he said.

After President and Mrs. Cárdenas left, Cam used the pen to write his friend a letter in which he reviewed "some of the qualities of the best Friend I have."

He also was a Ruler, but the most powerful one there could possibly be. He loved His subjects greatly but they, due to their rebellious-ness, did not wish to take advantage of His love. Not finding any other way to release them from the dreadful situation into which their rebelliousness had dragged them, He disguised Himself and lived among them as a poor carpenter. He was so poor that He had not where to lay His head. . . . He gave assistance to as many people as asked for His aid. He never denied help to anyone. His patience was inexhaustible toward all types of people except the hypocritical religious leaders whom He called a "generation of vipers." . . .

In the long essay letter Cam movingly summarized the character and life of Christ, climaxing with His death, resurrection, and presence with believers. Then he added a short personal testimony:

Mr. President, is it any wonder that I have dedicated my life . . . to such a Friend? At least I can assure you in the most categorical way that in Him I have found everlasting joy and peace, because He has the faculty of imparting His own abundant and eternal life to His followers . . . *

Two weeks later the Mexican Supreme Court ruled in favor of the workers and against the oil companies. When the companies refused to obey the court, the workers pressed Cárdenas for action. He responded by expropriating seventeen companies, declaring that the nation's economy could not stand a strike. Cárdenas pledged to pay back the money invested, but the companies demanded 400 million dollars on the basis of expected future earnings.

The impasse deepened the crisis. The companies called for "gun-boat diplomacy." Terribly concerned, Cam prayed to be shown how he might help improve relations. He wanted to show Cárdenas that there were Americans who cared for Mexico. An idea came: Why not a corps of American young people to help with Mexican social projects. They could both demonstrate fraternal friendship and take

---

* Ethel E. Wallis and Mary A. Bennett, *Two Thousand Tongues to Go* (New York: Harper & Bros., 1959) pp. 85–86. Used by permission.

back home a true picture of Mexico. It was similar to the idea that two senators would suggest to presidential candidate John F. Kennedy twenty-two years later which led to the Peace Corps. But there was one key difference. Cam's "Inter-American Brigade" would be paid small salaries by Mexico.

When he presented the proposal to Cárdenas, the president liked it. Cárdenas was also agreeable to a discussion with the oil companies on indemnification. Cam offered to go to Washington and New York and plead Mexico's case, and at the same time recruit some young people for the social projects.

Cárdenas expressed his appreciation, adding only one stipulation. "You must allow my government to buy you a new car. I don't want your sick wife riding in a bus."

Cam thanked the president and accepted a $1,000 check. Then he went to the American Embassy and discussed the trip with Josephus Daniels. The ambassador wrote a letter of introduction to President Roosevelt's appointment secretary, and Cam and Elvira left immediately for Arkansas where they purchased a new Chevrolet. Elvira remained with the Basts in Sulphur Springs, while Cam drove on to Washington.

Unable to see Roosevelt, he went to Standard Oil headquarters in New York. John D. Rockefeller, Jr., was too busy, but a company executive saw him and promised to discuss the "possibility" of a settlement with his superiors. Cam waited and the response was that the company intended to continue fighting to get the properties back.

Cam refused to quit: He presented Mexico's side of the controversy at clubs and to any group of educators and businessmen who would listen. He stressed that the Mexican government was willing to pay a reasonable price and that even poor people had donated jewelry, chickens, cabbages, and other sacrifices to a fund for payment. But he got nowhere.

Calls at the New York offices of two large Protestant mission societies were equally discouraging. After hearing Cam tell about Camp Wycliffe and the challenge of the tribes, both responded in effect: "We already have more than we can handle."

A record enrollment of thirty students at the 1938 Camp Wycliffe was heartening. Seven of the group were volunteers for the Inter-American Brigade. Elvira gave them special lessons in Spanish and Latin American culture. Her lectures were later printed in a helpful book called *Latin American Courtesy* and distributed to all members of the Summer Institute of Linguistics (SIL) before they went to Latin America.

Pike and Nida were mainstays on the faculty. Pike had already completed initial study for his doctorate at the University of Michigan and Nida was planning graduate work also. Near the close of the session, Pike and Evelyn Griset, Cam's niece, delighted everyone by announcing their engagement.

Cam had stayed tuned in to the continuing diplomatic tug-of-war between the U.S. and Mexico over payment of the oil claims. When the U.S. State Department pressed for payment of an old ten-million-dollar indebtedness while the oil companies pushed a boycott of Mexican petroleum products, Cam fired off a telegram of protest to Secretary of State Cordell Hull.

WHY PLAGUE MEXICO ABOUT A SMALL DEBT WHEN EUROPE OWES US SO MUCH? THE FRIENDSHIP OF LATIN AMERICA IS WORTH MORE THAN TEN MILLION DOLLARS. JAPAN, GERMANY, OR ITALY WOULD GIVE MORE THAN THAT FOR IT. FURTHERMORE THE AMERICAN PEOPLE ARE NOT SHYLOCKS TO EXACT THE LIFE BLOOD OF MEXICO'S UNDERNOURISHED MASSES. LET THEM PAY WHEN THEY GET THEIR BREAD AND BUTTER PROBLEMS SOLVED. I PROPOSE THAT A COMMITTEE OF CITIZENS BE ORGANIZED TO DISCUSS DIRECT WITH COMMITTEE OF MEXICAN CITIZENS ALL OUR PENDING PROBLEMS.

Secretary Hull merely acknowledged the message.

By the time camp ended Cam was tired and drained emotionally from his frustrating efforts to help Americans better understand Mexico. Those around him sensed that the big-stick diplomacy was driving him to closer identification with Mexico.

When they crossed the border back into Mexico his spirits seemed to lift. There were now thirty-two in the Mexico SIL group, plus the seven Brigaders Cam had recruited. The first linguist had been sent to the southernmost state of Chiapas which had an 80 percent Indian population.

The expansion was gratifying to Cam, but it meant more work for him as the director. He chose to delegate responsibilities. The experienced Max Lathrop helped the new linguists get outfitted for primitive living. Pike and Nida advised on linguistic problems.

Cam's expertise was in government relations. He usually took any linguist who happened to be in the capital with him on calls. This trained the linguist in the fine art of diplomacy, and gave Cam the opportunity to use the linguist as Exhibit A of the work. Cam usually carried along some practical result from the work: a primer, a vowel chart, or an article on some Indian language.

While feeling ran high against the foreign oil companies and their allies, SIL continued to be well received. The National University invited them to participate again in the annual "Linguistic Week," the highlight of which turned out to be a banquet given in honor of SIL.

All this took time away from tribal work. When some of the linguists grumbled, Cam reminded them that good relations with officials and educators was making it possible for them to translate the Bible. "If some of you are getting impatient over slow progress," he wrote in a circular letter, "remember Noah and his 120-year foolish task, or David's extra wait of seven-and-a-half years after the death of Saul."

Cam himself continued efforts to build understanding between the U.S. and Mexico. When he heard that Cárdenas was planning a trip to Baja, California, he suggested a "Good Neighbors" picnic near the border. Cárdenas thought this a grand idea and reserved an old hotel building near Tijuana for July 7, 1939.

Cam hurried to Santa Ana and presented invitations to friends and relatives around southern California. He asked Will Nyman to coordinate transportation from Los Angeles. About two hundred American guests came and everyone ate at long tables spread along the patio. As master of ceremonies Cam read 1 Corinthians 13, the "Love Chapter," and thanked President Cárdenas for help given to SIL. Then he asked parents who had sons or daughters serving among Mexico's Indian tribes to stand so the president might know who they were. All stood, except Cam's father who had not heard the request. Will was now very feeble, but had gotten out of his sick bed, eager not to miss the occasion. Cam asked his sisters to have him stand. Will stood as tall and straight as he possibly could. President Cárdenas took one look at the determined eighty-four-year-old man and stood to his feet in tribute, thanking "the man who has given his son to serve Mexican peasants."

Europe was heating up for a major conflagration when the 1939 Camp Wycliffe met at Siloam Springs. The Townsends, Nida,

Lathrop, and Legters served as faculty. Ken Pike arrived late from his study at the University of Michigan.

Acting on a suggestion from Brainerd Legters, Cam asked Dr. Eric North, General Secretary of the American Bible Society, if the A.B.S. wished to take over the training school as its "official center for training Bible translators. It has grown so and the prospects are for much more growth. Some of us wonder if a larger and more experienced organization shouldn't run it," he wrote. "There is no dissatisfaction with the Pioneer Mission Agency [which was continuing to channel support funds] whatever, but all concerned merely want the best plan possible to hasten the giving of the Word to all the tribes of the earth."

North declined, but sent a small gift from the Society for operating expense.

Legters ran on at full steam during his two weeks at camp. On the Camp Day of Prayer Cam asked, "Couldn't you give us more time next year, Mr. Legters?" The old warrior looked wistfully at him and replied, "I'd like to, Cameron, but the Lord hasn't given me liberty to take any appointments beyond next May. I don't know why. Maybe He's going to promote me to Glory by then."

After camp the Townsends went to stay with friends near Brownsville, Texas, while Cam completed a booklet on the oil controversy. The eighty-five-page *Truth About Mexico's Oil* was published the next year by an Inter-American Committee which Cam set up, and copies were sent to all members of Congress.

After emphasizing Mexico's willingness to pay a fair settlement, he asked, "When are we going to pay for that land grab (2/5ths of all Mexican territory) of 1848?" He wished that "American citizens *en masse* would serve notice on American companies abroad that henceforth and forever they will have to use their brains to get out of their difficulties and not expect a single gunboat . . . or diplomat to pull their chestnuts out of the fire." He pleaded for the legislators to resume silver purchases, cut off by Secretary of Treasury Morgenthau, and stop trying to "starve Mexico into submission." Then he proposed in a letter to President Roosevelt, included in the book, that a high level "Good Neighbors' Committee" be formed by U.S. and Mexican citizens to find friendly solutions to their problems.

On Christmas Eve Cam received a telegram from his sisters telling of his father's death from kidney failure. He didn't have the funds to attend the funeral so he wrote a eulogy praising his father for

His faithfulness in pointing me to God and His Word.
His habit of telling the truth at all costs.
His practice of resting on the Lord's Day.
His advice to do something until it becomes second
  nature.
His principle of delegating responsibility.
His courage in espousing the cause that he felt was
  right whether there was any chance for it to win
  or not.
I am truly grateful that Will Townsend was my father.

The following May the SIL group was having the annual business meeting in Mexico City when the news came of L. L. Legters's fatal heart attack. Less than two months later his wife Edna died. Cam had lost another pair of dependable helpers.

15. Wycliffe Bible Translators

It was Cam's idea to give a banquet in Mexico City to celebrate five years of service to Mexico's Indians in cooperation with the Ministry of Education and the National University. Among the guests were Ambassador Daniels, the ambassador from Guatemala, and two Mexican cabinet officers, but a poised young woman doctor stole the show.

Elena Trejo told of her struggles to get an education from the time she had been brought to the Townsends in San Antonio, Guatemala, as an illiterate Indian girl. "All that I am I owe to God and to my spiritual parents, Mr. and Mrs. Cameron Townsend."

After the banquet, Cam presented "Fifth Anniversary" Spanish New Testaments to various officials. With the name of each recipient stamped in gold, the Testaments were eagerly received in places where only a few years before employees had been under pressure to deny their religious faith.

The group was becoming well known and respected among Mexican educators for their work among the Indians. Cam made it a point to remember numerous Mexican friends at important milestones in their lives. He might attend a wedding or a funeral, or if someone was gravely ill hurry to his bedside.

For example, when he heard that Silva y Aceves was afflicted with cancer, he and Pike went and read Scripture with him. Later Cam returned to find him sinking fast and his nun sister at his bedside. She listened attentively as Cam quoted Scripture. Then after Cam led in prayer, the nun followed him outside the room where she threw her arms around his neck and sobbed her thanks for "giving us the Word of God."

He also kept trying to be of service to President Cárdenas. While the oil dispute simmered, he continued writing letters to help Americans "understand Mexico's side." When the conflict was finally settled by a joint Mexican–U.S. commission that awarded the companies payment for their investment only, both he and Cárdenas felt relations would improve between their respective countries.

On one visit with Cárdenas, Cam dreamed with the president about a united hemisphere. Deeply moved by the thought of what a closer relationship could mean, Cam took pen and wrote a "Hymn of the New America," which he dedicated to Cárdenas. A sampling of stanzas reads:

> We sing to one America,
> United Hemisphere,
> Blest harmony of nations!
> The world our song must hear.
>
> Nor Latin, now, nor Saxon,
> We'll one another call;
> Henceforth we're one America,
> With equal love for all!

In Guatemala and now in Mexico Cam had noticed that some missionaries identified constantly with the American community— too closely, he thought. Cam himself spent his energies cultivating Mexican friends, with the primary exception of Ambassador Daniels. The two genuinely liked each other and Daniels privately agreed with Cam on many policies.

While Cam was grateful for opportunities for friendships with the president and other high officials, criticism arose among his associates over "secular involvements." He was charged with "not doing Christian work." One translator even resigned from SIL and left Mexico so he could "evangelize."

Cam was further criticized for his policy toward church work. He had encouraged the linguists to attend evangelical churches when in the capital, but he cautioned against passing out "doctrinal" tracts. They should stick to translation, avoid sectarian involvements, and witness only on a personal level to friends.

When the criticism persisted, Cam spelled out his position in a crucial policy letter to all SIL members.

It seems to me there are three policies which might be followed by Christian workers in Mexico. The first is frank cooperation with

and commendation of the government projects which we can heartily endorse while carefully abstaining from anything that could be
considered as opposition. The second is strict neutrality concerning
government policies, neither commending nor criticizing them. The
third is opposition, either actively . . . or only verbally as is involved in open censorship. Those few of our number who cannot
follow the first should . . . consistently follow the second to avoid
getting us into trouble, and that is what I am now pleading with
them to do—just to be consistently neutral. Let us realize that
censorship may become deadly opposition and if we cannot com-
mend, let us be careful not to oppose.

We are in Mexico to serve and not to dictate policies to the government. If it wants to teach the children of Mexico to share with
one another as sincere socialists should, that is Mexico's lookout and
not ours. We should be more anxious than ever to give the Word of
God to the people, for it is the best preparation in the world for
sharing. If you and I lived in Russia we would find that the life and
love of God in our hearts would be ample preparation for living
under that regime and it would be less exacting than the Sermon on
the Mount. If they would let me teach the Bible in Russia, I would
gladly abstain from censorship of their policies that I did not like.
After all who called us to pass judgment upon rulers? Are we not
commanded to obey and pray for them? Let us be consistent. If
anyone feels obliged to hold himself aloof from government as regards cooperation, let him also hold himself aloof as regards criticism.
. . . There is too much at stake for this [criticism] to continue.
Twenty million Indians in Latin America wait to see the spirit of
the Gospel demonstrated in a way they can comprehend and to read
the Word in a language they can understand. Our linguistic group
must make both the demonstration and the translations. Is there
any other way we can do it than by patiently following by faith the
humble path of cooperation in which God has blessed us signally
thus far?

He was more blunt in a second letter:

I don't blame you for getting a wrong slant on things, for you
have more contact with the American colony, which is generally
very alarmist in its views, than you do with the Mexican element
that is responsible for the laws, and furthermore, many of you read
the _____ [an antigovernment newspaper], and that
is like trying to get a fair view of Martin Luther from reading
histories compiled by Jesuit fathers.

However, I find it absolutely necessary to point out to the ones who went off half-cocked in their criticism . . . that it was very unbecoming of us who have received so many courtesies from the government of Mexico. . . . Will you not respond to this in the right spirit, recognize your mistake and look up with a new faith and trust in the One who is going to visit Mexico with a great spiritual awakening if we but continue faithful.

Most of the SILers went along with a minimum of grumbling. But Max Lathrop and Brainerd Legters argued loudly against the director's "nonsectarian policies." Cam convinced Lathrop, but young Legters finally resigned in favor of general missionary work.

With increased responsibilities as SIL director, Cam began spending less time in Tetelcingo. There were now thirty-seven translators (including five pairs of single girls) in eighteen tribes. He was particularly frustrated over spending so little time in translation himself. *Don* Martín, the former mayor of Tetelcingo, was now pastor of a congregation of sixty, and longed for the New Testament in Aztec. When Dick Pittman, a young teacher from Wheaton College, and his wife Kay offered to serve wherever needed, Cam gratefully assigned them to Tetelcingo. They moved into a little house near the orange grove and began language study.

With the Pittmans in Tetelcingo and Pike willing to help in "diplomatic emergencies," Cam and Elvira felt free to accompany Dr. Elena Trejo to Guatemala. They longed to revisit the beautiful land of their first missionary endeavors, and this seemed the ideal opportunity.

While in Guatemala Cam had the opportunity to talk with President Jorge Ubico who was still in power. The president expressed opposition to anything that would accentuate or perpetuate existing distinctions between Indian tribes and the rest of the population. Cam interpreted this to mean that he would be displeased with publications in the Indian languages which did not have parallel columns or pages in Spanish.

Cam returned from Guatemala with a renewed conviction of the need for a corps of workers large enough to handle the entire task of working on the Indian languages. The neglect of the Cakchiquel New Testament by other missionaries indicated to him that linguistic needs were being overlooked.

At the business conference of SIL in Mexico City in 1941, how-

ever, pesos were so slim that they voted on whether to have coffee
in the morning or the afternoon. Financial support had always been
borderline, but with the death of Legters, their number-one fund-
raiser, some workers began suffering real hardship. Cam encouraged
them to continue "in the same heroic spirit . . . remembering that
Paul himself was not unacquainted with want." He suggested that
"we all try to interest our own friends more vitally in Bible translation by frequently writing them interesting details."

There were encouragements though. Will Nyman, the California
businessman who had given hospitality to SIL's first students, came
to Mexico and was overwhelmed. Although he had a heart condition, Nyman eagerly volunteered to take over the mailing of the
circular letters to home supporters. And by time for Camp Wycliffe
to begin, the rough draft of the Mazatec New Testament—a first
in the history of Mexico's Indians—had been completed by Eunice
Pike and Florence Hansen.

While the new recruits were settling in their tribes in the fall of
1941, Cam mulled over a request by an official to send workers to
the Lacandons, a tribe of only two hundred in the rain forest of
Chiapas who were considered the bottom of the cultural barrel.
Another official had mentioned the Seris, a smaller band of Indians
living along the Pacific coastline of Sonora.

Pike's Mixtecs numbered 200,000 and the various dialects of
Aztecs included two or three times that many. But did tribes of 100
and 200 merit the life work of educated linguists? Cam thought
again about Jesus' parable of the shepherd who sought out the one
lost sheep. Yes, the small tribes also needed the Word, he decided.
But would there be volunteers for them?

In October, Cam and Elvira were with the Lathrops on the shore
of Lake Patzcuaro. Cam rose early for devotions and sat watching
some Tarascans throwing their fish nets. The scene reminded him
of Jesus watching other fishermen at Galilee and saying, "Follow
me, and I will make you fishers of men." He took out pencil and
paper and began writing to the now forty-four workers under his
leadership: "Will each of you be responsible before the Lord for
one new recruit for Bible translation? . . . I'm sure He would give
us six extra for good measure."

Fifty new workers would more than double the force. But where
would the training school be held to accommodate so many? Where
would they get the supporting funds? Cam prayed long and hard.

Back in Tetelcingo he and Elvira met a new friend, A. M. Johnson. He had heard about the work and was curious. The Townsends welcomed "Uncle Al" into their home. Cam devoted the morning to telling him the history of their work and filling him in on future plans. They learned that Al Johnson was a widower who had retired from his post as president and board chairman of the National Life Insurance Company. "Guess the most interesting thing I ever did was to build a Moorish castle in Death Valley, California," he told them. "Built it for an old prospector friend of mine named Scotty who once saved my life when I was sick. But if you folks ever get up that way, I'd be pleased to have you stay there awhile. Or in my Hollywood home if that's more convenient."

When Uncle Al left it was with the promise, "You'll be hearing from me."

When the Pioneer Mission Agency in Philadelphia heard of Cam's call for fifty new recruits they wrote, "We can't handle double your number. You should organize your own office." The letter made it clear the decision was final, so Cam wrote three key friends about the possibility of opening an office for SIL.

All three quickly responded. Dr. Stephen Slocum, father of a Wycliffe member, estimated an office would cost $15,000 the first year—"money we don't have." Will Nyman said, "Sounds like a big assignment. If I can help, let me know." And Clarence Erickson, pastor of the Gospel Tabernacle in Chicago, asked, "What do you have in mind?" He invited Cam to speak at a missionary rally in his church and sent a $200 advance for expenses and honorarium. The money was a godsend, since the Townsends were almost penniless at the time.

Shortly after Pearl Harbor Cam and Elvira drove to California to discuss with Nyman a home organization. At the same time they decided to accept the invitation of the Board of Regents of the University of Oklahoma to hold their summer training sessions there, with full academic credit. The invitation had come through Della Brunstetter, a language teacher at the university, who had attended Camp Wycliffe to help her in her study of Cherokee. The university had long been a center of study for American Indian cultures. Definite plans for an office were left until next summer, to go over with Nida and Pike at Norman, Oklahoma.

After presenting a recruiting program at the Bible Institute of Los Angeles, Cam fulfilled the assignment to speak in Chicago, then went on to Philadelphia to arrange for the transfer of SIL records and files from the Pioneer Mission Agency office.

While in Philadelphia he received an invitation to visit a New York farmer who had read of the request for fifty new recruits. He took a bus to see the farmer and was given $250. This paid the first month's rent on an additional office in Mexico City, for they had long since outgrown the space shared with the American Bible Society secretary. Then he and Elvira started off again in *"Don Lázaro,"* the '38 Chevrolet given by Cárdenas, with a load of linguists for Norman.

There, Nyman, Pike, Nida, and Cam met in a motel to chart the future. They took the 1936 Mexico SIL constitution as a guide. "We don't want a U.S. board telling the field workers what to do," Cam insisted. "Direction must come from the field."

All felt that the name Summer Institute of Linguistics would not carry a Bible translation image to Christians in the States. "Why not have two organizations, then?" Cam suggested. "SIL can handle our training and contracts with foreign governments and universities. The Bible translation organization can do what the Pioneer Mission Agency did—receive funds and publicize the field work." After considerable discussion they agreed on this plan. Adopting a suggestion from Eunice Pike, passed along by her brother, they called the new organization Wycliffe Bible Translators.

The twin organizations would have interlocking directorates, and in most cases the same officers. Cam was elected general director. Nyman, who agreed to manage the home office, was to be the first secretary-treasurer. Pike was given the responsibility for academic affairs, with Nida as his associate.

The constitution for Wycliffe Bible Translators (WBT) had one unique feature. All monies received would be allotted directly to members who would assign back a tenth for the administration of field and home offices. As under the old SIL constitution, the general director would be elected by the board every four years. He would be responsible for "maintenance and expansion into new fields" and opportunities for expansion, subject to limitation by the board. Board members' terms would be staggered with some being elected by the member-linguists in business conference each year.

They adopted intact the doctrinal statement of the China Inland Mission which Cam had long admired. It included belief in the divine inspiration of the Bible, the Trinity, the fall of man, the atonement of Christ, justification by faith, the resurrection of the body, eternal life of the saved and eternal punishment of the lost.

The purposes of Wycliffe Bible Translators should center on "putting the Word of God into all the tribal tongues of earth in which it does not yet exist." This included assisting evangelical missionaries to get special linguistic training and other aids in Bible translation.

With their ideas on paper and agreed upon, Nyman looked squarely at his colleagues. "My health isn't good, as you know. I don't know how many more years the Lord will allow me. But I believe the Lord is in this thing. We'll have trials, but we can weather them with His help and if we stick together. I propose that we four covenant to stick together a minimum of five years. Then if one of us wants out, he's free to go."

All agreed.

Nyman returned to California to have the legal documents filed for incorporation. Cam and Elvira stayed on for the training institute, now called Summer Institute of Linguistics as well as Camp Wycliffe. Cam watched with great satisfaction as Pike, Nida, and six other linguistic veterans kept the 130 students interested and learning. However, the founder himself presented the greatest challenge in his chapel messages. His quiet, folksy stories made the young listeners want to pioneer in Bibleless tribes at whatever cost or sacrifice it might require.

By the end of 1942 Cam had his fifty new volunteers for Bible translation, plus one more for good measure.

"If I have been devoted to my Lord's service in the past, by His grace my devotion shall be a passion from now on."

16. Tears Do Not a Vision Dim

SIL '42 was challenging and exciting, but the war news was grim. Axis forces were sweeping across North Africa. Around U.S. shores German submarines were torpedoing Allied ships. In the Pacific Japan had reached the Aleutians and New Guinea. But Cam was dreaming advance.

"Who will open Tibet, or claim the last acre of the Amazon, the hills of central India, the jungles of Borneo, the steppes of Siberia—the merchant or the missionary?" he asked the SILers. "When the war is over, let us take up the Sword of the Spirit and march."

But it was not enough to dream. There were mundane things to do. There was the Wycliffe office to be set up in the apartment over Nyman's garage. Nyman took no salary and donated the space. The only paid employee was a secretary, and since they bought a minimum of supplies, the cost of running the office was only $150 a month at the beginning.

While Cam and Elvira were there helping, Nyman mentioned that only $105 was lacking for the field workers to receive 100 percent allowance during the current month. Cam raised his eyebrows questioningly at Elvira. They had $105 set apart for a refrigerator. She nodded and Cam said, "We'll give what's lacking."

That same day the Townsends received three separate gifts totaling exactly $105. Later, on the way back to Mexico City, a motel owner in New Mexico presented them with a check for $200 instead of a bill.

Back in Mexico, Cam greeted Dawson Trotman, the founder of the Navigators, who had come down for the annual business conference. "Win a convert and train him to reproduce spiritually" was the motto of Trotman and his Navigators. Trotman was captivated by Cam's dream. "The burden of reaching whole tribes who had never had a single sentence from the Word of God translated into their own tongue gripped me," he wrote to his servicemen who were serving on over a hundred ships. Before leaving, he assured Cam that he would recommend Wycliffe to Navigators seeking further opportunities of service.

About this time a new problem arose among the WBT/SIL members. It dated back to the last summer's training school when Cam had stirred criticism from the independent fundamentalists by inviting a member of the Presbyterian (U.S.A.) Board to study, and had invited a woman with "Pentecostal leanings" to speak in chapel. The Pioneer Mission Agency, which had continued to funnel some funds to WBT/SIL, threatened to cut off support. Also, questions had been raised about students and some new translators who did not adhere to the doctrine of eternal security generally held by old members.

The founders of Wycliffe had discussed the question of admitting Pentecostals, and others who believed healing was provided in the atonement, to the summer school. Nida, Pike, and Nyman wanted to exclude those holding "doctrinal differences." Cam wanted them in, if, as he said, "the differences are in nonessential matters." They had tabled the issue, with the serious division of opinion remaining.

On February 23, 1943, Cam summed up his reasons to Nyman in a key letter. WBT/SIL was not dedicated to propagating any system of theology or to extending existing denominations, but to give the Bibles to tribes that did not have it. Members should be as careful about "matters of purity, love, mercy and humble service" as about nonbasic doctrines.

We can't take ourselves as a standard, nor the organizations from which we come. Let's stick to the Bible as our gauge—no broader and no narrower—as exclusive but with a love that is inclusive. What we know, or think we know, about that Book and the way we live it should not be the mold we pass on to the world, but rather the Book itself.

In the scientific world we are supposed to accept facts even though they go against our theories, but in spiritual things we tend to discount all the virtues a man has . . . if we hear that his connections are under ostracism. Four of our new workers came out under such a cloud last summer. All four have fitted in beautifully.

He then suggested that the accepting of candidates be left to the staff at the summer sessions, who would know the students from their studies at SIL, rather than being submitted to the directors.

He stressed again that they were doing something new and departing from old methods. Looking to the future he saw Wycliffe with a thousand members in all parts of the world "serving evangelical missionary organizations which have all kinds of doctrinal peculiarities. The more we can serve them, the more accurate and efficient their work will be. Let's not limit our sphere of service by officially condemning their pet theories."

In a follow-up letter, Cam suggested to Nyman the distribution of responsibilities in the Wycliffe work:

You should have complete charge of business matters, Nida of public relations in the States as regards Boards and schools, Pike as regards scientific connections, and I of advances on the field. We can each be like generals in our particular field, the Board will be like Congress and the missionaries like soldiers with voting power that gives them ultimate control.

. . . You need sub-councils in different parts of the country composed of men whose hearts God has touched to the point where they have already rolled up their sleeves and gone to work for us. When God, Himself, has chosen the men, we can trust them with jobs. We don't need to be afraid of their lack of reputation or even that they aren't accepted in the inner circle of certain doctrinal groups. . . . Here in Mexico we've seen God work through men we would have thought to be most unlikely. Let's never try to cramp the Lord by setting up our judgment as over against His.

Then Cam outlined the "distinctive features" of Wycliffe work as he saw them:

1. We specialize on giving the Scriptures to tribes without them.
2. We pioneer, going preferably to closed fields.
3. We cooperate with missions, governments, scientific organizations, philanthropic organizations, always cooperate and serve, never compete.
4. We follow the linguistic approach.
5. We dare to follow even when God leads along strange paths.
6. We are not sectarian or ecclesiastical, not even dogmatic. We don't try to force people into any type of denominational or anti-denominational mold.
7. We look to God to raise up the men and means and to open the doors.

8. We should use all the aids of science, including radio, airplanes, etc., when going to jungle tribes.
9. We expect to finish the task in this generation.

Throughout the war years, WBT/SIL kept expanding. A branch SIL summer school was started at Briercrest Bible School in Canada. An official bulletin-magazine called *Translation* was started with Max Lathrop as editor. Membership and finances steadily increased.

Cam wanted evangelical pastors to understand what they were doing and to get behind the work. At Muskogee, Oklahoma, Dr. W. A. Criswell, pastor of the First Baptist Church, invited Cam and some of the linguists to present a program. Afterwards Criswell commented, "I'm impressed. I'd like to help you."

Oswald Smith, the fiery pastor of the missionary-minded Peoples' Church in Toronto, Canada, was more encouraging. When he visited Mexico he told Cam, "You folks are on our wavelength. The world can't be evangelized until every tribe has the Bible in its own tongue. My church will be with you 100 percent." Peoples' Church was soon supporting almost a score of Wycliffe linguists.

With Cam's approval, Pike had joined the faculty part-time at the University of Michigan. He had also written a text on phonetics and had helped Dr. Charles Fries prepare textbooks for teaching English to foreign students at the university. Pike fretted at being away from his tribe, but Cam felt that in the long run he would be of more value "helping us get recognition in the linguistic world."

In 1943 Pike was in Mexico when the American Bible Society asked him to make a trip to Peru, Bolivia, and Ecuador to assist missionary translators with linguistic problems in the Quechua language. Cam was enthusiastic about the invitation. Pike wasn't so certain. "I don't know if we're ready for such an undertaking." Cam reminded him of the vision he had had of reaching the forgotten tribes of South America. Finally Pike agreed, saying, "I'm a little frightened at the magnitude of the project, but this could be the hand of God, so I am willing."

Upon reaching Lima, Pike called on the minister of education, Enrique de La Rosa, and gave him his book *Phonetics*. Impressed, La Rosa asked about SIL's work in Mexico. When Pike told him about the linguistic study, practical service projects and Bible translation, the high official said, "Why not do that for our Indians in the Amazon jungle?"

"We haven't been invited," Pike replied.

The minister talked briefly to an assistant, then said, "You're invited. Come back tomorrow and we'll have it official and in writing." When Pike returned he was pleasantly surprised to be "introduced" to one of his former students from the University of Michigan, now an official of the Peruvian government. Everyone seemed not only willing but anxious for SIL linguists to help the Indians of Peru.

Cam received Pike's report with elation. For twenty years he had been looking in this direction. Now it seemed to be the Lord's time for definite plans to be made to go. It also seemed to be the time to start the boot camp for translators going to the jungle that Cam had been dreaming of for so many years.

A site in the Chiapas rain forest near the Guatemalan border was recommended—as similar to Amazonia as it was possible to be in Mexico. And the Lacondon Indians there were just as primitive as some in Peru.

Cam went to Chiapas and bargained for a lease. The land owner agreed to build three huts for the first jungle camp set for the fall of 1945.

When he returned to Mexico City, several members told him something had to be done about more adequate housing. "We can't continue to live like gypsies in such overcrowded quarters." As a result, they rented an old downtown gray building called "Palacio Quetzalcoatl" that had once been a boardinghouse for tourists. Though twenty-five rooms at first seemed a lot, they were hardly enough for offices, printing facilities, and bedrooms. Furniture was sparse and many had to sleep on webbed rope beds while visitors were given cots. Still, "The Kettle"—as they affectionately called it —became a home for members who had to be in the capital.

With Mexico growing and Peru calling, Cam still found time to think of further advances. He and Elvira visited Mr. and Mrs. Turner Blount and Miss Faye Edgerton who were working on the Navajo reservation in Arizona. Although English-speaking missionaries had worked among the Navajos for years, they had had limited success, and there was little or no Scripture in Navajo. The trio had been working in the language for three years, and after attending SIL, wanted to join Wycliffe. On Cam's recommendation the board unanimously accepted the Blounts and Miss Edgerton into membership. Their acceptance was another milestone, for it marked the first work outside of Mexico.

Cam was eager to make a survey trip to Peru, but first he wanted to work on a biography of Cárdenas. Uncle Al Johnson invited him and Elvira to stay a few weeks at his Hollywood home where Cam would have solitude.

They had just gotten in bed on December 23, 1944, when Elvira started gasping, "There's no air! There's no air!" Crawling out of bed, she staggered to the window, took one deep breath and collapsed into Cam's arms. He got her back to bed and called Uncle Al to get help.

Through the night and on into the next day Cam sat by the bed, holding her hand and fearing that each breath was the last. He was only vaguely aware of relatives coming and going. After nearly twenty-four hours Elvira's breathing stopped altogether. But Cam still sat there until Uncle Al led him into another room.

At the funeral in Glendale, Dawson Trotman read a statement from Cam who was still too shattered to speak.

God gave Elvira as a love gift to the people of Latin America and to us. He used her by His power and now He has taken His handiwork to Himself. The task she served, however, remains; and we remain.

Face to face with that task, recalling our Loved One's devotion to it, recognizing the Power that works through weakness, and with greater longing than ever before to hasten the return of our Lord. "What manner of men ought we to be?"

My own answer to that question is as follows: If I have been devoted to my Lord's service in the past, by His grace my devotion shall be a passion from now on. . . . If I have permitted hardships, dangers, pleasures, and the powerful chords of human love to swerve me at times from full obedience, henceforth "none of these things shall move me," neither shall I count my life dear unto myself, so that I might finish my course with joy. . . .

This pledge is not taken lightly. It has been burned into my soul, and though the branding processes have not been easy, the pain now seems like nothing as I visualize the fruit and joy of a truly all-out effort for my Savior and the unevangelized tribes that need Him so.

The task of giving God's Word to all the peoples of the earth can be finished in this generation.

Cam had requested that, instead of flowers, Spanish New Testaments be given for distribution in Guatemala and Mexico. The Testaments were stacked around Elvira's grave. One of the few floral pieces was shaped as a large V in which were the words: "O grave, where is thy victory? Thanks be unto God which giveth us the victory through our Lord Jesus Christ."

Uncle Al paid all funeral and burial expenses and took Cam under his wing as a younger brother. Slowly Cam began to adjust and to accept the reality of his wife's passing. She had been his co-worker for a quarter of a century, handling their many social obligations with gracious hospitality in spite of her physical and emotional illness. He had seen her before at the apparent brink of death. Still, he missed her presence.

Cam was forty-eight years old. He had lost his parents and his three closest friends and supporters—the Cakchiquel Francisco, Robby Robinson, and L. L. Legters. Now his wife was gone.

Part II
WIDENING HORIZONS

"The job can be done . . . it must be done."

17. Amazonia—a New Frontier

As he had from previous heartbreaks, Cam quickly snapped back. The work was more important than his own feelings, and there was no time to feel self-pity.

He wrote Enrique de La Rosa, minister of education in Peru, accepting his invitation to work in his country. Describing the educational and social projects in Tetelcingo, he suggested that similar programs might be undertaken to help the Peruvian jungle Indians. The minister replied by return mail. "Cooperatives are of special interest to me. I will be happy to introduce you to scientific societies in Peru." But he added, "I will write you when I judge it the right time for your trip."

While he waited, Cam negotiated the purchase of the old hotel they had been renting in downtown Mexico City. And he made arrangements for leadership in Mexico, since he expected to head the advance into Peru.

Dick Pittman, Cam's successor in Tetelcingo, had functioned as director while Cam had been away during the past months. He seemed to have understood and followed Cam's policies, and had kept up contacts with the government officials. The soft-voiced, slow-speaking little American was also making good progress on the Aztec language, and this pleased the Indians as much as it impressed the Mexican officials. Cam felt that Pittman should continue to direct the Mexico corps.

John McIntosh, with the Huichol tribe, was another potential leader. He had listened to Cam on the radio in California back in the Thirties when he was still in high school. He had told Cam then that he wanted to be a translator, and Cam advised him to complete his education, then get in touch with him. He had. The determined young man had kept his eye on the goal of Bible translation until he made it. Cam felt that anyone with that kind of perseverence had possibilities, and he invited McIntosh to go with him on some of his rounds of government offices.

The young translator was pleased to be asked, but got a little fidgety waiting for Cam to get down to business. When they entered a man's office, Cam would never just tell what it was he wanted. First he would inquire about the man's family. Or he'd remember a sick child, a son in the university, or a hobby. Then he would ask McIntosh to say something in Huichol. Cam and the Mexican would talk and talk while the young American fidgeted. Finally when it seemed time to be going, Cam might say, "Oh, by the way, I have some papers that need signatures." Then he would hand them to the official. The man would do his best to cut bureaucratic red tape saying, "Happy to help you in your important service to my country's minority language groups."

Then it might take some time for Cam to get out of the building. He would stop and chat with minor officials, ask about their families, or remember someone to them. "Don't overlook anybody," he told McIntosh. "The man in charge who signed our papers was only a clerk when I first met him."

Once in a while Cam would be stopped by a traffic policeman. McIntosh noted that Cam would greet the officer as graciously as if he were the chief of police. Then he would pull out his briefcase. "Do you know we are working with Mexico's Indians?" he would ask. "I have some pictures. Would you like to see them?" Without waiting for an answer, Cam would pass a few photos of Indians and linguists to the policeman. And if the officer happened to spot a picture of Cam with some high official, it couldn't be helped. They might talk for fifteen minutes and end with the policeman gladly returning the license plate he had taken off. As they drove away from one such incident Cam said, "Never offer a bribe, John. That demeans them. Just tell them about our work."

Otis Leal was another translator Cam spent time with. When Leal returned to his Zapateco village, he told his wife Mary about the experience. "He just wouldn't accept closed doors," he recalled. "He might say, 'Let's see how God is going to solve this.' But he never doubted that God was going to work out a problem. He has an utter conviction that God wants every language group in the world reached—and that Wycliffe is His means of doing it."

The tall, good-looking Ben Elson, who had heard Cam and Gene Nida speak when he was a student in Los Angeles, also was taken around with Cam. So was George Cowan, one of the few seminary trained men, who had married Florence Hansen, one of the first two single girls. They had worked together in the Mazateco tribe. All of them found it so hard to keep Cam on a schedule that they had quit promising he would be in a certain place on a certain day. One suggested that he operated by a cloud in the morning and a pillar of fire at night.

Then in the spring of 1945 another letter came from the Peruvian minister of education. The time was "right" for Cam to come. Because of the restrictions placed on U.S. citizens during wartime, Cam had to apply to the State Department in Washington for a permit to go. While waiting for the permit, Cam heard that the globe-trotting literacy pioneer Frank Laubach was in Mexico City. In Laubach, ten years his senior, Cam found a kindred spirit. Laubach's "Each One Teach One" campaigns, using his alphabet and word picture charts had taught great numbers to read in many countries. Cam explained his psycho-phonemic method for teaching literacy and presented the challenge of the Bibleless tribes. Laubach was intrigued. Then Cam took him to meet the Mexican minister of education and arranged for a pilot project of the Laubach method.

Some time later Cam called on the commercial attaché at the U.S. Embassy, who had visited Tetelcingo. He was surprised to hear that Cam hadn't received his permit, since he had an official invitation from the Peruvian government. "Let me make a phone call," he said. When he hung up the receiver he told Cam, "Go see the Consul General. He might have good news for you."

The permission was waiting for Cam when he arrived at the Consul's office. The Consul made no explanation, but later Cam heard that an influential ultraconservative Catholic in the State Department had been sitting on his application.

Flying over the desert coastline of Peru between the Andes and the Pacific on his way to Lima, the capital of Peru, Cam thought back over the past two decades and his dreams of entering Amazonia. He remembered how he and Lynn Van Sickle had tried to persuade the Central American Mission to expand into Amazonia. When that failed he was still determined to go until Legters persuaded him that he should start in Mexico. But he had never lost the vision.

The very immensity of the area was staggering. The great

Amazon River drained an area almost as large as the continental United States, and covered large portions of six countries. Amazonia had been a graveyard for explorers and missionaries for four centuries. It would take recruits with some real gumption as well as special training and equipment to be willing to pioneer there. Peru seemed the natural starting place. The network of rivers that veined the forests and timbered highlands could accommodate amphibious planes. From Peru they could gain invitations to neighboring countries until every tribe in Amazonia had Scripture in its own language.

Cam felt confident since Pike had been received so cordially in Peru two years before. And Moisés Sáenz, the Mexican educator, had served there as ambassador before his untimely death in 1941 and had recommended the SIL program to Peruvian educators. Yes, Peru would be the next frontier.

Cam's host, the minister of education, welcomed him as an honored guest and sent him around to local linguists, anthropologists, and educators. In his careful courteous manner, Cam asked questions, realizing that his hosts were eager to help the Indians.

Dr. José Jiménez Borja, a prominent professor at San Marcos University, and the director of Indian affairs, was assigned to orient Cam. On a large relief map in his office he pointed out various strategic locations. "Here, near the Brazilian border is our largest jungle city, Iquitos. The Amazon divides a short distance upstream into the Ucayali, fed by streams out of our southern mountains, and the Marañón, fed from streams in the north and south. Most of the jungle Indians live along these rivers and their tributaries."

He fingered an area on the upper Marañón. "The proud Aguarunas and other warlike tribes live here. Our frontier soldiers have a mutual agreement to be friends from a distance. The Campas and Piros are down here to the south. They are not so hostile."

After making his preliminary contacts with officials, Cam flew across the Andes as the guest of the Ministries of Education and Aeronautics. His plane landed on the main street of Pucallpa which served as the air strip of the booming riverfront town that lay beside the muddy Ucayali. The acting mayor of the town met the plane, introducing himself as Joe Hocking, a Plymouth Brethren missionary. Cam spent the afternoon with him discussing the possibilities of translating the Bible for the Indian tribes of Amazonia.

Then he boarded a steamer that was to take him seventeen hours downstream to a Shipibo village.

The rest of his time was spent traveling to various Indian tribes, by plane, river boat, and canoe. "The Indians are dear people though primitive," he wrote back to Mexico. "I heard of four savage tribes that kill intruders . . . but those I met were friendly and were glad to give me, through interpreters, words in their languages. I saw much more, but best of all, I saw that there is *hope*, that the job *can be done*, that it *must be done.*"

Cam was deeply impressed with the need of providing workers with medical assistance in time of emergency. One missionary told him of a harrowing twenty-five-day raft trip on a stretch he had just flown over in a few hours. "I see why missionary work has been so very difficult," he wrote in his notebook, after a severe bout with stomach pains. "A few have weathered the storms like rugged oaks, but it is evident that the average worker will need modern equipment, health aids, efficient backing and good linguistic training."

Back in Lima Cam met again with the minister of education to go over the proposed contract in which SIL would study the Indian languages and prepare primers, translate articles of law, sanitation procedures, farm manuals and some literature of high patriotic and moral value. The latter, Cam explained, would include parts of the Bible. The government, in turn, would provide entrance visas, travel discounts, office space, licenses for planes and pilots, land for a base and other facilities.

When the contract was drawn up and signed, Cam bid farewell to the officials. Then in the few hours before his plane was due to depart, he went sightseeing in the fascinating capital. As he was crossing the central plaza he noticed a crowd milling about and went over to investigate. A thin dignified man was chatting with people in the park near the entrance to the presidential palace. "Who is he?" he asked a street vendor.

"*Es el Presidente*," the hawker replied.

Cam pushed through the crowd and bowed before President Manuel Prado y Ugarteche. "*Buenos dias, Señor Presidente*," he said with a smile. The president extended his hand and returned the greeting. Then the crowd surged forward cutting off conversation. But it seemed to Cam providential that the last man he met on his trip was the chief administrator of the land.

"God is my heavenly joy and you are my earthly joy."

18. Elaine

In Mexico, the response to Cam's report was enthusiastic. Everyone was glad to have Cam back, and he was glad to see them all again too. But the one he wanted to see most was the tall blue-eyed young educator who had been teaching the Wycliffe children at Tetelcingo.

Immediately after Elvira's death Cam had felt that he would not remarry—certainly not for several years at least. He needed to be free for pioneering. How could he ask a wife to tolerate his long absences from home?

But unknown to him WBT/SIL members had been busy speculating on who would make the best director's wife among the more than a score of single girls in the group. At least five separate groups had concluded that the ideal one was Elaine Mielke.

The daughter of a Chicago printer, Elaine had been named at twenty Chicago's "Outstanding Young Protestant" by a newspaper and was awarded a trip around the world. Six years later she was the supervisor for special education in 300 Chicago schools. She had promised the Lord that she would support four missionaries from her salary, then discovered that full commitment required the giving of herself. This she had done, coming to SIL in '42 and going on to Mexico a year later to become the first "support" member of the linguistic group.

She was a godsend for translator parents who could not provide education for their children in the tribes. The children whom she taught in the makeshift classroom in Tetelcingo loved her.

Cam was quite attracted to Elaine and spent as much time with her as he could, after the Peru trip, before leaving for appointments in the United States. He asked her to write him at stopping off

134

points on this journey. Unsure but hopeful of his interest, she promised to do so.

While in Los Angeles Cam stopped by Dawson Trotman's office. The only one there was a businesslike young lady who introduced herself as Betty Greene, a member of a new organization called Missionary Aviation Fellowship. "The Lord has called us to provide flying service for missionaries in remote places," she explained. "We're just getting started, so the Navigators let us use their office."

"*You* are a pilot?" Cam asked in amazement.

"I was a WASP—a Women's Air-Force Service Pilot during the war."

Recovering quickly, Cam began telling of plans for Peru. "We're going to need a pilot and a plane to start. I know of a plane in Texas we can get for $2,500. Will you come and fly it for us?"

Surprised at the quick invitation, Betty Greene promised to "pray about it and talk to my associates."

Whereupon Cam quickly dashed off a letter to Pastor Clarence Erickson in Chicago. "I've got a pilot, but no plane. Do you think your church could raise $2,500 for this most needy project?"

Cam then left for Norman, Oklahoma, and SIL '45. He taught no classes that year, but talked up Peru in the daily chapel. One of his most interested listeners was Dr. Kenneth Altig, a tall angular physician from San Gabriel, California, who promised to pray about joining Wycliffe.

From Oklahoma, Cam moved on to the Canadian linguistic school at Briercrest to scout for more Peru recruits. While there he heard that Elaine's grandmother had died and that she had gone to Chicago for the funeral. His first thought was to phone her. Then he reasoned that he needed to see Pastor Erickson about the plane, so he would go on to Chicago.

He took the train to Minneapolis and there between trains called from the station. It was good to hear her voice. He was tempted to voice his love, but there wasn't much privacy in the station. He hesitated to use Spanish, since some passerby might understand, so he tried Aztec. "Temitztlasohtla meac."

"Pardon?" Elaine asked. She had picked up a smattering of the Indian language. Cam repeated the message. "Oh, thank you," she replied. She wasn't really sure what he had meant. But she thought she knew.

In Chicago Cam saw Clarence Erickson, who promised to give the money for the plane. There was also time for some sightseeing with Elaine. Then Cam asked to speak privately with her father. "I want to marry your daughter," he told the printer who was less than ten years his senior. "I've observed her for three years, and I feel that she would make me a wonderful wife. Would you consent? I haven't a thing materially to offer, but I promise to love and cherish her as long as the Lord gives me life."

Mr. Mielke was a natural tease and was greatly tempted to make Cam squirm. But when he saw Cam sitting nervously on the edge of his chair, so intense and serious, he thought better and for once played it straight. "If that's what Elaine wants, you have our consent and blessing," he replied.

On his way back to Mexico, Cam stopped again at Norman where SIL was still in session. He confided to Dawson Trotman about how God had "greatly blessed—providing us with a pilot, a plane, a doctor, and a wife for the director." Trotman was enthusiastic until Cam mentioned waiting three years before marrying Elaine. "Whatever for?" he demanded.

"That would give me time to get things going in Peru."

"Well, that just doesn't make sense. You need a wife. She could be of great assistance to you in Peru. Besides, it seems to me that anyone marrying a tremendous girl like Elaine would want to spend as many years of his life with her as he could."

After the biennial conference in Mexico City in October 1945, Cam and Elaine had a little time together before she left on a literacy campaign in the far south of Mexico. But they wrote every day. While she was away Cam followed Mexican custom and asked approval of two special friends: General Cárdenas and Hazael Marroquin, the Mexico representative of the American Bible Society. Both gave enthusiastic approval, feeling that Elaine had the necessary educational background and training along with the natural charm, gregariousness, and leadership ability Cam needed in a wife.

Their encouragement was all Cam needed to push up the date. "Will you marry me in March?" he wrote. Her answer came quickly:

For years I have wondered whether the Lord would ever bring across my life a companion I could love with all my heart; one whose interests were the same as mine. One who is thoughtful, understanding, loving, patient, loves children, generous, hospitable, self-sacrificing, dynamic personality, a leader, a pioneer in the Lord's work, one who practices what he preaches, a man of prayer. All of these qualities, I have found in you, Dear, so in answer to your question I can gladly say, "Yes!"

As far as a home is concerned, just to be near you will be enough. Although we probably won't be able to have a permanent home for many years, if ever, I think we shall enjoy making a temporary home wherever we are.

As far as being willing to undergo hardships, let me assure you that I came to the mission field expecting to endure hardships as a soldier of Jesus Christ and I shall still be happy to do so. It will be a happy day in March when the Preacher asks me, "Do you take W. Cameron Townsend to be your wedded husband?" and I can tell the whole world, "I Do!"

With all my love to the one I love dearly,

Elaine

In Elaine Cam had found a loving and competent partner who never questioned his leadership. She enjoyed people and was always doing things for others. She loved him and never failed to show her appreciation when he expressed his sentiment in pet names and bits of poetry. Since cherry pie was (and is) his favorite dessert, it was natural that Elaine became "My Cherry Pie." "Beloved Joy," he called her in one letter, "because you are the Joy of my life." On Valentine's Day before they were married he drew a big heart on an old napkin and wrote across it, "JOY IS MY VALENTINE." On the inside fold he penned:

> For you I pine, my Valentine,
> For you I sigh, my cherry pie.
> For you I dream, whose eyes so beam.
> For you I wait, my helpmate great.
> And now I write my angel bride,
> To say I love you, Precious Dove.

Jungle camp for the Peru recruits came before the wedding. The Waco biplane which Erickson's church had purchased for Missionary Aviation Fellowship was not yet fully equipped, so Uncle Al Johnson chartered a local bush pilot to fly the twenty-three Peru volunteers, including six single girls, into the remote jungle area. For the next three months they took survival hikes, swam, hunted, rode canoes through breathtaking rapids, learned first aid, prepared maps, built individual jungle huts without benefit of hammer and nails and in general learned to survive and live off the jungle. Cam stayed busy supervising and planning the activities, which also included building palm-thatched buildings for the next contingent of campers.

When the jungle camp ended in February 1946, Cam felt that Elaine should continue with her literacy work in the hinterlands. "But the wedding?" she protested. "Who'll make arrangements for the wedding next month?"

"Well," replied Cam calmly, "after all the problems involved in setting up jungle camp, making plans for a wedding shouldn't be too much trouble. Please trust me to have everything tastefully done."

"Of course," she replied. "If you plan it .I know I'll be pleased with it all."

Letters flew back and forth between Cam and Elaine, jammed with details of their busy lives and plans for the coming ceremony, all spiced with endearments. "Your delightful letter from Yochib arrived today," Cam wrote on February 21. "You must bewitch those Indians to get them to study so long at one sitting and you cover so much ground! You'll beat Laubach's record. God bless you. You bewitch me, too." Three days later he waxed eloquent with, "God is my heavenly joy and you are my earthly joy. . . . Love, kisses and hugs, bear hugs, honey kisses and eternal joyous love to the most kissable, huggable and lovable person in the world."

General Cárdenas had already agreed to be best man, and his wife Amalia matron of honor. They wanted the ceremony held in their home on Lake Pátzcuaro, in the state of Michoacan, about ten hours' drive from Mexico City. Because of space limitations they asked that the guest list be limited to one hundred.

As the big day drew near Cam began to get a little apprehensive. Besides the invitation list, which included many high government officials, he had to make travel arrangements for guests from Chicago and California to get to Lake Pátzcuaro.

"I just know I am going to forget something," he told Adele Malmstrom, one of the twenty-three recruits for Peru who also happened to be his first wife's niece.

"What about the ring?" she asked.

"Uncle Al Johnson is bringing it," he replied. "He's also buying my wedding suit."

"And Elaine's dress?"

"She is going to wear her sister Millie's dress. It has arrived already."

"The wedding cake?"

"The Cárdenases are having it made; it will be delivered the morning of the wedding."

"Well, I can't think of a thing you've forgotten, Uncle Cam. Don't worry now. It will all come off beautifully."

"I just hope Elaine is pleased with the arrangements I've made," he sighed. "I certainly will be glad when she gets back!"

A death in the family of General Cárdenas caused the wedding to be postponed one week, to April 4. The big day dawned bright and sunny. The Nymans had come from California, Uncle Al Johnson was there, and so were several Mielke relatives, Mexico's leading anthropologist Dr. Manuel Gamio, six generals, and other prominent Mexicans. The orchestra played. Amanda Marroquin sang "The Love of God" in Spanish. The local mayor presided.

As Elaine walked toward him, Cam thought, "She is wonderful!" The short ceremony was soon over and they were *Señor* and *Señora* William Cameron Townsend. The reception seemed a blur of picture-posing and hand-shaking. Finally it was over and the bridal couple started toward the door.

"Oh no!" Cam blurted out, consternation on his face. "I know what it was I forgot!"

"What was it?" everyone wanted to know.

"It doesn't matter, dear," Elaine commented. "Whatever it was I didn't even notice."

"But—but," Cam stammered, "I forgot to get a place for us to spend our wedding night!"

After some good-natured teasing, Uncle Al came to the rescue by offering his room at the nearby Don Vasco Hotel.

Then Cam and Elaine left, arm in arm, filled with anticipation of the new life they were beginning together.

"We'll donate the gas tanks to the Peruvian Air Force."

19. Faith on a Shoestring

Cam and Elaine enjoyed only two brief days of honeymoon before plunging into last-minute preparations for Peru. There were supplies to be packed, crated, and shipped. And last-minute diplomatic ruffles to be ironed out for twenty-three members of WBT/SIL who had been assigned to Peru. Not until Cam was assured that everything was in order did he and Elaine take off ahead of the others for a planned stopover in Venezuela.

In Caracas they talked with President Betancourt and a cabinet member about beginning work in their country with its twenty or more languages the following year. Both officials were encouraging.

Joining their colleagues in the new "promised land," Cam and Elaine set up headquarters for the group in the Hotel Maury in Lima. Living accommodations were fine and all seemed promising when an audit of group finances in Mexico City showed that instead of having funds for three months, they had less than one month's living expenses. Cam quickly transferred them into a large unfurnished house. He and Elaine added over $1,100 of wedding gifts to the group's bank account. A supplementary check came from the Church of the Open Door in Los Angeles for $500. The Christian & Missionary Alliance Bible Institute lent them some used mattresses which they scattered about on the floors for sleeping. Even so they were going to be on short rations.

Prayers and optimism kept them going. "God brought us this far and He will see us on," Cam assured. But the girls were nervous whenever Cam invited government officials in to eat, for they didn't have adequate table service. One official broke a pewter ware fork trying to cut the meat. After he and other guests had left, Cam laughed. "At least they know we aren't a rich bunch of Americans. They realize we need their help and cooperation."

April 4, 1946, Cam and Elaine Mielke were married at the home of General Cárdenas on Lake Patzcuaro. *Above:* Before the ceremony General Cárdenas takes a boutonniere for his lapel from the bride's bouquet. *Below:* Lázaro and Amalia Cárdenas were best man and matron of honor at the wedding.

Cam gives Billy, Elainadel, Joy, and Grace a piggyback ride with Elaine's help in Lima, Peru, 1953.

One way the Peruvians helped was by allowing the group to attend Spanish classes in government schools free of tuition and providing equipment and medicines. Cam was careful to inform them about everything the group was doing and planning. This kept him in government offices almost daily. The American ambassador to Peru, the Honorable Prentice Cooper, and his mother, became friends of the group. The Mexican ambassador to Peru, General Adalberto Tejeda, an old acquaintance who had traveled through Sonora with Cam and President Cárdenas, was very helpful.

Cam's main push was now toward finding a suitable base in Peru's eastern jungle for a center of operations and a jumping off point for tribal linguists. It would need to be near a large river or lake to accommodate amphibious planes which would ferry workers and supplies to other water landing sites near tribal locations.

Then friends told him about an abandoned government-owned hotel on a high bluff overlooking the Aguaytia River, which is a tributary of the Ucayali, north of Pucallpa. After getting a go-ahead from Peruvian officials, Cam made a quick trip to check it out. The location seemed ideal. It was on the main road so supplies could be trucked over the mountains from Lima. It was near the juncture of two rivers, and there were tribes in three directions. Although the unfinished building needed rewiring and carpentry repairs, Cam felt it was usable. Planes would have to land and take off under the longest suspension bridge in Peru, but that problem could be overcome, Cam felt. Perhaps an air strip could be built on an island down the river.

Returning to Lima, Cam got permission to use the abandoned building. He then sent Ralph Sandell and Sylvester Dirks to prepare the base for occupancy, while he worked on tribal assignments. He was glad to welcome Doc Altig and his wife Lucille who flew in after a stopover in Panama City to pick up a couple of old radio transmitters which Cam had arranged for. "One for the new jungle base and one for Lima," Cam said. "The Lord provides."

He took Altig downtown to the Ministry of Health that afternoon and obtained a medical license. The only stipulation was that the first Wycliffe medic must restrict his practice to the back country. "But first," Cam told the new doctor, "you're needed at the new base to do a little rewiring and patch up a generator. And while there, you can set up one of the radio transmitters."

Altig protested that his experience with wiring and motors was limited. "You can do it," Cam assured him. "Later on the Lord will give us some real electricians."

The linguists were anxious to get into tribes and begin work. Gloria Gray and Olive Shell were assigned to the Cashibos near Aguaytia, Esther Matteson and Irene McGinnis to the Piros in the south, Ellen Ross and Lulu Reber to the primitive Machiguengas, Titus and Florence Nickel to the fierce Aguarunas along the Marañón River in the north.

The Nazarene Mission had an outpost among the Aguarunas, but the language barrier limited their outreach. "Our pioneer, Roger Wynans, lost his wife out there," a Nazarene warned the Nickels. "It's a rugged two-week trip overland and by canoe." But the Nickels were not to be discouraged, even though they had funds for only four weeks' rations.

"We've got to get an amphibious plane," Cam told them. "But go ahead overland if you feel this is what the Lord wants you to do."

He was still hoping for a plane and pilot from Missionary Aviation Fellowship when a young Army Air Force lieutenant called at the house. Larry Montgomery, a pilot, had heard about the work, and he knew of an old surplus amphibious double-winged Grumman "Duck" plane. "The Navy is selling it for $3,500. It needs some repairs, but that's a fantastic price. I'd say it has a lot of life left."

"We're interested. Would you be interested in flying it for us?"

"W-w-well, I have a few months left in the service," Montgomery stammered. "But my wife and I will certainly pray about it."

Cam sent a letter to MAF describing the plane and how badly they needed it. The reply was disappointing. MAF doubted the wisdom of purchasing such a powerful plane. But Cam refused to close the door. "If the Lord wants us to have that plane, then He'll provide the funds for its purchase!"

With growing concern for the Nickels and others who had left for tribes, Cam talked to Ambassador Cooper. The diplomat offered to help negotiate the purchase of the plane.

Next Cam sent three cables to friends in Philadelphia, Chicago, and Santa Ana, California, saying, "Plane available for $3,500 if we act immediately." To the first two messages he added, "Please pray." On the third to Herbert Rankin, a merchant friend in Santa Ana who had encouraged his dream of missionary aviation nearly twenty years before, he left off the prayer request.

Responses were quick in coming. The first two promised prayer and nothing else. Rankin replied, "Your cable came as an answer to prayer for . . . I was having to decide how to distribute some contributions. I'll give $3,000."

The next day an invitation came for Cam and Elaine to attend a cocktail party honoring Minister of Education Luis Valcarcel. Elaine worried that their missionary friends might "misunderstand" their going. But Cam felt it was very important for them to be at the function. "We'll just politely decline alcoholic drinks."

At the party Cam sat next to the head of the antileprosy division of the Ministry of Health that maintained a leprosarium in the jungle. When the official heard about their plans and need for a plane, he said, "My department will help you. We'll give one-fourth of the cost of the plane."

Thrilled and grateful, Cam passed the good news on to Dr. Valcarcel. "Well, then," he responded, "the Ministry of Education will pay one-fourth also."

"Great," Cam declared in exuberance. "Now we'll all donate the gas tanks to the Peruvian Air Force. They're interested in the jungle Indians also."

Cam conveyed all this to the MAF people in California who now agreed that the Lord must want the linguists to have that plane. The president of MAF wrote that their pilot Betty Greene would be coming immediately.

Cam planned a program for the plane's christening which was set for Saturday, July 27, just two weeks after his fiftieth birthday. Lt. Montgomery flew the plane for a demonstration. Ambassador Cooper gave a speech delivering the plane to Peru. The Peruvian minister of health spoke eloquently about the help the U.S. had given through various service institutions and accepted the plane. The American ambassador's mother and the minister of education's daughter christened the plane. Then Cam spoke briefly about how the craft would be called the *Amauta*, an Inca word meaning "a wise man at the service of the people." He ended by quoting Jesus: "I have not come to be served, but to serve."

That afternoon the ceremony was front page news in Lima. Now it was urgent to get the repairs done, for there were eleven pioneers out in the jungle needing flight services. As yet there had been no word from the Nickels in Aguaruna land.

Meanwhile Elaine had been lecturing on literacy methods, especially the psycho-phonemic system, at San Marcos University in

Lima. She had been well received and the Peruvian-American Committee on Cultural Cooperation asked her to train literacy teachers at a seminar to be held close to Lake Titicaca near the Bolivian border. This would entail a trip to Puno, high in the Andes, but the opportunity couldn't be missed. She worked with a Peruvian professor to prepare a basic primer in the Aymara language. Although both she and Cam dreaded the separation, they both knew that her experience in Chicago's public schools, her literacy campaigns in Mexico and her knowledge of his psycho-phonemic method made her uniquely qualified to share her experience and knowledge with the fifty-six government teachers who were about to set up literacy campaigns among the Aymara and Quechua Indians. And they would write.

Before Elaine left Lima, they suspected she was pregnant and while she was gone Cam worried about how she was faring in the high altitudes. He had gone to Aguaytia to work with Dr. Altig on the campsite. Although he would have liked to be back in the capital before she arrived, duty held him there.

Doc Altig and the others were trying to convince him that Aguaytia was not the most desirable location. Cam felt they could "make do" with the situation as it was, even though the facilities were terribly crowded. But the most serious problem facing them was the river. A pilot might have difficulty landing and taking off under the suspension bridge. Then, too, the currents were quite strong, and the Indians told them the river sometimes flooded in rainy season.

"It would be nice if we could have a location that was nearer the center of the tribal areas," Cam agreed, "but we just can't afford to move elsewhere. Maybe we could build a landing strip on that island downstream. Let's get a canoe and paddle over."

Although Altig was far from enthusiastic about it, he went along. But on the way to the island, their canoe hit a submerged log and split open, dumping them into the water. They were only about fifty feet from shore, but the water was too dangerous for swimming through the swift current. Clinging to the sides of their disabled craft, they were swept rapidly downstream.

Fortunately two Indians saw them, paddled their dugout out, and rescued the two drenched men. When they finally stepped on dry land, Cam agreed that a new base site would be required. But it would take time.

"Well! I'm a father. And I wasn't there."

20. Dedication in an Embassy

Cam stayed on at the jungle base to work on the "Nestle Inn"—
a hut he hoped would give him and Elaine the privacy they had
lacked since their marriage. In his thinking, it would be four years
at least before they could leave Aguaytia for another jungle base.

But one night Joe Hocking, whom Cam had met at the central
river town of Pucallpa on his 1945 trip, stopped by. Hocking
dreamed of recording the gospel in tribal languages so that Indians
could hear the Good News in their own tongues even before the
written Word became available to them. He, like Cam, was a
visionary, and the two enjoyed swapping ideas for the future.

When Hocking learned of the disadvantages of Aguaytia, he
suggested a site near Pucallpa. "There's some land you could get
on high ground overlooking Lake Yarinacocha for a reasonable
price."

"We don't have the funds," Cam responded, "but maybe I should
go look at it when the plane is fixed. I should have the information
just in case someone in the States wants to make a special investment for the Lord."

Cam worked a few days longer after Hocking left, then left the
"Inn" still unfinished to hitchhike across the high mountains to
Lima. There was a weekly lecture series he had promised the
University of San Marcos. With Cam, duty—especially to foreign
governments and educators—always took precedence over personal
concerns.

It was so good to be with Elaine again. She had finished her
literacy teaching and had gotten back to Lima before him. She was
indeed pregnant and the baby was due in January. But there still
had been no word from the Nickels who had been isolated in the

jungle for almost five months. The *Amauta* Duck plane, unfortunately, was still not ready for a flight over the Andes.

When Cam went to the university to lecture on American Indian languages, he was welcomed by a dark-haired secretary with an unusual air of competence and authority. He thanked her courteously. Soon they were old friends. Rosita Corpancho had been born and raised in the jungle and had a lively interest in the welfare of the jungle tribes. In briefing her on WBT/SIL's plans for the future, Cam candidly admitted the group had a few problems. When she offered to help, he expressed his appreciation for "any bit of assistance you can give."

Not long afterwards Cam received a call from an important Lima businessman. "My friend Rosita Corpancho told me about your good work among the Indians," he said. "She gave such glowing reports I felt I had to call and offer my help."

"Rosita," muttered Cam, straining to place the name. "Rosita Corpancho. Oh yes! The secretary for the linguistic department at the university!"

The calls kept coming. From businessmen, newspapermen and politicians. They all said, "Rosita thinks we should help you."

Cam discovered that the unassuming secretary was a member of one of Lima's outstanding families, and her brother was an important member of Congress. Rosita's position in the social elite of the city gave her entree into important government and diplomatic circles. Thus began a friendship that was to prove extremely helpful to the Institute and the work among the Indians over the years.

At the time Cam needed encouragement. Repairs on the plane were subject to faith-testing delays. Betty Greene was frustrated at having come all the way to Peru and not being able to fly.

The plane was finally ready in December. Cam felt obligated to make a flight into the interior to allocate two teams. Although Elaine was eight months pregnant, the doctor assured him that he could get back before the baby's birth.

Cam, Betty, and translator Sylvester Dirks took off in the single engine *Amauta* on December 20, 1946, to fly across the high mountains. They climbed to a height of 17,000 feet and then dropped to the foothill town of San Ramón, gateway to Amazonia at that point. Here they were weathered in until Christmas Day when the clouds cleared, permitting them to fly to Pucallpa on the Ucayali where ships docked over 3,000 miles from the mouth of the Amazon.

Betty landed smoothly on the local air strip—the main street of the town. Joe Hocking pushed a wheelbarrow through the crowd for their luggage and took them to his house where his wife waited with refreshments. Without realizing it, they were celebrating an event of historic significance: Betty had been the first woman to pilot a plane across the Andes.

After greeting them, Joe handed Cam a rumpled note scrawled in crude Spanish by an Indian chief.

Dear Mr. Hocking: We have made a school house. We want to follow your commandments. Come and teach us. I will not go anyplace until you answer me. We await you. Come.

"I have too much to do here. I can't help him, but maybe your people can. And in his own language," Joe explained.

"That's why we're in Peru. We'll help him. Now let's go see that base site."

They struck out along a trail that led through timbered lowland past Indian huts. "Shipibo Indians," Joe said. "They're all around here. You could build a road along here from Pucallpa."

After about five miles they reached the high bank above Lake Yarina and looked out at the half-moon of water around an island. A long straight stretch of lake could handle float planes, and there was space to build a landing strip.

They tramped along the lakeshore, disturbing four- and five-foot iguana lizards that slithered off into the high weeds. Monkeys chattered in the trees above them. "Gators are in the lake," Joe casually said. "But they won't harm you, and there's an occasional boa."

Cam was impressed. "This may be what we need, though I would prefer not to be this close to civilization for the sake of the Indians whom our folks will be bringing in for language study. How many acres could we get here, Joe?"

"Well, there are several parcels. You could buy ten or fifteen acres on the lakefront now and later get more adjoining as the need arose."

"Good! Then we'd have enough room for individual homes, a clinic, a sawmill, a printing plant, a radio tower, and hangars at the air strip."

"You really like to plan big," Joe commented.

"Let's claim this land for God, and the Indians," Cam responded.

They knelt under a giant ceiba tree. "Lord, you know we don't have the money to buy this place," Cam prayed. "But You can provide it. We ask You to sanctify this land, that it might be set aside for Your glory."

The next day Betty landed the *Amauta* on the lake, then flew back to Pucallpa. Cam radioed Elaine from the Peruvian Air Force's station. "Everything's fine," she reported. "You'll be happy to know that Titus and Florence Nickel just arrived from Aguaruna land. Safe and sound and full of great stories. Took them twenty-one days of nearly impossible traveling to get out, but they did it."

"Well praise the Lord," Cam exclaimed. "I can hardly wait to hear their report."

Cam, Dirks, and Betty took off the following day for Atalaya, a small town at the junction of the Urubamba and Tambo Rivers where Dirks intended to start a survey among the Campa Indians. The first to welcome them on landing was a short, stocky, Franciscan missionary priest. Padre Pascual Alegre cordially invited them to tea.

Dirks gave the cheerful missionary monk a book of D. L. Moody's sermons in Spanish. "Thank you very much," the little Franciscan said. "I'll preach these." And he did.

When they returned to the military post on the 28th, the commanding officer met them grinning. "You've had a radio message, *Señor*," he told Cam. Cam looked around at the other soldiers whose smiles indicated they were also in on the secret.

"Congratulations, Mr. Townsend. You are a father," the C.O. announced ceremoniously. "Your daughter was born yesterday, December 27. Both she and your wife are doing fine."

"But—but—it isn't time," Cam stammered. "Well! I'm a father. And I wasn't there. A daughter! They're both fine, you say? I have to get back to Lima. Where's Betty? I have to go meet my daughter!"

Betty flew him back to Pucallpa where he caught a commercial flight across the Andes. In Lima, he went directly to the hospital to see his wife and daughter. When he marveled that she was so tiny, Elaine laughed. "Babies that are so impatient that they can't wait usually are small. She weighs only six-and-a-quarter pounds. But she's perfectly normal. As a matter of fact, I think she's just perfect."

They named her Grace Lillie—Grace for "God's unmerited favor" and for Grace Fuller of the Old Fashioned Revival Hour radio broadcast, and Lillie for her Grandmother Mielke. Cam thought she looked very much like his own mother.

Announcements went to friends at home and in Lima. Many of the Peruvians expected to be invited to a christening, always a big event in Lima. As five weeks passed and no ceremony was held, the Townsends started getting questions from their Peruvian friends.

"Oh, we'll wait until she is old enough to make her own decision," Cam told them. "When she accepts the Lord as her Savior, then she'll be baptized."

"But if she dies," a distraught official's wife worried, "she'll go to limbo. You should have a ceremony now."

When Cam and Elaine realized the problem, they began to think of having a dedication service. But they realized that their friends in officialdom would be reluctant to attend a service in a Protestant church. Cam was telling the Mexican ambassador and his wife about his problem one day. "Have the ceremony for your baby in our embassy," Ambassador Tejeda responded. Cam gratefully accepted the offer. Invitations were sent to about thirty people, including the Peruvian ministers of education and defense and their wives and the American ambassador and his mother.

The day before the ceremony, the first secretary from the Mexican embassy called Cam. "We've been discussing your ceremony," he said. "It's against Mexican law to have a religious service in one of our government buildings. You must not bring a clergyman."

Cam agreed. "But can I say a few words?" he asked, "And perhaps a friend who isn't a clergyman could read selections from the Bible?"

"Surely!" the diplomat replied. "Just so we don't have clergy."

At the last moment it was decided to include Bob and Lois Schneider's infant son, Jonathan, in the ceremony. John Twentyman, an unordained representative of the Bible Society, read carefully selected Bible verses. Cam told how proud the group was that Grace and Jonathan were Peruvians. They were links that bound the two countries together. He then talked about how the love of Christ motivated young pioneers to go to the jungle to teach the Indians to read and write and give them the Bible in their own language.

He looked at Ambassador Tejeda who had been listening intently. "Could we have a minute of silent prayer for little Grace and Jonathan and for our workers in the jungle?"

The Mexican dignitary nodded.

Everyone went away happy. Now no one would worry about the

babies going to limbo, and they were also now better informed about what the translators were trying to do.

Two days later on February 16, 1947, Cam and Elaine and baby Grace boarded a Panagra plane to begin the trip to Mexico. They would stop off at jungle camp in Chiapas, check on operations in Mexico, move on to the summer SIL campuses and attend the group's biennial conference. At the same time Cam would be recruiting, trying to raise interest in an aviation program for Peru, and if he "happened" to find someone willing to make a large investment for the Lord, he could tell them about the property at Lake Yarina.

He left Bob Schneider in charge of government relations in Lima, and Doc Altig in command at the jungle base at Aguaytia, where they were struggling along in spite of the many difficulties.

The week in jungle camp in Mexico was busy. Everyone was properly impressed with little Gracie. Cam and Elaine told Peru stories around the campfire each night, fanning interest among the campers.

When it was time to leave for Mexico City, Cam and Elaine climbed into the back seat of the tiny commercial Piper Super Cruiser in back of the bush pilot. Their scanty baggage was on a shelf behind. Gracie lay on a pile of fresh diapers in a long Mexican cane basket across Elaine and Cam's laps.

The jungle campers stood waving as the plane ran about two-thirds of the way down the 2,000-foot strip and then lifted off. They had started to turn away when the inexperienced pilot turned the plane downwind through a gap in the tree line, missing the treetops by inches. Suddenly—because it still didn't have sufficient speed—the plane lost altitude and crashed.

*"We are in aviation (by being in the jungle)
whether we like it or not."*

21. Jungle Aviation and Radio Service

The first to reach the crash scene was a Tzeltal Indian who had been working nearby. The plane had hit one side of a ravine, with the force of the impact causing it to bounce head-on against the other bank. Gasoline was streaming from the engine, drenching the passengers and baggage, but not a drop fell in the baby's eyes.

Although Cam's left leg was broken and blood was streaming from his left hip, he was clear-headed enough to hand the baby out to the Indian. "Take her away," he gasped in Spanish, fearing the plane might catch on fire. "Away, away from the plane." The Indian quickly moved the baby to safety.

Elaine's left ankle had been pulled out of its socket and was dangling by the flesh. Somehow, despite their injuries, they managed to crawl painfully out of the crumpled cabin. The pilot didn't move. His head was jammed against the instrument board, but he was still alive.

By this time the first jungle campers had reached the site. They started pulling out the unconscious pilot as Dr. Paul Culley, the camp medic, went to work on Elaine. He managed to stop the bleeding and placed her on a stretcher made from an old army blanket fastened over poles.

Cam was fully alert though in great pain. "Get your movie camera," he called to young Dale Kietzman, "and take pictures before they move us. People need to see how badly we need safe aviation for pioneering in the jungle." Kietzman got the pictures.

As soon as Cárdenas heard of the accident, he requested the governor of the state to fly in a doctor, an aide, and medical supplies. Harold Goodall made rustic crutches for Cam from two saplings. But it was twelve days before the doctor felt Cam and

Elaine could be flown out to a hospital in Mexico City where a metal plate was inserted in Cam's leg and Elaine's ankle was operated on. Both were fitted with casts. It was six months before Elaine could walk without crutches. During much of this time Grace was cared for by various Wycliffe members.

The confinement gave Cam time to think more about an aviation department, although he had no funds to count on and could only plan by faith. He was determined that the young translators must have the best pilots and equipment to provide transportation to and from tribes where there was no other way of going.

He was grateful for the fledgling MAF which had just begun services for missionaries in Mexico. But he questioned whether they could meet the special needs of WBT/SIL in Peru. Betty Greene, MAF's one pilot there, was as brave and capable as they came, but she could not handle the job alone. "We should have our own flying program," he told Elaine. "Larry Montgomery is finishing his tour of duty for Uncle Sam. We can start with him."

Cam was confident that God would have someone to spearhead the aviation program that was still only a dream in his mind. If not Larry, then there would be someone else. Only twelve years had passed since the first linguistic investigators entered Mexico in 1935, and the Lord had since provided key lieutenants for the other aspects of the ongoing program.

Heart patient Will Nyman, for instance, still going strong despite medical predictions, ran the home office efficiently, keeping administrative costs to less than five percent. Ken Pike, who now had his doctorate, was heading up the academic arm, SIL. Gene Nida was pushing ahead as Pike's associate. Dick Pittman had been elected Mexico branch director with George Cowan as assistant. Otis Leal, another of Cam's Mexico "Timothys" had been formally elected candidate secretary. Certainly there were disagreements— that was to be expected. But they worked together as a team.

Besides these, there were many others showing leadership potential. For many years Cam had prayed for each member by name every day. Now there were so many involved in the total program that Cam no longer knew everyone personally. He was aware, too, that the greater numbers had resulted in new demands: a residence home for the children whose parents were out with tribes; a translation center in Mexico where translators could come apart from village distractions and work intensively with informants; literacy campaigns to produce more readers for the translations; and no less essential, an enlarged jungle base in Peru and the aviation program which he considered essential. This would be only taking care of the current situation. With the hundreds of new recruits and the opening of new fields which he anticipated, other challenges would arise.

As if all this were not enough to occupy his mind, Cam felt that he owed it to the world to finish the biography of Lázaro Cárdenas, whom he considered one of the most remarkable men of the century.

Because he felt constrained to work on the book, and because Elaine was still having difficulty walking, Cam accepted an invitation from Uncle Al Johnson to stay at his castle in Death Valley.

Some members questioned the wisdom of taking time off to write the biography of a radical statesman at a time when demands from expansion were so great. Furthermore, they felt Cam might become involved in political matters, which was against WBT/SIL policy. Cam, however, felt it his duty to inform the American people about Mexico's remarkable friend of the common man. While drafting the biography, he sandwiched in a trilogy of articles for the then influential *Sunday School Times* (January 24, 31, Feb. 7, 1948). In them he pointed out how WBT/SIL was overcoming three barriers to reach Bibleless tribes:

1. The barrier of a closed door to evangelical missionaries. He cited Robert Morrison, who had translated the Bible into China's major dialect when Chinese law forbade foreigners even learning the language. He started as an interpreter for the East India Company and later for the English ambassador.

2. The barrier of learning unwritten languages. Wycliffe members, he noted, are trained linguistically at SIL to hear difficult sounds, and to find the logic and symmetry of complex languages.

3. The barrier of geographical inaccessibility. This, he said, could be overcome by aviation.

After making good headway in the writing projects, Cam took Elaine and Grace to Santa Ana. There an appendicitis attack put him in the hospital for immediate surgery. This meant more time recuperating, when Cam was anxious to get back to Peru. But if he couldn't leave the country for a few weeks, he could recruit.

Dawson Trotman put him in touch with one of his top Navigators, Don Burns, who told Cam of his desire to attend the University of San Marcos in Lima and live Christ before the students. Cam sold Burns and his wife Nadine on the idea of going to Peru as Wycliffe members with Don attending the university and both serving as houseparents for the group in Lima.

While visiting with Nyman in the Glendale office, Cam took a call from Ernie Rich in nearby Downey where Cam had lived as a boy. "I've had four years of college and three of Bible college," the inquirer said. "My mission board wants me to get three years of seminary before going to the field."

"What's your skill?" Cam asked.

"It isn't preaching. I've been a mechanic for Standard Oil. I like working with tools and my hands."

"The Lord must have wanted you to call," Cam said. "Can you come down here tomorrow?"

Rich could and did. Cam asked him a few quick questions, then suggested he get some training in aviation mechanics.

Encouraged, Rich said he could get a license in a year.

"Fine. When can you start? Oh, by the way, you and your wife will need a summer at one of our linguistic schools."

Rich reported back to his wife, "That Townsend is just like a vacuum cleaner. He sucks you right in."

About this time disturbing reports began coming from Peru. Some members were complaining about operating procedures, and funds were scarce. Rations were so short at the base at Aguaytia that they were almost counting out the peas on each plate. Then there had been two near tragedies with translators. Ralph Sandell and Harold Goodall had almost drowned in a river rapids. And Harriet and Dale Kietzman were taking a raft down a swift stream when they had slammed into a log and were dumped into the river with their baby. Other translators were having to wait for days and weeks for the one plane.

As soon as they could, the Townsends headed south. Cam left Elaine and Grace in Mexico since Elaine was expecting again and the trip to Peru would be too much for her.

From Lima he went directly to the base at Aguaytia. "We must move to a new base," Doc Altig and Larry Montgomery insisted. "We've tried, Uncle Cam. We've given it all we can. This is just an impossible situation."

Cam agreed and left immediately for Pucallpa. He and Joe Hocking went to see the man who owned the thirty-five-acre tract bordering Lake Yarina. Cam settled on thirteen acres for $375.

Cam then turned his attention back to the aviation challenge. Larry Montgomery was flying the old Duck four and five days in a row. That was too heavy a schedule even under ideal conditions, which they certainly didn't have in the tropical rain forest.

Betty Greene could only help part-time, since MAF asked her to fly their plane for other missions in Peru, too. Also, they did not agree with one of Cam's basic principles, flying for the Peruvian government. Cam felt that they should seek opportunities to serve the government. To him, serving was a privilege, since service was the major means by which political barriers were overcome.

Cam was now even more convinced that WBT/SIL must have its own aviation program with a fleet of planes, hangar facilities, and pilots and mechanics to ensure regular, dependable service.

Meeting in Santa Ana without Cam, however, the board didn't see it his way. They knew they were lacking in the know-how for running an aviation program, whereas MAF had technical experts. WBT/SIL was also walking a tightrope financially. There was no money whatsoever to buy even the first airplane.

When Cam learned the board had declined to act, he began writing letters to everyone he thought might help change their minds. In a letter to Evelyn Pike, he said:

We are in aviation (by being in the jungle) whether we like it or not. The thing to do is to look to God to enable us to handle it in the most efficient way possible. This means a department manned by the most capable and consecrated men possible and concentrating on our Amazonian problem rather than on a lot of other fields as well, as is the case of MAF's vision.

I believe God can and will raise up a technical aviation secretary for us who will be just as outstanding [in his department] as Ken [Pike] and Gene [Nida] are in theirs.

Between writing letters Cam tried to build the morale and strengthen the faith of his young colleagues now attempting the seemingly impossible. Living in primitive tribes, learning the languages and customs, some were even beginning to translate Bible passages. "I wish I could do what you're doing," he said sincerely. "But God has called me to be your leader. Please trust me as I try to follow Him."

He had been back in Peru for only a few weeks, but he needed to raise funds for the new base as well as more support for the

Peru pioneers who were living on a shoestring that kept breaking. More recruits were needed, and there was the Cárdenas biography to finish, and he had to convince the board that they must have an aviation program. So he flew back to Mexico and Elaine and Gracie.

In the Cárdenas's home on beautiful Lake Pátzcuaro where they had been married only two years before, he polished his book for publication.

In the concluding chapter, Cam revealed his concern for new U.S. initiatives toward its smaller Latin neighbors. He called for:

—A counterpart of the Marshall Plan for Latin America with Cárdenas as chairman.

—Appointment of athletic attachés at U.S. embassies in Latin America. "People in the habit of playing together are more apt to work together."

—Increasing cultural exchange.

—Tourist offices in U.S. embassies.

—A New America, Amerinova, "free from prejudice, exploitation, imperialism."

—Acceptance of the principle championed by Cárdenas of non-intervention in a neighbor's affairs.

Then in the final paragraph Cam called for Amerinova to "consider the record of this Mexican democrat":

He ruled without shedding blood. He made no political prisoners. He welcomed home all political exiles. He opened the doors of Mexico to political refugees from other lands. He gave liberty of expression to the press. He restored liberty of worship. He took the government to the people. He exalted the dignity of the common man. He combatted vice, ignorance, selfishness and prejudice. He sought the welfare of the Indians. He respected other nations and secured their respect for his own. He worked for peace and for a western hemisphere united as "one great spiritual fatherland." This he did and then retired to work, fight and work again in obscurity that Mexico might be democratic.*

With the manuscript in the mail to a publisher, Cam turned his mind to rethinking policies for future advances. Against the background of problems in Peru, he wrote to the Wycliffe workers:

---

* *Lázaro Cárdenas, Mexican Democrat* (Ann Arbor, Mich.: George Wahr Pub. Co., 1952), pp. 370 ff.

The first five years in a new field are very critical. In critical situations democracies are accustomed to give extraordinary authority to the leaders they have chosen. In the future we will have to give the man who leads a new advance full authority until his teammates are in a position to exercise their democratic privileges wisely. And of course if the leader makes bad mistakes, the board in California can step in and either correct or appoint a new man.

It will still be a team effort. Like a well-trained football team, the quarterback calls the signals, but the plays have to be carefully and enthusiastically carried out by the team if they are to be successful. Every team must have a quarterback. It's not that he's infallible, but simply that he does his best and everyone follows without a moment's hesitation.

The spelling out of Cam's "advance" policies was not premature. Pike was now making arrangements for a third SIL training school, this one in Australia where aboriginal tribes needed linguists. (Pike had turned down an invitation to teach linguistics at Yengching University in China because of his commitment to WBT/SIL.) Contact had been made with New Guinea where numerous languages awaited translation. Cam sensed that the vast Pacific area would soon be opening to Bible translation and he wanted WBT/SIL to be ready.

Their "Mexican" daughter was born May 5, 1948. Cam was pleased that she chose to arrive on a Mexican patriotic holiday. They named her Joy, Cam's pet name for Elaine and the name of their missionary recording friend Joy Ridderhof, and Amalia, in honor of Señora Cárdenas. They dedicated her as they had Grace with the ceremony observed at a hotel in Mexico with many Mexican friends present.

Coming after news that Uncle Al Johnson had died, the financial statement for June reported less than $10,000 total gifts for all 160 WBT/SIL members, with less than $2,000 for Peru. There was understandable questioning by some members of Cam's plans for an aviation program and advance into the Pacific.

Cam refused to be discouraged. He kept writing letters. He wrote to every evangelical leader he knew in the U.S. and some he knew only through third parties. He did not mention the low receipts nor did he solicit directly. He emphasized the "open doors," the biblical injunction to take the gospel to all nations, and the necessity of aviation and radio for reaching the remote tribes.

The replies were mixed. One said he had bought another Christian radio station and was under a "heavy load." Another thanked him for "acquainting me with the particular needs of Wycliffe" but "could not" make commitments.

J. D. Hall, an executive at Moody Bible Institute was the most encouraging. Hall had visited the first Camp Wycliffe and had been an "admirer" ever since. He persuaded the missionary committee of Moody Church to send a donation and talked to Henry Coleman Crowell, vice president of the Institute. Crowell, son of the founder of Quaker Oats, thought WBT/SIL might receive some surplus government equipment which Moody had secured.

At the board meeting in the States, five of the seven members present did not readily approve Cam's plea to begin "our own aviation and radio program in Peru." Cam, Nyman and Pittman voted in favor; Pike and Nida said no. Then Pike consented to go along *if* $40,000 came in by the next biennial conference in 1949. Cam was certain it would.

Traveling on to Chicago, Cam spoke to the students at Moody Bible Institute, interviewed young mission majors, and talked missionary strategy with President William Culbertson and a few faculty members.

J. D. Hall had already arranged for him to meet Henry Coleman Crowell. Crowell was enthralled with Cam's report and promised that any war surplus equipment the Institute couldn't use would be set aside for Peru. He also accepted Cam's invitation to accompany Paul Robinson, head of the Institute's missionary technical department, on a visit to Peru.

After holding a rally to arouse interest in the aviation program, Cam drove his family back to southern California where he kept speaking engagements and met with a JAARS (Jungle Aviation and Radio Service) committee that had been formed as a subsidiary of WBT/SIL. A member of the committee, San Diego grocer Earl Miller, donated a small plane. It was sold and the money put toward the purchase of a four-passenger amphibious Aeronca to be delivered in the spring.

Jim Price, one of the men who had volunteered to help fly the Aeronca to Peru, mentioned to Cam that he was also a carpenter. Cam invited him to stay awhile in Peru. "You can help us build the new base."

"Well, my wife and I aren't members yet," Price noted, "but we plan to attend SIL next summer."

"Good. Then you're planning on joining."

"We hope to. If your group will accept members of the Assemblies of God."

Cam was quite aware that WBT/SIL had no Assemblies members at the time. Still he did not hesitate in promising, "We are nonsectarian, so of course, we'll accept you. If you can accept us and our doctrinal statement."

"How can we deny tribes the Bible while we debate minor issues."

22. Compatible vs. Incompatible

Confident that the additional pilot was on the way, Cam and his family returned to Peru after almost a year's absence. In Lima they were pleased to see Don and Nadine Burns. They were house-parents at the Lima group house, and Don was already enrolled in San Marcos University.

The short wave radio transmitters and receivers had been set up while the Townsends were away. To Cam it was confirmation of his vision to be able to talk to translators, and to hear Doc Altig prescribe for a patient three hundred miles away.

Cam was pleased that Acting Director Bob Schneider had kept up government contacts. He took Cam around to see various officials. The Air Force promised more gasoline, the Ministry of Health free medicines. Cam was in rare spirits. "They're helping us because we're helping the Indians," he exulted.

In the spring of 1949, Crowell and Robinson came from Moody. Cam met them at the Lima airport and they flew with Larry in the Duck first to the new base site at Yarinacocha, and then to a Piro village where Esther Matteson, a graduate of Moody, and two other girls were living in a thatched hut.

After Cam saw the visitors off in Lima, he commented to Don Burns and Bob Schneider, "This is the way to give people a vision of the need. Get them here to see for themselves. We're going to hear more from Crowell and Robinson."

Funds were trickling in for the new base now and an all-purpose building was going up. Cam was there building a shelter for his family which was due to increase in December. For its walls and roof Elaine sewed together mosquito cloth and canvas from five tentlike jungle hammocks to hang over a wooden frame. Doc Altig shook his head. "You'll either suffocate or the mosquitoes will eat you alive," he warned. Cam shrugged and remarked it would have to do until they could build a better house.

When it was finished, Elaine and the children came to the new base. It was the first home of their own, but just as Doc predicted it was hot and was a haven for jungle critters. Still it was better than trying to crowd into the all-purpose building where four families were already living.

Candidate secretary Otis Leal wrote that new recruits weren't coming fast enough. Cam replied that he could not understand this. Might they be rejecting some borderline candidates who with a little help might make the grade? "It's been four years now since the president of Venezuela asked us to come to his country. Without an adequate number of recruits I'm sad to confess that we might have to further postpone that advance."

It was with this concern that further advance not be slowed that Cam went to the biennial business conference in Oklahoma in September 1949. The good news was Nyman's report of a quarter-million-dollar net income for the past year, which included $41,000 designated for the aviation work, JAARS. This seemed to convince everyone that the Lord wanted them to do their own flying. And Ken and Evelyn Pike would soon be going to Australia to help missionary leaders there set up an SIL school.

The bad news for Cam was that the question of accepting Pentecostals had become a touchy subject. The subject had been discussed six or seven years before, but had been tabled. This time the issue brought an extended floor debate. The application of Jim and Anita Price which had initially provoked the controversy was forgotten as opponents talked mostly about members as "compatible" versus those who were "incompatible." Suppose they mixed people from the Assemblies of God in among Baptists, Methodists, Presbyterians. Wouldn't that cause dissension? There must be harmony among the WBT/SIL workers.

Cam countered that to reject the Prices and other applicants from the Assemblies of God would be violating the group's nonsectarian policy. "How can I go on telling governments that we're nonsectarian when we won't even accept true believers who disagree on nonessentials?"

He also argued that in rejecting candidates, the conference was keeping the tribes of Peru from receiving the Bible. Money couldn't do the job alone, nor airplanes. The tribes had to have dedicated, Bible-believing workers, and the Prices certainly were all of that.

He acknowledged that Assembly people didn't believe exactly as those at the conference did, but the differences were really minor. Certainly, he went on, Wycliffe shouldn't delay giving the Bible to people who had never heard while its members sat and debated minor issues.

Cam continued to argue and plead, even threatening to resign if the Prices were not accepted, while his colleagues sat distressed. Then the highly respected Nyman said that what really bothered the objectors was that some Pentecostals believed no one has the Holy Spirit unless he has spoken in tongues. But then he emphasized that not all Pentecostals believed that. "Why don't we define 'incompatible' as someone who believes speaking in tongues is essential for the indwelling of the Holy Spirit?" he proposed. "Then we can continue our policy of accepting candidates on the basis of compatibility versus incompatibility."

The members voted their agreement and Cam had his pilot and construction worker, with his capable wife. Then he hurried out and sent a telegram to the Prices in California.

REGRET HARDSHIPS CAUSED YOU. IF YOU CAN FORGIVE US, WE WOULD WELCOME YOU FOR PERUVIAN ASSIGNMENT. LOVINGLY, UNCLE CAM.

One other item of controversy on the agenda was the timing of a translator's New Testament. Gene Nida felt the linguist should strive first to win tribesmen to Christ and not complete his New Testament until the latter part of his missionary career. Cam, Pike, and some others disagreed. Finally Pike presented a motion calling for a completed New Testament within ten to fifteen years after the work began. This passed.

From Oklahoma Cam went on to Chicago where he was a guest at the Crowell estate on Lake Michigan. In talking to the Moody executive about equipment for new recruits and the base at Yarinacocha, he proposed a stateside organization be formed to facilitate the equipping of missionaries. It would certainly save a lot of time and trouble and money to those on the field. Crowell thought this a great idea. Eventually he got a committee together which started

Missionary Equipment Service. It has served thousands of missionaries overseas.

After speaking to the Moody students several times, Cam moved on to Dallas for recruiting at Lewis Sperry Chafer's seminary. Then it was Glendale, California, for the board meeting. There Cam jolted everyone with his announcement, "We ought to make a film. A real top-notch, professional-type movie that will demonstrate to audiences across America just what we are doing and why. It will be the next best thing to visiting the base."

"What would such a project cost?" asked Treasurer Nyman. "And do we have anyone who is qualified?"

"Mr. Crowell has recommended Irwin Moon who has done the Moody Science films," Cam said. Most of the group had seen at least one of those films, and were enthusiastic about his abilities.

"And the cost?" Nyman persisted.

"About $5,000 expense money. Moon has offered to donate his time for the two or three months it will take him to shoot the footage in Mexico and Peru if Moody would get first use of the footage."

"When could he go?"

"Right away."

There was a long silence. Five thousand dollars seemed like a fortune.

"We've never spent much for promotion," one of the board members conceded. "We could scrape up the money somehow," another agreed. "If you think we should do it, Cam, I'll go along," Nyman said. "I make the motion . . ." The motion carried.

After a brief visit with friends and relatives, Cam flew to Lima and over the Andes to Yarinacocha and home. As he walked around the base with Elaine he saw that more homes were up. With their palm-thatch roofs, the base now looked like a semi-modern Indian village. Quite a difference from the first time he had seen the patch of solid jungle with Joe Hocking, and claimed it for the Lord.

Irwin Moon arrived shortly and shot film around the base and nearby villages. Larry flew him to Aguaruna country far to the north for pictures of tribal life, and then he left for Mexico to film among the Tzeltals.

Elaine and Cam's third child who was supposed to be "Junior," but turned out to be a girl, was born December 28. They named

her Elainadel (for her mother and Adele Malmstrom). Their friend
Padre Alegre (or "Happy Pappy," as the WBT/SILers sometimes
translated it) was a proud witness for the official registration of
her birth in Pucallpa.

Cam was brimming over with happiness. Not only was he a
father again, but a gift of $10,000 had come from Crowell. Three-
fourths of the amount was marked for a clinic at the base, with the
remaining $2,500 to be spent for a "decent dwelling" for the Town-
sends. Crowell had seen pictures of the tenthouse and wanted Elaine
and the children out of it.

Cam was eagerly awaiting announcement of a date when Moon's
film would be premiered when a letter came from Nyman saying
there was no money to pay for professionals to edit and narrate the
film. What did the general director want to do with the raw film?

Cam read the letter thoughtfully, then turned to Elaine. "Well,
Sweetheart, it looks as if you and I are going to have to enter the
motion picture business."

"We have purposefully restricted ourselves to translating the Bible."

23. Advancing Through Service

Cam and Elaine packed up their three "stairsteps" and flew to California. For the next five tedious months they worked on the film at the Moody Institute of Science Studios near Los Angeles. Moon and his associates advised as their time permitted, but the final responsibility fell on Cam.

Cam was encouraged to keep at the laborious task by reports from Ken Pike that the first SIL in Australia had enrolled thirty-nine students from eight denominations and sixteen mission boards. Pike had also visited New Guinea. "There are at least three hundred languages there waiting for Scripture," he told Cam, never dreaming there were actually over twice that many.

One day when Moon was with Cam, the scientist mentioned a Catalina "flying boat" at a nearby airport, which some executive was using for fishing expeditions.

As soon as Cam could get away he headed for the airport, taking along Crowell's son John, who was then working with the Institute of Science. The squat, two-story, twin-engine amphibian had room enough to carry two tons of freight plus passengers. Cam thought it ideal for Amazonia. He and young Crowell stood under a wing and prayed that God would give JAARS a Catalina.

The film "O, For a Thousand Tongues" was finally completed in July 1950. Radio preacher Charles Fuller recorded an introduction and Cam did the narration. Fuller premiered it at the Long Beach Auditorium for his Sunday afternoon audience. Many said it was the best missionary film produced up to that time.

Cam later showed the film to the SIL students at the University of Oklahoma, then went on to Chicago where he left Elaine and the girls with the Mielkes while he and Amos Baker went for showings in the East and Canada. Elaine premiered the film at Moody Church the same night Cam gave the first showing in Boston. Cam even had the privilege of showing the film in the main auditorium of the Department of the Interior in Washington before a distinguished group of officials from the Bureau of Indian Affairs.

He hadn't forgotten about that Catalina. At his request Larry Montgomery, home on a short furlough, located a used one in Newark, New Jersey, that he felt was a good bargain.

Armed with information about the plane Cam headed for Mexico to see his good friend, Dr. Ramón Beteta, the tennis champion who was still serving as Mexico's minister of finance. Cam wondered if Mexico might not give the plane to Peru in memory of the late educator Moisés Sáenz. "He first invited me into Mexico," Cam recalled. "Here is an opportunity for Mexico to promote international friendship and to help us help the Indians of Peru."

Beteta had been close to Moisés Sáenz and liked the idea. "Go see his brother, Aarón," he suggested. "The family and friends will want to participate. Then I'll call a meeting of key people."

Aarón Sáenz had retired from leadership in politics but was still an outstanding civic leader and industrialist. He promised his family's help. Beteta then called a meeting of Minister of Education Gual Vidal; Head of the Inter-American Indian Institute Dr. Manuel Gamio; Head of the National Indian Institute Dr. Alfonso Caso; Peruvian Ambassador to Mexico Dr. Oscar Vasquez Benevides, and Aarón Sáenz to discuss the project with Cam.

They all agreed that the work of the Summer Institute of Linguistics in Mexico was so meritorious that a grant toward an airplane for its work in Peru was highly justified. Then Beteta spoke to President Alemán about the government's participation. The president endorsed a substantial grant. This, plus the gifts from the private citizens, was enough to buy the plane.

Now only $5,000 was needed to put the plane in first-class flying shape. Then it could be ferried to Mexico for dedicatory ceremonies, and from there on to Peru. Crowell gave the amount, telling Cam, "Even if it shouldn't be of much service to you, the diplomatic good will is worth all the money."

On April 5, 1951, an impressive entourage of officials and diplomats assembled at the Mexico City Airport for dedication ceremonies. Besides President Miguel Alemán and three Mexican cabinet members, there were five ambassadors. The widow of Moisés Sáenz, stately and gracious *doña* Herlinda, christened the plane, and Aarón Sáenz thanked everyone for the honor paid his brother. The ambassador from Peru spoke in appreciation of the gift from Mexico.

All three major newspapers of Mexico City gave the ceremony front-page coverage, and there was also a television special. The Mexicans were pleased and freely talked about Cam's latest accomplishment for international good will.

Then the plane was flown to Lima for another ceremony with President Manuel Odría and other Peruvian officials.

The final lap took the "Cat," with a load of textbooks and school equipment for Spanish language schools in jungle towns, to Yarinacocha for maintenance and equipping for tribal flights. There it sat in the lake for a while because some of the members thought it too big and too expensive. Someone even dubbed it "Uncle Cam's Folly." However, Cam and Larry Montgomery finally convinced the objectors that the plane should be put into service.

There were other planes in use in Peru. One had come from Texas, a six-passenger amphibious Norseman. An Aeronca had been given by Crowell and another by missionary students at the Bible Institute of Los Angeles. There was still a need for another plane, Cam felt, one that could take off and land on extremely short runways. At the time he didn't know such a plane was available.

With four planes, the aviation program moved into high gear and the pilots had all the flying they could handle. But some months gifts for aviation totaled less than $100. Fortunately, the policy of serving everyone which Cam had continued to insist upon turned out to be the fiscal lifesaver. The gifts were supplemented with modest revenues from flying government officials, businessmen, missionaries, anthropologists, and other jungle travelers. Protestant and Catholic missionaries received a discount and WBT/SIL members flew at subsidized rates of 4½¢ a passenger mile.

Cam continued to keep the WBT/SIL family on both a Christian and nonsectarian course. When he spoke to the Peru group in the new assembly room that was used for base meetings, Sunday services, and a schoolroom, he cautioned members about "stepping out of bounds. We have purposefully restricted ourselves to translating the Bible," he said. "If we pass out tracts, hold meetings, and do other things regular missionaries do, the door could be closed in our faces. I'm all for witnessing in their mother tongue as friend to friend. But let's do it by inviting neighbors into our homes, visiting them, and building friendships."

The philosophy was easier to follow at the base than in Lima where the members attended local evangelical churches. One weekend when Cam was in the capital he attended worship services at a nearby church, where he found that Don Burns led the singing. Afterward Cam pointed out to Burns that only one Peruvian was on the platform in the church service. "Perhaps you should step down permanently," he suggested. "The Lord will give you enough to do without your taking a church job that a Peruvian should fill."

Cam also felt the evangelical churches in Lima were patterned too closely after their counterparts in the States. When the gospel singer Anton Marco, a former opera star, came to Lima, Cam suggested to Peruvian friends that they sponsor a benefit concert for the Indians in the Municipal Theatre. Over 2,000 Peruvians came, most of whom would never have entered a Protestant church. They heard Marco present a selection of classical songs, then listened attentively when he sang a hymn and told how he had become a Christian. "It just goes to show," Cam told Burns afterward, "that you can reach many people outside of church buildings on neutral ground."

Every few weeks Cam flew over the mountains from Yarinacocha on group business and to help Bob Schneider with public relations. But his trips became less frequent as he saw how well Schneider was building friendships and keeping up contacts with officials and educators.

Back at the base Cam now had a full-time secretary whom he kept busy with his prodigious correspondence. Cal Hibbard had been recruited during a previous trip to Chicago. Having a male secretary was customary for Latin American officials.

When time came for the 1951 biennial conference that followed the SIL training schools in the U.S. and Canada, Cam felt that the work in Peru was running smoothly enough for him to be away for awhile.

With total Wycliffe membership nudging three hundred, the conference voted to switch to a delegate system. Peru was voted in as a chartered branch. Cam was unanimously reelected to another five-year term as general director.

Dick Pittman had recently returned from a visit to the Philippines and reported that the country had been saved from near civil war by the new Secretary of Defense, Ramón Magsaysay. He hadn't been able to see Magsaysay, but he felt an invitation would soon be coming to begin work in the scores of languages spoken on the islands.

In his report Cam expressed disappointment that the door to Venezuela had closed "for the moment." A new government had rescinded President Betancourt's invitation. "Keep praying," he requested.

Buoyed by Dick Pittman's prognosis on the Philippines, Cam called for one hundred new recruits. He also asked for an agriculturist to come to Peru. "My garden in Tetelcingo drew the attention of President Cárdenas. He liked my idea of serving the Indians with practical projects. We need a man who will help us raise food for the base and also train Indians in scientific agriculture." Afterward a muscular recruit came up to Cam. "I'm Herb Fuqua. Just got my degree in agriculture. My wife and I are ready to go."

There was some criticism of the methods Cam had used to raise funds to buy the Catalina. Had he departed from the original principle of complete trust in God with no solicitation? "No," he replied, "I've never asked anyone to contribute to personal support. But when the Lord leads me, I'm willing to ask one government to help another. Or for a wealthy man to help buy an airplane for the people of another country."

Another matter concerned twenty acres of valuable land on the edge of Santa Ana, donated to WBT/SIL by a ranch combine. A majority of the delegates wanted to return the land and concentrate on developing a main center in Sulphur Springs, Arkansas. Cam didn't agree. "The Lord had something in mind when He led them to give us that land." But they still voted for the land to be given back.

An amendments committee proposed that the doctrinal statement calling for belief in the "divine inspiration of the Bible" be amplified to make it stronger. Cam stood to object. "I've only had three years of college and don't understand a lot of these big theological words," he said with a Will Rogers grin. "I believe we should keep it simple. If we add things, people will start quibbling. No one believes any stronger in God's Word than I do. Just to say it's inspired, as the China Inland Mission doctrinal statement has it, is good enough for me."

Nevertheless the members voted the change.

The next report was about the Bible Society. "They've declined to publish the Mixteco New Testament," Cam explained. "They say there aren't enough believers. But we want the Word not only for the believers but for the whole tribe! God has put it on the hearts of some Christian farmers in Canada to back publication. We want to continue working with the Bible Society, but when they won't publish, we'll have to go elsewhere."

After the conference the Townsends stayed on in the States to read proof on the Cárdenas biography. They spent the Christmas holidays with Elaine's family in Chicago, and kept busy speaking and showing "O, For a Thousand Tongues" in area churches. Soon after New Year's Cam received copies of *Lázaro Cárdenas: Mexican Diplomat*. He sent Pittman a copy for mailing to Ramón Magsaysay, the Philippine minister of defense, and sent review copies to magazines and newspapers. The *New York Times* called the book "significant." The *Washington Post* and the *Chicago Tribune* also praised the book. *The Saturday Review* termed it a "friend's-eye biography."

In February Cam spoke at a meeting sponsored by the Latin American Council. The main speaker was Dr. Alberto Lleras Camargo, former president of Colombia and the current head of the Organization of American States. Cam gave him a Cárdenas book, and he appeared interested in SIL's methods and goals. They agreed to keep in touch.

Driving back to the Mielkes, Cam told Elaine, "I have a feeling we'll see him again. Maybe he will get us an invitation to work among the tribes in Colombia."

Cam was glad to get back on the "firing line" at the Yarinacocha jungle base early in 1952. Here he could keep his finger on the pulse of advance in Peru. He felt that to be more important than to be close to the home office. Nyman faithfully sent him minutes of all board meetings so he could keep up. He studied them carefully and responded when he felt his opinion should be heard.

A discussion in 1952 on non-Caucasian members roused his interest. Cam immediately wrote to the board that he had been praying for years for Negro members. He recalled that a Negro doctor had once asked for information about attending SIL and had been steered to the school in Canada. The doctor had never filled out the application, possibly because of age. Now, Cam noted, the

University of Oklahoma was open to admitting Negro students.

"Our organization has never suffered from race prejudice," he continued. "Our constitution has nothing that savors of discrimination. You won't find it in the New Testament either. Please send along all the non-Caucasian workers you can, if they make out good in courses."

Meanwhile Dick Pittman had finished his doctorate at the University of Pennsylvania and was in Philadelphia when a hard-to-understand phone call came from the Philippines. He caught only "thank you," "book," and "important for my people." When the caller had hung up, he asked the operator who had called. "It was a Mr. M-A-G-S-A-Y-S-A-Y," she spelled.

Pittman realized the caller had been the Philippine secretary of defense. He quickly wrote Magsaysay thanking him for his expression of appreciation for the Cárdenas biography, and telling him more about the work of WBT/SIL. That summer Pittman led the newest SIL held at the University of North Dakota, where he offered a course in Tagalog, a major Philippine language, and an orientation to the Pacific area and Filipino culture. After the session he and his wife Kay took a ship to the Philippines. When the boat docked, Secretary Magsaysay's personal aide was there to meet them, and told them that Magsaysay had just been nominated as a coalition candidate for president.

Pittman and Magsaysay became good friends, and a contract to bring in a translation team was soon signed. One day after the election, President Magsaysay told Pittman, "Townsend's biography of Cárdenas has given me a pattern for national reform."

This same year, 1952, Cam sent Don Burns to Guatemala. The little country with over half its population composed of Indians had been on Cam's heart since he had left twenty-two years before. He knew there were at least a dozen tribes still without the New Testament.

Cam felt the Guatemala program was in good hands with Burns. Since he had pulled the outgoing Scot off the church platform in Lima, Burns had buckled down to become Cam's kind of man. He had almost completed his doctoral degree in linguistics at San Marcos University and some said he spoke the best Spanish of anyone in the group.

Then an Ecuadorian diplomat in the U.S. who had heard about the work in Peru wrote the University of Oklahoma an invitation for

SIL to "work with us." Cam wanted to go himself, but pressures in Peru were mounting. He sent Bob Schneider with careful instructions to keep the linguistic work in the foreground, and not give the impression of being ecclesiastics.

"Explain that we are anxious to find ways of serving in each country we work. That's where literacy and medical help come in. While we are evangelical in faith, we are not fighting anybody, not even the witchdoctors. If people are in need we will serve them, be they Catholic, Protestant or pagan. They in turn will serve us. All we want is an opportunity to give the Word of God to the Indians."

Schneider followed Cam's suggestions and soon obtained the contract. He found that Radio HCJB and Missionary Aviation Fellowship also worked under contracts with the government. They proposed that the Wycliffe base be located near Shell Mera where other missions were established. Cam felt this location would tie the group too closely with ecclesiastical groups. But the minister of education thought it a good idea, so Schneider and the new workers who had arrived began operations on a river a few miles from Shell Mera.

With so many new fields of service opening, new tribes being entered, and the number of recruits rising, Cam looked forward to the future with great anticipation.

"It's like Pharaoh's daughter paying Moses' mother to nurse her own baby."

24. Bilingual Schools

Evangelical educators in the U.S. were now recognizing that Cam had cut new niches in Christian service abroad. Successively, Seattle Pacific College, Wheaton College, and Biola College offered him honorary doctorates. Cam had high regard for each school, but he declined the honors. He was proud of Wycliffe members who had earned Ph.D.s but he feared that some potential recruits might believe a degree was necessary to translate the Bible. By holding no degree of any type, Cam could help refute that notion.

In Peru Wycliffe was experiencing growing pains. Translators equipped with two-way radios were now in fifteen tribes and being served by five planes, including the big Catalina which had been overhauled and modified at the Air Force arsenal in Lima. It was used to fly out supplies to central points from which the small planes ferried them to smaller rivers near the translators' stations. When costs were compared, Peru treasurer Watters found that although the Cat cost more per flying hour, its larger payload made it cheaper than any of the smaller planes. Cam's vision had been vindicated!

Esther Matteson's Piro New Testament was moving along ahead of schedule. Other workers were publishing primers and Gospels. But what good were they without readers? Cam maintained his optimistic outlook. He knew the Indians would learn to read, if they only had a chance in their own language. He invited General Juan Mendoza, the new minister of education, to dinner with the group in Lima to discuss the need.

"We've never been able to have a school system for the jungle Indians," Mendoza observed. "Most are too remote and in a few places where we've tried, the Spanish teachers don't understand their language. This language barrier is a real concern to us."

175

"An Indian understands his own language best," Cam mused. "What you need are Indian teachers. But they'd have to be trained." General Mendoza smiled. "Townsend, the solution is bilingual government schools! Your linguists could pick out sharp young men in their villages, bring them to the base, and we could give them a training course. They could go back and teach what they learned, then come back for another course."

"That's right, General," Cam responded enthusiastically. "If you establish a training course, our linguists will help your educators train the selected tribesmen to teach. Indians will teach Indians, first in their own languages, then in Spanish. That would be a natural bridge into the national culture."

"Catholic doctrine would have to be taught," General Mendoza observed. "That's a requirement in all public schools."

"Well, we're nonsectarian Christians," Cam noted, "but we would be happy for Indian teachers to give lessons from Scripture in the tribal languages."

The General liked that idea. The proposal went through channels with gratifying speed. Afterward, President Odría invited Cam for an interview and praised the work of SIL.

With help from Rosita Corpancho, Cam lined up a *patronato* committee of important Peruvians interested in the welfare of Indians to serve as unofficial "sponsors" of SIL. One of the *patronatos'* first projects was the sponsoring of a program in the Golden Hall of Lima's Municipal Palace. With many high officials in attendance, Cam showed pictures of a trip across the jungle in the Catalina. Tribal dances and customs were demonstrated. *Patronato* members gave speeches expressing appreciation of SIL. The next day the Lima newspapers ran laudatory articles.

The minister of education appointed Dr. Martha Hildebrandt, a brilliant Peruvian of German descent and the youngest faculty member of the University of San Marcos, to direct the Indian teacher training course at Yarinacocha. Linguists in the tribes recruited prospective teachers and sent them to Yarinacocha by raft, boat and plane for the first teacher training course. Cam radioed his old friend Padre Alegre to send a Piro student from his Franciscan mission. Padre Alegre wrote Cam:

My highly esteemed friend,
You and I do not belong to the same religion, but nevertheless

we ought to be united by the common purpose of every Christian, which is to "love our brethren as Christ has loved us." Oh, how can this union in love become a reality; love toward that Lord who gave His life for all of us . . . For my part, you can be sure that whatever I can do for others I will always do without laying down conditions, for this is my obligation as an unworthy disciple of the one and true Master.

About twenty trainees were flown in for the first class. Some didn't know how to hold a pencil. Many had never seen the Peruvian flag. After singing the national anthem, and saluting the flag, the school day would begin. They studied primers in their own languages prepared by SIL linguists, Spanish, the three Rs, and principles of teaching. At night the linguists helped the Indians with their homework in their own tongues. The miracle of it was that young tribesmen, whose fathers had been sworn enemies, ate, studied, and played together.

Naturally there were questions from skeptical members. Wasn't this going a bit too far? Wouldn't literacy classes in the tribes do just as well? "No," Cam declared emphatically. "It's the government's responsibility to provide education for the jungle Indians as well as its other citizens. I am very gratified that Peru recognizes this obligation, when very few other countries of the world are doing it for their minority language groups. We ourselves haven't the means to provide such training. And we have a biblical precedent. It's like Pharaoh's daughter paying Moses' mother to nurse her own baby."

January 20, 1953, was an epochal day at Yarinacocha, because that was the day the Townsends had a son. William (for Will Nyman) Crowell (for Henry Coleman Crowell) Townsend weighed in at nine and a half pounds, and his proud father was overjoyed.

The Peru branch had elected Harold Goodall director, but Cam still carried the main responsibility for JAARS. Besides keeping on top of maintenance and repair problems, Cam had to indoctrinate new pilots in his policies.

The biggest hurdle for some newcomers was doing favors for Catholic missionaries. Cam wanted mail and newspapers picked up in Pucallpa and dropped off at Catholic mission stations. He also sent special delicacies which Elaine made for the padres and nuns. Some of the pilots thought this unnecessary trouble at best, and helping the "enemy" at worst.

Merrill Piper of Park Ridge, Illinois, was one who said no. He had been told to drop off something for Padre Alegre. "Go talk to Uncle Cam about it," Larry Montgomery said when faced with the refusal. "It's his order."

Cam listened until Piper had wound down, then quoted some love passages from the Bible. When Piper still wasn't convinced, Cam said forcefully, "The newspapers and pickles must be delivered!"

Grudgingly, Piper landed at Padre Alegre's station. When he stepped ashore he looked up into a smiling face. "How about some cold lemonade?" the padre said, extending a glass.

Piper couldn't stay long, but the next time through the padre persuaded him to spend the night. After supper, they moved to the cool veranda. Curious villagers had gathered outside to see the newcomers. Padre Alegre pointed to a short-wave radio. "Like to hear something from the outside world?"

Piper dialed HCJB, the evangelical station in Ecuador. He turned up the volume and for the next hour the padre and a hundred villagers listened to a gospel message. When he returned to the base, Piper told Cam, "I've learned my lesson. If I hadn't done the favor, those people would not have heard that message."

With advances pushing ahead in three new fields, Cam kept his secretary, Cal Hibbard, busy with correspondence. Dick Pittman, heading up the advance in the Philippines, wrote that he needed travel money which hadn't been budgeted. Cam asked Nyman to take it from the "director's fund." This fund, provided mainly by the foundation established by the A. M. Johnson estate, was solely for Cam's use and discretion in financing special projects. The advance in Ecuador was also moving along, but Cam anticipated problems because of the base location. And Don Burns wrote from Guatemala that he needed Cam's help in diplomacy.

Cam responded to Burns's appeal by flying to Guatemala City, where he conferred with two cabinet members on four separate occasions. One, the minister of education, had been a student leader at Antigua during Cam's days with the Cakchiquels. Residence visas for the Wycliffe workers were cleared, and the minister promised to pay for the reprinting of Cam's old Cakchiquel primers. Cam left feeling the signals were all green, and returned to Lima where the government had loaned SIL half a block of choice residential property for a group house. The Air Force pledged 16,000 more gallons of aviation fuel.

Then news came that some Christian leaders in England had invited Ken Pike and George Cowan to conduct a linguistic training course in London. Cam's spirits leaped higher and higher. In his "Director's Letter" to the membership, he declared:

The movement to the small neglected tribes is gathering momentum every day. . . . Tribes-people are getting the opportunity to read God's Word in their own language. Seven thousand translators and supporting personnel (aviation, radio, literacy and supply) will be needed to complete the task of reaching all the tribes . . . including those behind the iron curtain. Faith knows no barriers!

Then came the storm that threatened to wipe out the entire SIL operation in Peru.

The first indication that trouble was brewing came during a teacher training course. Alarmed at Protestant growth in Peru, the Catholic hierarchy objected to what they considered "ecclesiastical activities" carried on by the linguists. Officials showed the complaints to Cam.

"These are not our members," he said. "Some are Adventists, and one is a former member who left Wycliffe and later came back to represent his church in Peru. We have no authority over what they do." The officials seemed satisfied.

A few days later the leading newspaper in Lima published an article by a jungle missionary priest saying that the linguists were Protestant missionaries in disguise. Orders went out from the hierarchy to the jungle priests and nuns to decline any lifts from the "Protestant pilots." The order sparked a wave of grumbling as Catholic missionaries returned to slow boat travel that required a week of sweat and mosquito bites instead of an hour or two in a JAARS plane.

More anti-SIL articles appeared in the newspapers. Privately, officials passed word to Cam that behind-the-scene pressures were being applied to "get rid of your organization. We know you're nonsectarian," they said, "but we'll need proof."

Cam came up with a new twist on the aviation program. He proposed that JAARS become, in effect, an adjunct of the government airline. The planes would carry commercial passengers, baggage, and mail, and would charge commercial rates, but planes and pilots would primarily serve to carry out the cultural and educational agreement between SIL and the Ministry of Education. All operations would be controlled by the Ministry of Aeronautics. The generals liked the idea and the papers were signed which solved the flight controversy.

Forced to change strategy, the attackers now charged that SIL was endangering the unity that existed between the government and the Catholic church. One critical bishop insisted that the summer school in Oklahoma was not affiliated with the university, but was in reality a Baptist institution. The university president, Dr. George Cross, quickly replied that SIL was affiliated with the university, and nonsectarian linguistic courses were being taught. A Catholic faculty member backed him up.

Cam took a week off to prepare his "one reply" to the opponents. His four-thousand-word letter to the editor of Lima's leading newspaper *El Comercio* must stand as a classic in Christian diplomacy.

He quoted endorsements and praises of SIL from numerous officials, educators, and Catholic clergy. He traced the history of SIL in Peru, with "each successive government enlarging our original agreement." He noted that SIL was cooperating with four departments of the state: education, aeronautics, health, and the army. "Our planes and radio stations are at the service of Peru," he said. "All our operations are controlled by competent government authorities from whom we have at no time tried to hide anything."

He described the faith and practice of SIL members in several incisive paragraphs, pointing out that all were true believers in Jesus Christ, but none could be an ordained minister. All had dedicated their lives to serve primitive Indian tribes.

I, your servant, do not belong to any denomination. I respect them all, however, and try to be a good neighbor to all. The Summer Institute of Linguistics, founded and directed by me, does not protest against anything and does not attack any. On the contrary, endeavoring to promote a spirit of love and brotherhood, we try to serve all. We don't call ourselves Protestants, but simply believers in Christ. . . .

Our nonsectarian attitude does not mean that we do not recognize and accept the Christian's duty of making Christianity known to the primitive peoples whose languages and customs we study. The great majority of the Indians live in fear of the witch doctors, and continue in their worship of the spirits of the forest, the whirlpools, and even in some cases, the boa constrictor. Many Indians suffer and even die because of witchcraft and their primitive beliefs, and a true believer who speaks their language cannot, and should not, show indifference to such situations. On the contrary, it is his duty to explain that God is love and that He desires to make us His children, and therefore, brethren, through faith in Jesus Christ. We do not go beyond the teachings of the Catholic Bible nor do we propagate any ritual or ecclesiastic system. . . .

If some of them [the Indians] meekly desist from accepting all the ritual and discipline of the State Church, it is expected that they will accept at least a basic Christian faith and this is the most difficult step. Because of our nonsectarian nature, we are not responsible for the teaching of rituals and ecclesiastical systems of any nature. The missionaries, whether Catholic or Protestant, are the ones to care for such. . . .

We love Peru. When we shall have completed our linguistic investigation, then we shall go, taking with us very pleasant memories and leaving behind our Base at Yarinacocha with all of its buildings, for a center of Indian education as we have said from the beginning. We shall also leave behind for the archives of the Peruvian Ministry of Education . . . and for the National Library, dictionaries, grammars, primers and articles concerning the languages of the jungle. I expect that in time these works shall come to be nothing more than souvenirs of the past because all tribes that now speak those languages will have been incorporated linguistically, and in every other sense, into the national life of this delightful land which we love as our adopted fatherland.

The conflict came to a head in early September 1953 when President Odría convened a special session of his cabinet. They voted to continue backing SIL and increase financial aid. A short time later President Odría had Cam decorated for "distinguished service" to the country.

Afterwards, a *Time* reporter who had been covering the controversy cornered Cam and asked him pointedly, "Are you people missionaries or linguists?"

Cam smiled and replied, "What would you get if you crossed a grapefruit and an orange?"

"[SIL] . . . is familiarizing the Amazon Indians
with the rudiments of modern civilization and,
as a result, is preparing them for gradual incorporation into the national life of the country."
—Arnold Toynbee

25. Family Fun and Practical Service

The gift from Henry Crowell to the Townsends had made possible a
new residence at Yarinacocha. Elaine designed the plans and Cam
hired Peruvian workmen, scrounged materials and fixtures, and
planted mangos, avocados, and Brazil nut trees in the yard. Some of
the WBT/SIL members living on the base helped as time and
talents permitted.

When the two-and-a-half-story house was finally finished, it was
large enough to accommodate the steady stream of distinguished
overnight visitors who were coming to the base. Elaine welcomed
government officials, military officers, anthropologists, missionaries
(both Catholic and Protestant), professors, writers, and various
home supporters who came to see the work. One night when they
had seventeen guests, Cam and little Joy slept in a closet.

It was Cam's custom to ask a guest to read Scripture at the
breakfast table, regardless of his religious affiliation or belief.

One night a week they invited members in for refreshments and
socializing. The evening usually ended with Cam challenging them
to keep advancing. "The greatest missionary is the Bible in the
mother tongue," he would often remind them. "It never needs a
furlough, is never considered a foreigner, and makes all other
missionaries unnecessary."

While the Indian teacher training school was going on, the
Townsends invited students and faculty in for fun and fellowship on
Friday nights. Elaine served warm Kool-Aid (cold drinks hurt the
Indians' poor teeth) and salty delights like popcorn. The Indians
loved skill games such as darts and dropping peanuts in the bottle.
They proved to have better memories than the linguists, and usually
won when playing games such as "Going to Jerusalem."

Doc Altig became concerned. "Your family is liable to catch germs from the Indians," he warned Cam. "Maybe so," Cam admitted, "but we have to be with the tribespeople. That's the very purpose of our being here."

Doc grinned. "I knew you'd say that. But please be careful."

Cam had his own ideas about health and medicine. When visiting tribes he neglected to swallow the amoeba pills which Doc insisted visitors take. His cure-all for whatever ailed the children was hot lemonade with salt. For himself he prescribed raw egg in coffee for a quick boost of energy.

He frequently asked the base medic what he thought about certain Indian remedies. Doc was usually patient with him, but one day he snapped, "Uncle Cam, you believe in Indian medicine more than mine!"

The Piros gave Cam the name "Yawuro," meaning "stork." One evening an old Piro, José Domingo, told Esther Matteson a story.

"One day I stood near the house of Yawuro, your chief. I watched him receive the governor. He took him into the house, seated him in the best chair, and gave him a drink of lemonade. Then he sat down and talked with him. Yawuro was not in a hurry. He had all the time the governor wanted.

"A few days later, I asked to visit Yawuro. He came outside the house to meet me. He took me in and seated me in the best chair and brought me lemonade. Then he sat down and we talked together. He was not in a hurry. He had all the time I wanted.

"Yawuro, your chief, is a great man. He is my friend."

Because Cam had to be away so much, Elaine made the domestic decisions and handled most of the discipline, but Cam deeply enjoyed the time he did get to spend with his family. When he was home he usually cooked breakfast—almost always oatmeal—as his father had done. They read a chapter from the Bible and recited memory verses, followed by prayer. Evenings, he would romp on the floor with the children. When "Billy Boy" and "Dell-Dell" grew sleepy, he would sing them a lullaby.

When in Lima they would visit the children's zoo or go swimming in the ocean. Cam always brought little presents when he returned from trips—things like licorice, candy, and can-can slips for the girls.

Cam lamented his frequent absences from home, and so did Elaine and the children. Once seven-year-old Grace greeted him on his return by saying, "Daddy, you're never home. Please stay longer this time." Another time he found a big sign on the door made by the children: "WELCOME HOME, DADDY, BOY." But the separations were bridged with loving letters full of homespun details. Cam was always lavish with praise and expressions of love for his children:

Precious Gracie:
It was good to hear your voice over the radio today. Thanks so much for the promise to make a cherry pie for my return home next Saturday. I'm so glad that you know how to make good pies. I'm very happy, too, over the good progress you are making in music. Do you remember that I gave you your first piano lesson? It was "Peter, Peter, Pumpkin Eater."
Well, my darling daughter, it's getting late so I'll close. Kisses and hugs from your Daddy.

Darling Joy Girl:
You gave me a wonderful thrill over the air today. I'm still walking on air. When you and Mommy gave me the news that you were first on the honor roll, my heart filled with gratitude to God for enabling you to do it.
Good night, now, precious girlie of mine. . . . Hugs and kisses from your Daddy.

The separations were also eased because the whole family was encouraged by the common goal of Bible translation in which they were caught up. Unlike many modern families where children are not close to their father's work, the Townsend youngsters were surrounded during their formative years by evidences of their parents' accomplishments.

Cam needed the all-too-brief times of refreshment with his family, for his responsibilities were now heavier than ever.

After the Catholic criticism quieted in Lima, he was confronted with news that Gene Nida had declined to run for reelection to the board. He was heavily involved in his work for the American Bible Society, and he continued in disagreement with certain WBT/SIL policies. He was, however, willing to "continue serving [the group] . . . for I appreciate the excellent work which many are doing, but not as a board member."

Cam had always considered the American Bible Society an or-

Cam taught Bill to read Spanglish—English written phonetically using the Spanish alphabet. Cam proposed in his book, *They Found a Common Language* that English be changed to some form of phonemic spelling—as Spanish—or failing that, that a system of bilingual education be established in the U.S. to enable the many minority language groups to learn to read and write effectively.

Loving Greetings from Cameron and Elaine Townsend, June 1960.

Grace 13, Billy 7, Joy 12, Elainadel 10

The 1960 family picture.

In September 1973 the family gathered for a reunion: *L. to r., back row:*
Robert and Elainadel Garippa, David and Joy Tuggy, Bill Townsend,
Grace and Tom Goreth. *Seated:* Elaine, Christopher Tuggy, Cam.

ganizational brother in the work of giving the Bible to all tribes, but he felt that Nida was too valuable a man to lose from the board. He tried in a series of letters to reconcile some of their policy differences, but they were both strong men and neither moved the other. Still, they continued to admire and respect each other personally, with Cam praising Nida's contributions to Bible translation and assuring him, "All of us love you greatly."

The slackening of the clerical criticism from Lima caused Cam to feel he could go to the States for the group's business conference. Returning, he stopped in Mexico, Guatemala, and Ecuador for various appointments.

In Mexico he found a publisher for the Spanish edition of his Cárdenas biography, saw and shared his faith with the former president four times, and handled a diplomatic chore for the Mexico branch's new director, John McIntosh. The Mexico branch seemed to always have some matter for Cam to handle with officials. And Cam enjoyed helping out, for he was the nostalgic type who tried to keep old friendships alive.

In Guatemala Cam joined over a thousand Cakchiquels in celebrating the thirtieth anniversary of the Robinson Bible Institute. His address to the large assembly was in the tribal language, even though the others had spoken in Spanish. Afterwards the Indian pastors came around and said, "Nobody speaks our language as properly as you, *don Guillermo.*" It was the highest praise they could give a linguist.

From Guatemala he flew to Ecuador to make a few official calls with Bob Schneider. One appointment took them and translator Rachel Saint to see President Velasco Ibarra. "She wants to go translate the Bible for the Auca tribe," he informed the Ecuadorian leader.

Velasco admired such dedication. But he warned that the Aucas were "very dangerous. I once flew over them and they threw spears at the plane."

Cam and Schneider also called on the Colombian ambassador to Ecuador and explained the SIL program to him. "When will you help us with our Indians?" the ambassador asked.

"We would like to immediately," Cam replied. "But we'd need a base and some planes."

After a few months at home in Yarinacocha, Cam flew south to La Paz, Bolivia, the highest capital in the world, for the Third Inter-

American Indian Congress. Francisco Arellano Belloc from Mexico was in Bolivia on an errand for the United Nations and took Cam to see the president of Bolivia. They talked about SIL serving the jungle tribes of his country. President Paz Estensorro showed keen interest in his country's Indians. He knew about Cam's biography of Cárdenas and was following some of Cárdenas's ideas. He put his stamp of approval on the SIL contract with only minor changes. When Cam talked to the head of the Brazilian delegation to the Indian Congress, Dr. José de Gama said he knew of the missionary group. "Too bad you aren't scientists. We could use you in Brazil."

Cam replied by acknowledging their concern to translate the New Testament, but went on to list the group's scientific and scholarly accomplishments, and expressed his desire to serve the Brazilian government.

Dr. de Gama gave no invitation, but when Cam returned to Yarinacocha he sent Esther Matteson to attend the Congress of Americanists in Brazil to demonstrate her linguistic accomplishments with the Piros. When she returned, she told the group that an invitation was in the offing, and Cam asked Dale Kietzman, one of the early Peru translators, to begin to gather a task force for that advance. The new workers in Guatemala were mainly from Mexico, but Ecuador had drawn largely from Peru and Cam anticipated that Bolivia and Brazil would use Peru workers also.

There were problems to be faced, though. Cam felt that the ratio of support personnel to translators should be about two to one. A steady supply of new linguists was coming from the States, but pilots and mechanics were in very short supply. The best source was the aviation training course of the Moody Bible Institute. Cam wrote Henry Crowell, whom he now addressed as "Kilo Kid," a joking reference to his friend's expanding girth. "Send me three mechanics and I'll give you a dispensation to eat all the oatmeal you want without gaining more weight."

Ecuador required a plane badly. Planes were also needed in the Philippines and for the Bolivian advance. But one month the total contributions for JAARS was only $21.67. Only the income from paying passengers and cargo kept the planes flying in Peru. There was nothing for new parts and planes. "We need $100,000 right now," Cam wrote Nyman.

The mail brought only a flow of criticism from those who objected to the group's "helping" Catholics. Day after day Cam dictated letters to Cal Hibbard, courteously giving the same answers he had spelled out to previous critics. He always tried to include a spiritual story about a tribesman, a government official, or even a priest. In his folksy way, he was plain, but never vindictive.

The news from the tribes was good, though. One morning he was called to the radio tower for an important message. Lorrie Anderson and Doris Cox from the Shapra tribe were on with the exciting word that Chief Tariri had received the gospel! "He's stopped warring against his enemies and no longer prays to the boas. He's a new man."

Cam was thrilled. News of the head-hunter chief's conversion spread across the jungle and over the mountains to Lima. Cam flew out to Shapra land to meet Tariri, who greeted his visitor as a fellow chief. Lorrie and Doris interpreted as the chief described how he had stopped killing and sent peace offers to all his enemies.

Dramatic stories were also coming in from other tribes. Hundreds of Piros, Aguarunas, Campas, Machiguengas, and other once superstitious jungle Indians who had lived in fear of the elements and witch doctors were turning to Christianity as they heard Scripture in their own languages. The news from Mexico was just as gratifying. Marianna Slocum and Florence Gerdel reported over five thousand new believers in the Tzeltal tribe.

The teacher-training course for Indian teachers was still being held each year, and a planeful of dignitaries came to the base for the 1955 graduation ceremonies. After the graduation Cam flew to Lima at the request of the Peruvian president to report on the work. In Lima, he gave a luncheon attended by many officials and a highly esteemed Catholic bishop. Members of Congress praised SIL in speeches before their colleagues. Afterward the vice president was reminded, "Don't you know they're Protestants?"

He replied, "Don't talk to me about Protestants and Catholics. The truth is that if Christ came to Peru today as He did to Palestine, He would choose Townsend for one of His apostles."

Historian Arnold Toynbee, visiting Yarinacocha in Cam's absence, gave a testimonial to the newspapers. SIL "enjoys the favor of the Peruvian government," he said, "because it is familiarizing the Amazon Indians with the rudiments of modern civilization and, as a result, is preparing them for gradual incorporation into the national life of the country."

Cam was grateful for the verbal bouquets, but he told the min-

ister of education quite frankly that the very transformation of the
Indians was causing other problems.

"They want a higher standard of living. The old hunting and
fishing economy is not enough. They need cattle, chickens, fruit
trees, new crops and land titles. This will require an agricultural
course.

"In some areas they need justice. A few big landowners abuse the
Indians, keeping them in virtual serfdom. Couldn't some Indians
from each region be trained as local authorities?"

The minister promised to do all he could. "Will the Institute
help us provide an agricultural course?" he asked.

"With God's help, we'll do all we can to serve," Cam pledged,
sticking his neck out again.

To encourage the group at the base he mentioned his little garden
in Tetelcingo until some grew weary of hearing about "Uncle Cam's
cabbage patch." He would quote James 2:15, 16 quite often, adding
that "we prove our love by service to the Indians in practical ways."
He hinted to the new agriculturist Herb Fuqua that "we may be
needing you for something more than growing vegetables for the
base kitchen."

While Cam was laying the groundwork for the agricultural project,
the invitation came to enter Brazil. Esther Matteson's visit, plus
subsequent visits by Pike and Rosita Corpancho, had convinced the
Brazilian Indian service that SIL could make a scientific contribution.

Dale Kietzman, as Cam had requested, led the advance team.
About the same time Dick Pittman reported feelers from New
Guinea and Vietnam. But the work in Guatemala, the Philippines,
Ecuador, and Bolivia was still in the infancy stage. There were so
many needs, especially a plane for Bolivia. From where would the
money and personnel come to open these and other new fields?

Cam didn't know. "Our policy thus far," he explained to Harold
Key, another promising young leader, "has been to advance without
waiting for much more than a one-way ticket. Because of that
policy, we've had some trying moments in Mexico and Peru. But I
don't think anyone wishes we had delayed."

Key listened, agreed, and led a group to Bolivia under the same
conditions. Another advance had begun. *Adelante! Siempre adelante!*

"I recommend that we ask for these planes, not for ourselves, but for the governments whom we serve."

26. International Goodwill Planes

One spring day in 1955 Cam was driving back to Sulphur Springs, Arkansas, from a visit to Tulsa. This was a furlough year for the Townsends, but Cam seldom rested even on furlough. He had been to Tulsa to try to interest Oklahoma citizens in providing a plane for Bolivia.

Suddenly he was jolted out of the future into the present. In front of him he saw a single-engine plane—not a helicopter—hovering overhead, almost at a standstill!

Hurrying to the nearby airport, Cam found and questioned the manager. The new Helio-Courier, he was told, could slow to 40 miles an hour without stalling, and could land at 30. It could get airborne in 50 feet. Yet cruising speed was 150 mph.

"This is just what we need for short land strips in the jungle," Cam exclaimed. "Where is it manufactured?"

"In Pittsburgh, Kansas," was the reply.

But before he could head for Kansas, there was the business conference to attend in Sulphur Springs. There an Australian missionary's report on New Guinea made the plane seem even more of a necessity. In calling for WBT/SIL to enter New Guinea, Robert J. Story passed around mimeographed tabulations of tribal groups on the island. "We now believe there are 1,300 different languages there and in the other islands of the South Pacific. Most have not a single verse of Scripture."

Cam sat agape. He had been talking about 1,000 languages to be reduced to writing. There must be over 2,000, he realized. And New Guinea was reported to have rougher terrain than Amazonia. Planes like the Helio would surely be needed.

With the conference over and the children enrolled in school in

Sulphur Springs, Cam took Larry Montgomery, Don Burns, and Lawrence Routh, a contractor from North Carolina, to the Helio-Courier factory in Kansas. Larry tested a model of the little four-passenger plane and pronounced it "a beaut. This is *the* plane, Uncle Cam."

Dr. Lynn Bolinger, president of the corporation and chief developer of the revolutionary new plane, smiled appreciatively. "How many can you use?" he asked.

"We could get by with six for now—four for South America and two for the Philippines," Cam said, with hardly more than lunch money in his pocket.

They went into Bolinger's office to talk. "We're not a business organization," Cam began. "We're helping poor Indian tribes," and he went on to describe the work, showing newspaper clippings, telling about interviews with presidents. "Once they see them in use, I'm sure some of the governments and other businesses will want Helios. I'm sure we could help sell some."

Bolinger's interest was caught. "Considering the work you do and that you'll help us with other buyers, we could sell the planes to you at our cost—$25,000 each. We could deliver one a month."

"That'll be fine," Cam replied.

Back in the car, Burns said, "Uncle Cam, I marvel at your faith. But where will we get the money?"

"Hasn't the Lord always provided, Don? He's given me a new idea which I'm going to present to the board."

Writing to the board about the Helio-Courier, Cam suggested that the latest Crowell gift apply toward a Helio for Ecuador. His new idea was about raising money for the six planes. He would like to use the planes as international goodwill symbols, and do that by raising money both in and outside the evangelical community (through commercial firms and possibly foundations)—the method they had used in South America which had proved successful there in fostering understanding and goodwill.

Cam envisioned christening ceremonies with speeches by the mayor of each city whose citizens had raised the money for the plane, and by the ambassador of the receiving country, along with demonstrations of the plane's capabilities. The publicity would promote good international relations. Further, he proposed naming the fleet of planes "Flotilla de Amistad Inter-Americana" (Inter-

American Friendship Fleet), with each plane named for the city, state, or company that helped buy it.

The first ceremony was already planned for Chicago.

The board found Cam's latest recommendations breathtaking, but voted approval. "Uncle Cam has always been a step ahead of us," Pike said. "He may be again."

December 17, 1955, was a cold, blustery day in the Windy City, but an impressive group of dignitaries was on hand for the first goodwill plane ceremony. Mayor Daley welcomed Ecuador's Ambassador Chiriboga, who in turn praised Inter-American friendship and SIL, "expressing the sincere admiration my country feels for all members of the Institute." After Don Burns conveyed a message of thanks for the plane from Ecuador's President Velasco Ibarra, the crowd went outside and watched Larry Montgomery put the Helio through its paces. Then the plane was flown to Ecuador and received by the president at an airport ceremony.

Back in Sulphur Springs, Cam was planning more International Goodwill plane projects when news came in January 1956 that five young missionaries had been killed by Auca Indians in Ecuador.

Cam knew one of the men, Missionary Aviation Fellowship pilot Nate Saint. His sister Rachel, a member of Wycliffe, was already working on the unwritten Auca language with a woman named Dayuma who had come out of the tribe to live on an Ecuadorian ranch. Profoundly moved, he wrote Rachel, "When I heard of the report, I prayed that the time would come when you would be able to introduce your brother's killer to the president of Ecuador as a transformed man who through faith had become your brother in Christ."

The account of the slayings in *Life* stirred the world. Some church leaders deplored the "needless sacrifice" of the five young men. However, many young people volunteered to go in their place.

Cam was anxious that the challenge of the tribes be continued while the event was still fresh on the minds of Americans. He wrote Rachel asking her to come for speaking appearances, but she felt she should wait, in deference to the widows. "We might be intruding on something that doesn't belong to us," she said.

So Cam returned to his plane project. He and Amos Baker went to Tulsa where they showed businessmen a notebook of clippings and photos of the Chicago plane ceremony. Although Cam talked

194   UNCLE CAM

enthusiastically about the need in Bolivia and the goodwill an Oklahoma Helio project would generate between countries, the businessmen made only limited commitments.

Feeling nothing could be gained by pressing for more pledges, Cam went on to start a plane project in California that seemed more promising. In Santa Ana, he got his nephew Lorin Griset working on the "Friendship of Orange County." Lorin, now a prominent insurance man, had high political contacts and thought Vice President Nixon might speak at the christening ceremonies, since he was from Orange County.

Assured that the Orange County project was in capable hands, Cam left for more speaking engagements, first in Denver and then in Kansas City. Kansas City Mayor Roe Bartle, to whom Cam spoke, thought a women's international friendship group would get behind a plane project in his city. He would arrange for former President Truman to speak at the ceremony.

Boosted by Mayor Bartle's optimism, Cam went on to Washington, D.C., where he called at the Soviet embassy. He had heard that there were numerous minority languages spoken in the Soviet Union, although he realized that the Cold War plus the group's limited funds and personnel made entry into the U.S.S.R. seem like an impossible dream. Nevertheless, Cam's faith thrived on impossibilities, and he felt there was no better time than the present to acquaint Soviet officials with the group's services.

Lawrence Routh, his contractor friend from Greensboro, North Carolina, accompanied Cam on his visit. The Soviet counsellor welcomed them cordially. He liked Cam's idea of cultural exchange: Soviet linguists coming to lecture at SIL and SIL people going to the U.S.S.R. "Could you go to Moscow and talk with our Academy of Science?" the diplomat asked. Much as he wanted to, Cam couldn't see his way clear to go just then. There were too many loose strings dangling. One worry was the stymied plane project in Tulsa.

Back at the hotel Cam handed Routh his worn Scofield Bible. "Read the story of Joshua marching around Jericho."

When Routh finished, Cam said, "You know why the Lord asked Joshua to march? I think it was to teach him obedience. To see if he would carry out the Lord's command. He's commanded me to march around Tulsa. I'm going back there and march until the Lord tells me to stop!"

He went to Tulsa and "marched"—patiently explaining Wycliffe's methods and purpose. And the wall came down.

The second Helio was christened at the University of Oklahoma. President Cross of the university presented the keys to Bolivian Ambassador Victor Andrade, who accepted the gift in behalf of his country and immediately turned over the keys to Ken Pike, who was representing SIL. A naval colorguard gave a nineteen-gun ambassadorial salute and Mrs. Cross christened the plane "Friendship of Oklahoma."

Funds for the "Friendship of Orange County" came much more quickly. Vice President Nixon had agreed to speak, and the Peruvian ambassador, Fernando Berkemeyer, was coming from Washington, along with other dignitaries. Then a few days before the ceremony, Nixon's father died, and an aide called to cancel the appearance.

The manager of the Santa Ana Chamber of Commerce was upset at the cancellation. "If the vice president doesn't show up, we won't have a crowd," he told Cam. "We've already spent hundreds of dollars."

"We'll pray," Cam replied.

The day before the ceremony, Nixon sent word he would be coming after all. The Chamber of Commerce man was so impressed by the answer to prayer that he later committed his life to Christ.

The plane presentation went beautifully. Cam gave a tribute to Peru and a pledge of service. Nixon spoke and the ambassador received the plane. The charming wife of the consul general of Peru in Los Angeles, Señora de la Fuente, christened it. Charles Fuller prayed. Then Pike intrigued the crowd by demonstrating with an American Indian how to begin to learn a language using gestures.

The Townsend's furlough year was up in the summer of 1956. Seeds had been planted, faith rewarded, and the campaign to reach all the tribes had increased in momentum. Cam was anxious to get back to Latin America.

"We can't control what they [journalists] write, but generally they are fair. And they tell the world what we are doing."

27. Tell the World

The years 1957–1960 were full and busy for Cam and for WBT/SIL. The work of Wycliffe increased and became more widely known, culminating in the 25th anniversary celebrations starting in 1959.

Two more goodwill planes were christened in 1958. The "Spirit of Kansas City" was dedicated for work in Ecuador on January 19, 1958, with former President Truman and the former president of Ecuador, Galo Plaza, speaking. The "Spirit of Seattle" was dedicated in Washington, D.C., in June 1958 as a gift to the Philippines; the mayor of Seattle and President Garcia of the Philippines participated in the ceremonies. A second Catalina went to the Amazonia countries where SIL worked from Orlando, Florida, in 1959, and another plane was sent to the Philippines from Pontiac, Michigan, in 1960. Cam was at each of these ceremonies, and had done a good bit of the legwork to raise the money.

Early in 1957 the first couple went to Vietnam, through the recommendation of President Magsaysay of the Philippines. "A further result of your Cárdenas book," Dick Pittman wrote Cam. Translation teams were in Alaska and had set up an Arctic training camp. Africa was beginning to call for translators. Cowan and Pike, just back from a visit to Germany, felt Europe was a potential gold mine for new recruits. And Cam was hoping to get contracts with Colombia and Venezuela.

In Peru things were going well. Enrollment in the bilingual Indian schools kept increasing, blessed by the special presidential decree calling for Indian Bible translations to be taught every day to the students. Agriculturist Herb Fuqua was teaching classes in scientific agriculture for the Indian teachers. That pleased Cam.

196

"We need cattle projects, too, and classes in carpentry and mechanics," he told Fuqua.

Herb threw up his hands in mock despair. "Give us time, Uncle Cam!"

When news came from Ecuador that Rachel Saint and Dayuma, the first Auca translation helper, would be flying to the States to be honored by Ralph Edwards on his television program "This Is Your Life," Cam had an idea. Rachel Saint had worked among the head-hunting Shapras before going to the Aucas. Shapra Chief Tariri could also appear on the program. He could tell about Rachel's living in his tribe and about his leaving his headhunting ways to serve the true God. Rachel and Dayuma were going from California to New York for an appearance at the Billy Graham Crusade in Madison Square Garden, and Cam was sure Billy Graham would welcome the chief to his platform also.

When Cam broached the idea to Lorrie Anderson and Doris Cox, the translators with the Shapras, they were opposed at first. Cam assured them that the intelligent, observant tribal leader would be a strong demonstration of what Bible translation could accomplish. The girls finally agreed to accompany Tariri, his wife and baby, to interpret for them and to protect them from civilization.

Attired in full tribal regalia of feathered headdress, beads and exotic beetle-wing earrings, Tariri was a great success in the Hollywood TV studios. After the program, the chief, his family, and Doris and Lorrie flew to New York for the appearance with Billy Graham. Then Lorrie brought the Shapras back to Peru.

"I talked to your countrymen," Tariri told Cam on his return. "I said, 'Let your ears listen to me. I used to think only of killing and cutting off many heads, but I quit that custom. Now I love Jesus and live well. Let's all stop killing and live well.' "

In sending Tariri to the States, Cam aroused a great deal of publicity, though there was some criticism for "exploiting raw savages," and some for giving a distorted idea of the citizens of Peru. Cam, however, was pleased, especially when the Reader's Digest wrote saying they wanted to do a story and would send senior editor Clarence Hall down. Harper & Brothers was interested in a book. On both projects Cam offered full cooperation. When Clarence Hall actually arrived, Cam was on his way to the States, but he mapped out a jungle itinerary for the journalist.

Hall was not the only journalist to come to Yarinacocha in those days. To each writer who visited the base, Cam always showed personal interest. He welcomed their questions and invited them to look around and talk to anyone. "We do everything in the open," he stressed. He realized this policy of press relations entailed risks of inaccuracies, and reminded supporters, "We can't control what they write, but generally they are fair. And they tell the world what we are doing." And that was always worth a great deal.

The *Reader's Digest* article appeared in August 1958. Cam flew to New York at the magazine's expense to check the article before publication, and was very excited at what Hall had done. In fact, he hoped that Hall would do the book that Harper wanted. However, Hall's feeling was that Wycliffe was too complicated for an outsider to do them justice; a Wycliffe member should do the book. Cam accepted Hall's explanation. He had a member in mind who just might do as the author, and she was in the States.

Ethel Wallis was an experienced Mexico translator who had already shown writing ability. Cam talked with her in San Francisco—after stops in Washington, D.C., Kansas City, and Seattle to work on fund-raising and ceremonies for goodwill planes. Ethel was somewhat taken aback by the request to write a history of WBT/SIL—it would be a tremendous task.

"How long would I have?" she asked.

"Harper's wouldn't need the manuscript until September."

"September? But it's already May, Uncle Cam. I'd have to do so much research." But Cam's expectancy broke down her objections. "I'll try," she said. "And I have a librarian friend, Mary Bennett, who might help. She's a good researcher."

Cam suggested they go on down to the Glendale office immediately, because a lot of the information was there. But when he phoned for reservations, everything was full. "Let's go to the airport, anyway," he suggested.

The ticket agent sold them open tickets—the planes were full for the day. Tickets in hand, Cam and Ethel started toward the gates. "But Uncle Cam," Ethel protested, "the man said there were no seats!"

Cam never slackened his pace. "Ethel, the Lord has taught me never to take no as a negative."

At the gate two passengers failed to show up and Cam and Ethel were seated in their places.

While in Glendale, Cam attended the 1958 board meeting, and

challenged the group to pray and work for 200 new recruits for their 25th anniversary year starting in 1959.

As Cam knew she could, Ethel Wallis with Mary Bennett did get the research and the writing of Wycliffe's history done. *Two Thousand Tongues to Go* was published in 1959, coinciding with the beginning of the 25th anniversary.

The impact of the *Reader's Digest* article continued to make itself felt throughout 1959. Over a thousand letters and about $15,000 in gifts came as a result, making 1959 the best financial year on record. Contributing to the increase in giving was the traveling of the 25th anniversary speaking teams, including Cam, Pike, Cowan, Burns, and others, who fanned out across the country holding round-tables and rallies in churches and auditoriums. And membership went over 1,000, including the first second-generation member—Dick and Kay Pittman's daughter Marilou.

For the first time, member "quotas"—minimal allowances estimated necessary for comfortable subsistence—didn't drop under 80 percent a single month. And this was the year the board reluctantly decided to resign membership in the Interdenominational Foreign Missionary Association. The reasons for this step had been building up for several years.

*"If I were condemned to hang, I'd ask God to
enable me to love my hangman."*

28. The Language of Love

The same years that brought mounting recognition and publicity
for Wycliffe also brought increased criticism both at home and
abroad. The main area of attack was Wycliffe's relationship to
Catholic missionaries. Abroad, the problem was primarily in Peru.
In the States, the criticism centered in the Interdenominational
Foreign Missions Association (IFMA), although questions were
raised and judgments leveled from other quarters also.

Wycliffe had joined the IFMA at the suggestion of Oswald
Smith, pastor of the People's Church in Toronto, who felt it would
aid the young organization in being accepted by the Christian
public. But when Cam returned to Yarinacocha, Peru, in July 1958
after his visit to the States for the *Reader's Digest* article and the
Harper book, he found a number of problem letters waiting for him.

The one from Clyde Taylor, head of the Evangelical Foreign
Missionary Association,* asked questions in a fraternal spirit. He
wanted to know, "So you consider Catholics to be true Christians?
And what about giving translations to Catholics?"

Cam replied:

*You might also ask if I equate membership in a Methodist, Presby-
terian or some other denominational organization with truly knowing
Christ. I've known people in all those organizations who seem to be
trusting the Lord . . . but, I've known many other members who
did not impress me as being true believers in Christ. It's possible to
know Christ as Lord and Savior and to continue in the Roman
Church. . . .*

---

* The EFMA, as part of the National Association of Evangelicals, allowed
individual churches to be members, as well as denominations. The IFMA is an
association of evangelical mission societies only—both denominational and interdenominational groups.

200

We shall be happy indeed if the translations are used by anyone and everyone. God's Word will not return unto Him void. We stake everything on its power in the lives of those who feed upon it.

Just yesterday morning at the breakfast table I handed it to a high government official to read. He read part of John 21 and then I read from Isaiah 53. The hearts of all present were touched. My advice to missionaries in these lands is to proclaim the Word more and argue about it less.

The letter from the director of a U.S. mission which had missionaries in Ecuador was more critical and judgmental. "I beg your missionaries to change their attitudes toward priests," Cam pleaded in reply. "The language of love is service. If I were condemned to hang, I'd ask God to enable me to love my hangman."

It was Dr. Ralph Davis's letter, however, that caused the greatest concern. Davis was president of the IFMA, and he cited charges from "anonymous" persons that the primary purpose of Wycliffe's work was scientific and cultural, not spiritual. And they used their airplanes to help the Catholic church.

Cal Hibbard, Cam's secretary, expressed his concern. "This could really mean trouble, Uncle Cam. A lot of folks support our work because we're in the IFMA."

"I know," Cam agreed. "I just wish some of these critics would come out in the open. But since they won't we'll just have to answer Dr. Davis point by point and invite him to come see the work."

Cam spent most of the next six months in his second-floor office overlooking the lake. The correspondence was tedious, but he tried to apply a reconciling touch in replying to each critic's complaints. And having an uncanny memory for little personal incidents that happened decades before, he might add a note in his tiny round-lettered script to a dictated letter.

Much of the heavy correspondence during the late months of 1958 related to the IFMA controversy. Cam kept suggesting to the WBT/SIL board that the best solution was for Wycliffe to resign from the IFMA. Nyman and company in California urged him to be patient. The keeper of the Wycliffe purse knew how precarious the financial support of the large growing membership was, with some existing on less than $100 a month. Resignation, or negative IFMA action, Nyman felt, could tighten the purse strings of many supporters in conservative churches.

Even the usually positive Crowell had a question. His concern was the use of the two names, SIL and WBT. "Why not declare yourselves as missionaries?" he asked.

Cam pointed to great missionaries of the past who had plied a trade.

Paul made tents. Carey cobbled. Morrison was a bookkeeper. The first missionary to Guatemala taught English. We enter countries as linguists, even though everyone knows we are missionaries at heart.

The classical missionary approach will not get the job done in this generation nor in ten. It almost seems that some people are so tied to the hitching post of custom in missionary activities that they would let the job go undone rather than adopt a different approach. . . .

That seemed to satisfy the practical Crowell.

Pike, who had differed with Cam in the past but had always loyally stood by, hoped Cam would see the seriousness of the criticism from their conservative brethren. In December 1958 he wrote Cam an explanatory note.

We are in for objection and criticism for a long, long time. You have been a very great innovator. Wycliffe, following you, is similarly a great innovator. But every innovator has to expect resistance from the people following the normal course of events. . . . Anybody with any sense of historical development knows that innovators cannot be replaced by law, committees, or by appointment. We need you horribly. Yet, please bear with us if once in a blue moon we act like normal human beings with normal conservative tendencies trying to preserve our normal useful social order!

But the IFMA leaders remained unconvinced that the group's innovations were proper, and decided to send an investigator to Peru. Cam replied that the IFMA representative would be cordially welcomed at the base, but asked: "How can he possibly see everything in eight days?"

A week before the IFMA man was due to arrive, a new problem arose in Peru that might have confirmed the IFMA's suspicions. The new Peruvian director of the upcoming Indian teachers' course told Cam, "I have orders to permit a priest to teach a class in Catholic religion for the Indian teachers."

Cam had thought that the Catholic criticism had been taken

care of. At the beginning of 1958 he had landed in Lima, after several months' absence, to be handed a collection of antagonistic press clippings from the Lima paper. "The SIL people are not really linguists, but Protestant missionaries in disguise. The Indians speak Spanish. They are Catholics and don't need help in their own languages. By being allowed to meddle with the Indians with government support, SIL is dividing the country."

Cam had discovered that some conservative prelates had been joined by a few plantation owners whose exploitation of the Indians had been hindered by the bilingual schools and the new agricultural projects. "You wouldn't believe some of the stories they are spreading," an SIL member told Cam. "All over the jungle, they're saying we take Indians to the base, kill them, and render them into oil to use in our planes!"

"How could anyone believe something like that?"

"Well, someone found a skull in the garbage—it had been taken from an old Inca mound—and took it to the authorities as proof we were killing Indians!"

"There really isn't much we can do about that kind of yarn," Cam had said. "Just ignore it, and try to love everybody. I'll try to talk to the prelates though."

He had gone directly to the papal nuncio, the Vatican's diplomatic representative to the Peruvian government. The nuncio received him cordially and listened courteously. "Your Excellency, we're bringing the country closer together instead of dividing it," Cam explained. "We're also trying to be of service to all the missionaries, Catholic and Protestant, and others who serve the Indians. Our goal is to put sacred Scripture into every language on earth."

The nuncio was new in Peru, and had not heard SIL's side. "Could you give me a written report on your services to Catholic missionaries?" he asked.

"Certainly," Cam smiled. "Now, your Excellency, would you kindly ask God's blessings on our brave young people who are translating the Bible in the jungle?"

The nuncio promised he would.

Cam's report had cited many examples of service performed by SIL to the Catholic missionaries, and also detailed how Catholic missionaries had often helped SIL linguists. "The gracious friendly things they do for us," he concluded, "do credit to the Lord who said: 'By this shall all men know ye are my disciples if ye have love one to another.' I believe they love us and I know we love them."

About the same time the director of the National Catholic Information Service in Washington had inquired about relationships between SIL and Catholics. Cam again had replied in typical style:

. . . Since we are nonsectarian and nonecclesiastical, we get help from Catholics, Protestants, Jews, Moslems, Buddhists and even atheists.

Our big problem is that we are a new type of crusader whereas people try to put us in categories with which they are familiar. Missionary-minded people think we are just a bunch of scientists and should look to scientific institutions for support rather than to Christian donors. Protestant zealots find we transport Catholic missionaries in our airplanes and . . . cut off contributions, saying we're helping promote Catholic missions. Catholic prelates who don't know us personally object because we aren't Catholics and don't tell the tribesmen, whom we help spiritually through the Bible, that they should join the Catholic Church when they give up worshiping the sun, the boa constrictor or the spirits of the forest.

You might think that so much misunderstanding would make it impossible for us to forge ahead, but when people find we are reaching primitive tribes, who, due to language barriers, have existed for centuries outside the pale of modern civilization, they help us. People like for the primitive underdogs to get a chance even though it comes through a rather off-color branch of missionary-scientists who believe in Christ and the Apostles' Creed, but aren't sectarian about it and try to love and serve everybody.

After receiving Cam's letter and checking to find that priests had been attending SIL summer schools, the Catholic press service had given a favorable report.

Cam had then invited several newspaper writers to come to Yarinacocha to cover the festivities at the graduation of the Indian teachers. He had felt the resulting stories would help clear up the misunderstandings, and to a large extent they had. Glowing articles had appeared in Lima's major newspapers.

But now it seemed the criticisms had risen again. So he went to see the local bishop, Monsignor Gustavo Prevost.

"What can I do for you, Uncle Cam?" the red-headed French Canadian asked. The SIL group had given Monsignor Prevost a reception when he had been assigned to the area, and he and Cam had visited back and forth.

"Someone in Lima has ordered a religion class in the next Indian teacher's course."

Prevost smiled. "Yes, I just got a request to send a priest over to teach twelve hours of religion a week. I did think it strange. We don't teach that much religion in the Pucallpa public schools."

"We just can't allow that at our facilities. We're nonsectarian," explained Cam. "I hope you aren't offended."

"No, no. Not at all. My priests have too much to do already."

"We could allow a priest to teach if attendance was voluntary," Cam suggested.

"If it were voluntary no one would come."

"I would," Cam declared. "Or perhaps you would be willing to come and give our workers some lectures. We're all plain laymen. Maybe we could return the favor by teaching one of your priests the Shipibo language."

Monsignor Prevost seemed impressed. "Perhaps I could come and speak. But I don't think I could spare a priest to work with the Shipibos. Our territory is so big and the priests so few that we can't adequately handle our Spanish responsibilities."

"Well, whenever you can come, let me know. And, before I forget, my wife wants you over for a home-cooked meal."

The bishop came and by the time they were to the cherry pie, their friendship was stronger than ever. "Come again," Cam invited. "If the rain bogs up the road, you can spend the night in our 'prophet's chamber.'"

Cam then went to report to the minister of education in Lima about the order. "This violates our nonsectarian policy," he told the educator. "How can we serve all groups if we cater to one?"

When the minister had heard Cam out, he said, "I'll cancel the religion class, but you must help me reassure the Catholics."

Cam promised he would.

The IFMA investigator arrived just after January 1, 1959. He walked around the base, looked at the hangar, visited a tribe, spoke at the Sunday services. He was cordial, affable and gave Cam an *abrazo* when time came to leave. "It's easy to criticize from eight thousand miles," he said. But he politely declined to tell Cam the identity of the complainers. Still Cam was encouraged and thought this storm would soon be over.

But in mid-1959 he received a disturbing letter from Ken Watters in California who had been helping Nyman handle correspondence. "The IFMA matter isn't dead by a long shot," Watters wrote. "Their president claims numerous people have complained about us."

Cam wrote IFMA headquarters: "Name one critic. . . . I doubt if many of them are working in an Indian language. . . . We feel very strongly that the way our critics want us to treat the monks and nuns is unscriptural. . . . We simply can't do it."

But the IFMA leaders still would not name the complainers. Instead they requested that the Wycliffe board present an official answer to the anonymous charges. Cam felt this would be wasted effort, but he agreed that George Cowan could draft a defense.

Nothing, however, could change the mind of the IFMA leaders. And so the decision to resign was made. Cam commented on it, "We can best serve everybody if we don't belong to anybody."

Cowan mailed copies of the formal resignation statement to missions which were members of the organization, adding, "We hope to serve you at home and abroad as in the past, and to experience the same cordial fellowship in the Lord's work." The result was that only a few Wycliffites lost support.

And back in Peru, Monsignor Prevost from Pucallpa occasionally went to Yarinacocha to the Townsends' home for tea or a meal. He and his priests began distributing Scriptures in the public schools in 1963. "Pope John is bringing us into a new era," he told Cam and Elaine. "He talks about love among all Christians."

The new decade had begun.

". . . it is important to make every effort possible to identify our work with the national interests of the countries where we work."

29. Patience and Fortitude

In Mexico the work was growing and relations with the government were on an even keel. But the increased number of workers put an added strain on the already overcrowded Kettle in Mexico City. Everytime Cam stopped in the Mexican capital on his way to or from Peru—which was quite often at the end of the 50s—Ben Elson, the director of the Mexico work, would remind him of the need for a new headquarters. But there was no money to buy land.

Cam had been to see President Ruiz Cortines in the summer of 1956 on his way back from furlough. But the answer to his question about a gift of land from the government had been "Not yet." In the fall of 1957 he was there again on an extended stay while he waited for plans to be finalized on the Kansas City plane ceremony When the land question came up again, Cam told Ben, "I'll pray more about it." The next morning he read from Ezra how the Lord stirred up the spirit of Cyrus to rebuild Jerusalem. "Lord, stir up some Cyrus here in our behalf," he prayed. Then, like the evangelist D. L. Moody, who believed in a prayer that "had feet and walked," Cam began calling on government officials. But again the answer was "Not yet."

Still, he challenged the group to believe and pray. One morning he spoke to them from Acts 11:1–2. "The early Christians prayed without ceasing for Peter while he was in prison. That's the way we should pray. With definite goals in mind. Suppose the Lord should suddenly appear and say, 'I'll give you all you ask for during the next ten minutes,' what would you ask? Well, the Lord's here right now, just waiting to hear our requests. Let's tell Him what's on our hearts."

Early in 1959 Ben Elson wrote asking Cam to try again. The new president, Adolfo López Mateos, was now in office. Cam flew in late in February and immediately started making the usual diplomatic rounds, calling on his friends in government circles.

He had been met at the airport when he landed with a cable to radio Elaine, but had not been able to get a good connection, so he could just barely make out that someone might be having surgery for appendicitis in Lima. Billy had been having stomach pains before Cam left—but not being able to communicate with Elaine was almost unbearable. "If weeping would do any good, I'd weep," he wrote her after trying to reach her again.

Cam was never one to sit and bemoan circumstances, however. In addition to making the rounds of the Mexican officials, he made an appointment to meet with the second secretary at the Russian Embassy. He couldn't get away from the idea of getting into Russia.

The Russian diplomat was impressed by the stack of grammars, dictionaries, and primers which the group had translated into Mexican-Indian languages. "How are you supported?" he asked Cam. When Cam explained, "We look to God to move individuals who believe in our work," the Russian murmured, "Incredible!"

Cam also enjoyed a warm reunion with Lázaro Cárdenas, who had just returned from a trip to Russia, China, and the U.S.A.

And he kept trying to see the president. When he finally got in, López Mateos poured lavish tribute on Cam and the SIL group. He also said he would see what could be done about a land grant for the headquarters.

And about the same time, Cam received an ungarbled message from Elaine. The emergency was over. Billy had had surgery and was recovering nicely. By the time Cam could fly back to Lima in April, Elaine and Billy had returned to Yarinacocha, where Cam joined them for almost a whole month before he had to leave again.

This time he was going to Guatemala to the Inter-American Indian Congress. Dr. Efrain Morote Best, a former director of the bilingual teacher training course, was going too—both were members of the Peruvian delegation to the Congress. Dr. Morote Best shared Cam's vision for the Indians. He had promoted the bilingual schools and also wanted Indians to receive more training in scientific agriculture, commerce, and technical and political skills.

In Guatemala, Cam spent a weekend revisiting familiar sites, including San Antonio, accompanied by Morote Best. But he spent more time in the present, planning for the future. He had several conversations with the head of the Colombian delegation to the Congress, Dr. Hernández de Alba. "We would welcome the scientific contributions SIL could make to our country," the anthropologist told Cam, "but the concordat we have with the Vatican would likely rule out translating the Bible."

Cam replied with something Monsignor Prevost had once told him: " 'Better the Indians be Protestants than continue pagan.' We promote Christian faith," he added, "and no special brand of it."

"I don't think you could get past the concordat," de Alba concluded reluctantly.

Just before the Congress closed, Cam and John Beekman, SIL's director for Central America, were given an audience with Guatemala's President Ydigoras. Beekman had been one of the translators of the New Testament into the Chol language in Mexico while afflicted with a constricted heart valve. Surgery had corrected the problem with one of the first artificial valves which contained a plastic ball that rose and fell in rhythm with the beat. Beekman literally ticked like a clock. Cam used the novelty to break the ice with the president, then went on to tell about his old work with the Cakchiquels and SIL's present program.

Ydigoras smiled. "You don't have to convince me. This work should be supported by everyone. How can we help you?"

"Well," Cam said, "we do need a little land here in the capital for a headquarters. We will put up a building, keep it up, and turn it back to the government when the work is done in your tribes."

The president turned and telephoned his minister of education. "I'm sending Townsend and his assistant over. They need land."

Cam and Beekman went straight to the minister's office, and in a short time the grant was made and signed. The Guatemalan headquarters had been provided for.

Later, at the rented group house, Beekman talked to Cam about his future. "You know Ben Elson wants me to head up a translation consultation program in Mexico," he said. "When can you get someone to take my place here?"

"I'll work on it," Cam promised. "What we need is a Center. I remember how much it helped me to get away to a quiet place with Joe Chicol and Trinidad Bac when I was finishing the Cakchiquel translation. I've long dreamed of such a center in Mexico where translators could take their Indian assistants for a few months and work with trained consultants."

After the Congress was over, Cam waited on in Guatemala City hoping that he would receive favorable word from Colombia for SIL's beginning work there. Finally, however, he decided that Colombia was not yet ready. He flew to Orlando, Florida, to participate in a plane ceremony, and then came back with the new plane to Yarinacocha and his family.

During the Townsend's year in the States (1959–60), another call came for help from Mexico. The headquarters problem there was far from resolved. Cam and Elaine and the two older girls flew in for a few days' visit, and Cam went immediately to work.

He and Ben Elson first went to see the new minister of education. Jaime Torres Bodet, Mexico's poet-statesman who had been head of UNESCO, gave Cam a warm welcome. "Next year will be our twenty-fifth anniversary," Cam told him, "and the place we began was Mexico. We would like to have a celebration and a conference of educators and officials from sister countries who are interested in the welfare of Indians. They'd like to see the great advances you've made here."

"How is your headquarters project coming?" the minister asked.

When Cam replied that SIL had no land for it yet, Torres Bodet phoned the controller of public properties, who agreed at once to see them.

In the elevator, Elson said, "I can hardly believe it. He said he'd get on it right away, and I'm sure he will! Praise the Lord! It's a real miracle."

The five acres which the government gave was in the Mexico City Tlalpan district and worth then an estimated $300,000. The agreement specified that SIL would construct suitable buildings to facilitate its program of linguistic research and Indian advancement. Land and buildings would be returned to the government in thirty years.

Before returning to California, Cam and Elaine had a lingering visit with Lázaro Cárdenas. The ex-president was worried over the start of a nuclear war between the great powers. He asked what Cam thought were the prospects of lasting peace.

"The Bible tells us the Prince of Peace will return to earth and end all injustices," Cam replied. "He will give everlasting peace."

Then, as he had many times before, Cam shared the inner peace Christ had brought to his heart. Cárdenas listened attentively. When the Townsends were leaving, he embraced Cam and said,

"Thank you my friend for your good words. You're the only one who talks to me about my soul."

The Townsends' return to the States plunged them again into the hectic pace of cross-country speaking engagements. At the same time Cam was helping raise money for the building program in Mexico City. He also had another headquarters problem on his mind. JAARS needed a central location and a headquarters building.

Lawrence Routh, the Carolina contractor, had suggested the Charlotte, North Carolina area. Cam had also met mercantile executive Henderson Belk, who lived in Charlotte and was keen on helping Wycliffe. Belk offered a nice tract of wooded and pasture land near the town of Waxhaw, about thirty miles south of Charlotte, for the new aviation center. Cam flew in to inspect. The tract was large enough for a landing strip, shops, hangars, and housing. There was even an old white-columned antebellum house that could be repaired and used until more adequate buildings were completed.

While in the Charlotte area, Cam met Melvin Graham, a farmer and Billy Graham's brother. Mel was an elder and teacher in the independent Calvary Presbyterian Church. The rugged outdoor type, Mel liked a tractor better than a platform. The idea of a world missionary aviation center near Charlotte excited him. When Cam asked him to be the chairman of a JAARS committee in Charlotte to work with Lawrence Routh, who would oversee the building program, he agreed willingly.

Then Cam put in a call to Jack Kendall in California. The retired telephone company engineer had already installed telephone systems at the Peru base. Kendall agreed to come to Charlotte and help with the engineering.

By this time the Townsends' year at home was up, and they returned to Peru, though Cam didn't stay at home long. In January 1961 a telegram came saying Will Nyman was dead. Cam flew immediately to California for the funeral. Though Nyman's death had not been unexpected, Cam felt as though a part of himself was gone. Nyman had been a faithful, loyal supporter for the twenty-five years of Wycliffe's existence, and even before that. Ken Watters and Phil Grossman, who had been carrying much of Nyman's load, would take care of things, but Cam would miss his old friend and his loyal support.

From Los Angeles Cam flew directly to Mexico City where Elaine met him for the 25th anniversary celebration of the work in

Mexico. Guests came from three countries to help celebrate. At a gala banquet presided over by Minister of Education Torres Bodet, Cam was presented with a handsome 694-page volume of 58 articles on Indian life and language from fourteen hemispheric groups prepared in his honor.

The Mexican scholar who spoke at the banquet characterized Cam in terms that could also describe the work he headed: "One of those mystics in whom two tendencies meet; one seeks the salvation of the soul, the other applies the positive good in our civilization so that not only souls but bodies may be freed from the horrors of sorrow, sickness, poverty, exploitation and premature death."

Cam on a visit to Jungle Camp in southern Mexico in the early 60's.

Cam at SIL Board meeting in Mexico City, at the "Kettle."

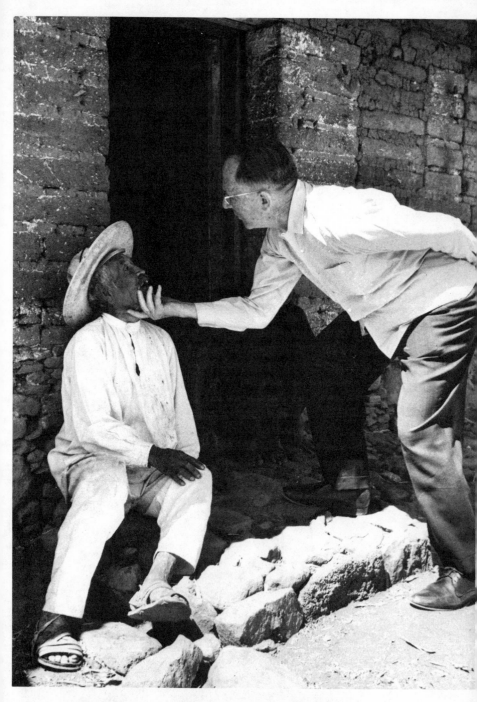

Cam was concerned about the physical needs of the Indians. He often helped care for their wounds and bad teeth.

Above: Cam embraces General Mendosa, Peru, 1963. *Below:* Cam with U.S. Senator Fred Harris of Oklahoma, on Bible Translation Day, September 30, 1966, in Washington D.C.

Above: In 1962 Cam and SIL leaders presented the printed Tzeltal New Testament to the Mexican minister of education. *Below:* Cam gives Testaments to the Tzeltal Indians at Jungle Camp.

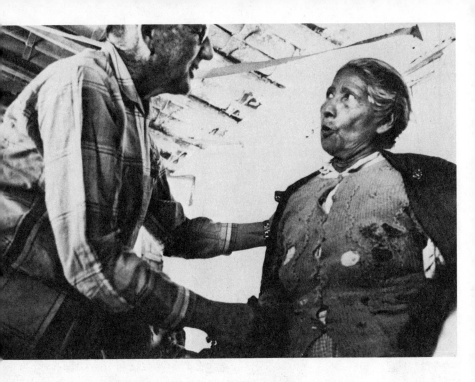

Cam often returned to Tetelcingo for a visit with old friends, including Josefina *(above)* and Refugio and Lola *(left)*, former landlords.

Cam parks his Texas hat, given him by his friend Bob Fenn, and his Mexican briefcase, given him by the Mexico SIL Branch, while he works.

"Don't apply unless you are willing to go an extra mile. . . ."

30. Colombia

In the two years since he had talked to Hernández de Alba about SIL's coming to Colombia, Cam hadn't stopped hoping and praying for an entrance. Actually, it had been nine years since he had met Lleras Camargo in Chicago, who was then head of the Organization of American States; now he was president of Colombia.

Cam knew the time would come when Wycliffe would be able to enter Colombia. In the meantime there was plenty to keep him occupied. When he left Mexico after the anniversary festivities early in 1961, he flew to Charlotte to look over the plans for the JAARS headquarters—hangars, shops, administration building, and a communications nerve center with radio contact to several Wycliffe fields.

Then there were plane projects in Greensboro, North Carolina, Philadelphia, and a speaking engagement on Long Island. There a ham radio operator conveyed a message to Cam from Bob Schneider in Ecuador: "President Velasco Ibarra is going to visit the base tomorrow to meet the Auca believers. Please come."

The message took Cam back five years to the killing of the five missionaries by Auca warriors. He had told Rachel Saint, whose brother was one of the five, that he would pray and believe that someday Rachel would have the privilege of introducing Nate's killers to the president of Ecuador.

Cam caught a flight immediately for Miami, where, in spite of being told he couldn't be cleared for Ecuador, he bought a through ticket, and caught the next plane, landing in Quito in time to join the presidential party at Shell Mera.

At the SIL base Rachel Saint introduced President Velasco Ibarra to Kimo, one of the Auca killers, who muttered something in Auca,

221

and reached out to touch the presidential pate. "I don't think he's ever seen a bald head before, Mr. President," Cam explained.

The president laughed heartily. "How were you able to teach such abstract conceptions as God and Jesus Christ to such savages?" he asked Rachel.

"May I suggest you ask Kimo, Mr. President?"

"Kimo, who is Jesus Christ?"

Rachel repeated the question in Auca. Kimo's face brightened as he replied, "Jesus Christ is the One who came from heaven and died for my sins. He made me stop killing and live happily with my brothers."

"Amazing!" the president exclaimed.

That night at a dinner banquet given by the SIL staff, Velasco Ibarra was still talking about the amazing transformation. "Mr. President," Cam assured him, "the same thing happens over and over again when primitive tribesmen hear the Word of God in their own language. Perhaps you see now why we are so eager to help the Indians."

"I think I do. Where will you be going next?"

"Back to Peru for the graduation exercises of the Indian teachers' course. Then to visit our work in Brazil."

"Ah, Brazil. Jânio Quadros, the new president, is a friend of mine. I will have my ambassador set up an appointment for you."

"Thank you, Mr. President."

"By the way, I've been hearing a lot about this preacher named Billy Graham. Would he come to Quito?"

"Dr. Graham is a good friend. He endorses our work. I'll ask him for you."

"Good. Good. I thank you. And I thank you for coming. My government will continue to back your work. Imagine, an Auca that has stopped killing and teaches the Bible. Amazing! I never would have believed it."

President Velasco Ibarra was true to his word. When Cam got to Brazilia in May of 1961, Jim Wilson, the new director of Wycliffe's work there, took him to see the Ecuadorian ambassador. The ambassador escorted them to the presidential palace where President Quadros courteously invited Cam and Wilson to his office for an audience. As a former teacher who had lived near the *campo grande* section of Brazil, Quadros was immensely interested in the Terena language primers which Wilson had brought with him.

"I know the Terena tribe," the president told them. "I lived near them as a boy. This is just what they need."

Cam and Wilson explained the work of SIL and the advantages of bilingual education. "It's a new day for the Indians, Mr. President, when they learn to read and write, first in their own language, then in Portuguese." Cam went on to describe how the Bible was changing the Aucas.

"How many tribes are you helping in Brazil?" Quadros asked.

"We have teams in nineteen tribes, Mr. President," Cam answered. "Some are single girls."

"Will you make primers like these for each tribe?"

"Yes. That is part of our agreement with your government."

"And there are young single women living among our Indians? They must be very brave."

"Yes, Mr. President, both brave and dedicated."

"How can I help?"

Wilson presented him a memorandum listing four requests. The president read them aloud, then said in a firm tone, "I will do it." He scribbled some notes across the top of the document, stamped it URGENTE, and handed it to an aide.

Cam flew back to Peru elated over the enthusiastic support promised by the Brazilian president, but his face dropped when he read his mail. Larry Montgomery wanted a leave of absence to work for the Helio corporation. His support had been dropping.

"I don't blame him for asking for a leave," Cam wrote Crowell, "but it's a hard blow when a partner, on whom you've depended for years, leaves you. I feel sort of lost without Will Nyman at home. Now I seem to have lost Larry's broad shoulders too."

Larry had been the dependable expert in aviation. Now Cam turned to Harold Goodall, Les Bancroft, a veteran mechanic, and Merrill Piper, an experienced pilot, who went to North Carolina to work on the JAARS project.

That summer—1961—Lima officials and educators gave a festive fifteenth anniversary banquet in Cam's honor. After the celebration, Cam and Elaine flew to Quito for a dinner with President Velasco Ibarra. From the high Ecuadorian capital, he wrote the membership a "Dear Gang" letter, reflecting on his sixty-fifth birthday.

My heart overflows with gratitude to God, to Elaine, to you and to our wonderful friends in Latin America, the U.S. and elsewhere.

Financially, I have almost nothing to show for my 44 years of labor on behalf of the Indians. We own an automobile that you folks gave us two years ago, a home in the jungles of Peru, five hundred dollars in savings for the education of our children and that's all. In the wealth of friendship, however, we are millionaires.

You live by faith the same as we. On faith accompanied by works, our organization has grown in 26 years to over 1,100. We get nothing (no personal support) from any government, nothing from the denominational organizations and very little from foundations or really wealthy people, but God has people send us enough food and clothing. It is the hand of God that feeds us as the mother bird feeds her fledglings. Our concerns therefore are even scantier than our savings. This is one of the reasons why we are such a happy group. True happiness comes through sacrifice for others.

It was biennial conference time again, and Cam took off for Sulphur Springs. The 1961 keynote continued to be advance. Otis Leal reported the acceptance of over one hundred new members. Ken Pike described linguistic workshops he had held in various fields. John Beekman felt that Pike's workshops, the Translation Center in Mexico, and technical aids would eventually cut in half the time required for translators to produce a New Testament.

John Bendor-Samuel, the Oxford-trained English linguist, was ready to start work in Africa. "Our supporters in England are expecting a visit from you, Uncle Cam," he told the general director. "You *must* come."

"I've been thinking of coming," Cam told him. "But lately the Lord has been speaking to me about Colombia. I want to be on stand-by when the opportunity comes there." This time it wasn't long in coming.

Cam was in Mexico City when Goodall phoned from North Carolina about routine JAARS business. "By the way," Goodall ended, "the Colombian ambassador is to be in Charlotte over the weekend to be guest of honor at the state fair, and will be staying with Henderson and Ann Belk." The statement electrified Cam. "I'll be on the next flight out," he declared. "Tell the Belks and pray!"

The weekend with the Belks was Cam's opportunity to orient Ambassador and *Señora* Sanz de Santamaria on the service of SIL. When they flew back to Washington, Cam was on the same flight, and they invited him to lunch at their home the next day. There, the ambassador gave Cam important letters of introduction. With the letters in his briefcase, Cam flew to Bogotá and looked up Director of Indian Affairs Dr. Hernández de Alba, whom he had met two years before at the Indian Congress in Guatemala City. Hernández de Alba gladly accompanied him as he delivered the letters.

The first was to President Lleras Camargo, who remembered Cam and his biography of Cárdenas from their meeting in Chicago nine years before. "We'll be glad to give you a contract," he said assuringly.

After they delivered the other letters, they visited Bishop Marceliano Canyes. He got to talking about his late brother, who had been both a priest and linguist. "I remember in 1937 your brother and I both had articles in the same linguistic magazine in Mexico," Cam said. "He was well known in linguistic circles."

"Yes, he always wanted to help the Indians. I have his manuscripts and books in my residence, but they've never been put in order."

Cam filed that piece of information in his memory, then outlined SIL's intentions. "In Peru we base our translations upon the Spanish *Nácar y Colunga* translation. We make them available to anyone who wishes to use them, evangelical or Catholic."

Bishop Canyes frowned. "This is a Catholic state, although Protestant missionaries are allowed in the Spanish-speaking areas. But the Church has an agreement with the government forbidding the Protestants to propagate their sects in the Indian territories."

"We should have no problem working with Catholic missionaries here," Cam said. "In other countries where we have government contracts, they help us and we help them when we can do each other favors. Our planes will be at your disposal at a moderate price just as they are to everybody else."

"Well, perhaps we can work together," the prelate concluded.

Cam left copies of SIL's constitution and contracts with other governments with Dr. Hernández de Alba. "I'll take it from here," the anthropologist promised. Cam went home to Yarinacocha and wrote the membership:

We need to be ready to start work in Colombia within six months. But how can we do it when we all have our hands full now? This morning we read Philippians 2 with our guests at the breakfast table and the 13th verse assured me: "For it is God which worketh in you

*both to will and to do.". . . . He will enable us. . . . Don't apply un-
less you are willing to go an extra mile in serving the monks and
nuns. Colombia's tribes will be reached only by loving service and
patient faith. Above all, pray. I'll let you know when the contract is
signed.*

Then while Cam awaited the execution of the contract, Goodall
returned to Peru to work on Peru branch business which had been
left hanging while he had been in North Carolina, and to start
closing up his house.

In January 1962, a letter came from Henderson Belk. "Either you
or Goodall," he wrote to Cam, "must come to Charlotte and super-
vise the JAARS construction." Fearing that the committee of businessmen might become discouraged, Cam decided to take charge
himself until Goodall could get away from Peru, which would be
about June. The Belks offered the use of their furnished river-front
summer home a few miles from Charlotte, so Cam moved the
whole family, enrolling the children in Charlotte schools at mid-
semester. Grace was a high school freshman, and the others were
in grade school and junior high. Elaine was glad to be closer to her
family in Chicago. Her crippled sister Shirley had died the preceding
fall and her father now had incurable cancer.

While they were living in North Carolina, the call from Colombia
came. Cam flew immediately to Bogotá where a smiling Dr. Hernández de Alba, greeted him with the news "The president and his
cabinet have approved the contract." Cam remained long enough
to work out final details for entry of the first SIL workers headed by
Bob Schneider. Then he flew back to Charlotte to assist in the
JAARS project.

When Harold Goodall arrived in Charlotte in the summer of 1962
to take over the leadership of JAARS, Cam felt he should go to
Colombia to help the Schneiders. Elaine and the three younger
children would return to Yarinacocha, Peru, where he would join
them later. This meant leaving Grace behind to attend high school
at Ben Lippen Academy, a Christian boarding school in the Great
Smokies just outside of Asheville. The parting was especially hard
for Elaine.

Cam was in and out of Colombia in the next few months. Bob
Schneider's first report was very encouraging. He had had good
cooperation from the Colombian government and from Catholic

missionaries. "We've put some teams in Catholic mission communities where they are enjoying beautiful hospitality. The Division of Indian Affairs has given us a fully equipped office in Bogotá."

In February 1963, however, Schneider made an emergency phone call to Cam, with the news that some of the bishops were beginning to have doubts about SIL. When Cam arrived Schneider showed him a newly published booklet that claimed to be a report of SIL activities in the country.

Cam's immediate reaction was "We must get this cleared up as soon as possible." First they called on Bishop Canyes, who greeted them with some reserve. Cam quickly asked permission to read aloud some of the charges in the booklet. Then he paused and said, "Bishop Canyes, the University of Oklahoma isn't a Southern Baptist school. The university might be very offended at this. And we certainly aren't translating a Baptist catechism. We translate only the Holy Scriptures and never even add doctrinal notes."

Bishop Canyes looked unsettled. "Evidently I have been misinformed," he admitted. "I'll take the little book off the bookstands."

"We'd be most pleased if you would," Cam said. I'm sure you want only the truth told. We need to know each other better. Perhaps you would tell us about your work in the jungle."

After a pleasant exchange, Bishop Canyes had an idea. "Why don't you speak to the Catholic missionary bishops who are meeting here in a few days. If you could tell them what you've just told me, I think they would understand."

Cam was only too happy to accept the invitation. After he and Schneider had been introduced and Cam had explained the work of SIL, a bearded Spanish bishop stood and said pointedly, "It's all right for Catholics and Protestants to be together in Bogotá with a Catholic church on this corner and a Protestant church on that corner. But out in the jungle it won't work. The Indians will just be puzzled at seeing two ways of worshipping God."

All eyes turned to Cam as he rose to reply.

"When I was in Brazil," he began slowly, "I heard how the Franciscans paddled a canoe for five days to take two of our linguists to a tribe. In Bolivia the good sisters nursed one of our radio men back to health. In Peru the monks and nuns have helped us more times than I can count. And of course we serve them too, when we have the opportunity, with our planes and other facilities. On the basis of our common love for God, we enjoy cordial relations.

"I'll admit we've never worked in a country where there were eighteen mission bishops as here. Doubtless we have much to learn in Colombia. But wherever we have worked thus far, the people see this loving cooperation, and say, 'That's true Christianity. That's the way it should be.' Furthermore, it seems to me this is what Pope John XXIII has been striving for."

"Yes, that's right," several bishops agreed.

"When we translate the Bible into the Indian tongues, we'll gladly provide copies for you," Cam continued.

"Would you include our footnotes?" one of the bishops asked.

"No, we couldn't do that. We're strictly nonsectarian. We can't prefer one group over another."

The meeting concluded amiably and the bishops seemed satisfied.

Anxious to keep their goodwill, Cam requested that SIL members in Colombia who were guests at Catholic mission stations attend mass "occasionally." When some members and supporters objected, he cited Paul's habit of attending synagogues as his precedent, adding, "I'm willing to attend any kind of worship, even a witch doctor's séance, if it opens the way to share the Word. We must not let old prejudices block the giving of the gospel to the tribes."

The next day Cam visited Bishop Canyes in his residence. Remembering the library of books and manuscripts the Bishop's brother had left him, Cam asked to see them. They were still in crates.

"Such books and manuscripts as these should be on shelves," Cam said. "Would you like to have one of our linguists catalogue them for you?"

The bishop was overwhelmed by the offer. "That would be marvelous!"

That afternoon Cam wrote Dr. Viola Waterhouse in Mexico, requesting her help in the special project.

After dinner Cam and Schneider talked a long while about the future of Colombia. "There are twice as many tribes here as in Peru," Schneider said. "We'll need lots of new personnel. Our rapid growth may bother the bishops."

"Well, if we follow the same policies that have worked in other countries, they'll see that we're here to serve, not to fight."

"Yes, Uncle Cam, but Colombia is different. We need you and Elaine. Peru is a chartered branch now; they could get along without you."

"Yarinacocha has been our home for seventeen years," Cam replied. "We love Peru."

"But we're just getting started here. Having the general director in Bogotá would encourage the group. Lois and I would stay on awhile and I'd work under you as we did in Lima."

"I'll pray about it," was as much as Cam would promise.

He wrote Elaine about moving to Colombia, and when he got to Lima he radioed her at the jungle base. "I've talked it over with the kids," Elaine told him. "They dearly love our home at Yarina. But if Colombia is what the Lord wants, then we'll move."

And so the decision was made. They would move, perhaps the hardest move they would make. At Yarinacocha they had had their first real home, the big house overlooking the lake where the children had spent their formative years. The fruit trees were just beginning to bear, and the hibiscus and bougainvillaea were never more beautiful.

Hardest of all was leaving friends. SIL members gave parties for them. Then Bishop Prevost and officials from Pucallpa came for a farewell tea. That was when it finally came home to ten-year-old Billy that he was really moving away, and he burst into tears.

Then there were farewell ceremonies in Lima planned by their Peruvian friends. Dr. Morote Best, who had directed the Indian teacher training course and was now rector of the University of Huamanga, granted Cam the title of Honorary Professor, and said of him, "You have given everything to Peru and taken nothing away."

There was a visit to President Fernando Belaunde Terry. And then a big banquet where the minister of education presented both Cam and Elaine Las Palmas Magisteriales awards, the highest honor Peruvian teachers can receive. The minister of foreign affairs pinned on them both Order of Distinguished Service awards.

The Lima newspapers published editorials about Cam. *The Expresso* called him "a truly extraordinary person," and went on to say:

He leaves the warm land of the Peruvian Amazon and his friends the Cashibos, Campas, Machiguengas, Piros, Culinas, and Amahuacas whom he taught to . . . know the existence of God and of Peru. . . . He came to give us his best. He takes with him the gratitude of thousands of dark-skinned men . . . and the heartfelt remembrance of Peruvian teachers who saw his work and had the privilege of working in the jungle at the side of a man of love and truth.

Even *Time* (the Latin American edition) took notice in its September 27, 1963, issue.

One day recently, Indians in the jungles of eastern Peru drummed a message on hollowed tree trunks: "Don Guillermo is leaving." Townsend was leaving Peru for Colombia, but 200 trained linguists and other personnel will carry on. His work had earned him Peru's Order of Merit, a warm farewell abrazo from President Fernando Belaunde Terry, and the affectionate title "Apostle of the Alphabet."

Close friends came to see them off on the steamer that would move them to Colombia. There was an emotional presenting of gifts and exchange of farewell *abrazos*. As the ship pulled away from the dock, Cam and Elaine stood at the rail waving until everyone was out of sight. As they turned to go to their cabin, Elaine saw tears streaming down Cam's face. She had never seen him so moved.

"God is calling us to take another step of faith."

31. The Pavilion of 2,000 Tribes

While the Townsends were living in Charlotte during 1962, Cam was introduced one day to a public relations man. After hearing a few stories about Wycliffe's work in Latin America, he said to Cam, "Your people ought to have a pavilion at the New York World's Fair. Even though it's a couple of years off, now is the time to start planning. And I have a friend on a Fair committee."

The idea stirred Cam's imagination. The publicity value of an exhibit there would be enormous. Not only would it bring Bible translation to the attention of the American public, but it would also introduce the work to foreign visitors.

"Yes, we might be interested," he responded. "Have your friend send me information and we'll consider it."

A few days later a packet came in the mail. Cam whistled as he realized a pavilion would cost at least a quarter of a million dollars. At the moment he had less than $250. It took so much to keep Wycliffe going. Still he felt there could have been something providential in bumping into the PR man. He would wait and see what else might develop.

He spent the rest of the summer on JAARS business, promoting the new headquarters in Mexico. He gave stories of the work to *Time*'s Jerry Hannifin in Washington, newspaper columnist George Grimm in Minneapolis, and world-famed photographer Cornell Capa in New York.

Cornell Capa had become interested in WBT/SIL after reporting the 1956 Auca killings for *Life*. He had visited Yarinacocha and seen the work in Peru first-hand. At the encouragement of Cam's friend Sam Milbank, Capa had teamed with anthropologist Matthew Huxley to produce a book on Peru's jungle Indians confronted by

231

twentieth-century technology and civilization. In *Farewell to Eden*, published by Harper & Row, Capa and Huxley showed the challenge and responsibilities of the dominant culture and its "agents of change." They found that WBT/SIL alone possessed the philosophy and attitude most understanding of Indians' needs and most useful in preparing the jungle tribesmen for the inevitable confrontation with approaching civilization.

Capa was so impressed by the work of the SIL linguists that he volunteered to give his pictures and edit a book describing the work. Cam gratefully accepted the offer and the result was *Who Brought the Word*, a pictorial presentation of Bible translation.

At the board meeting in February 1963, held in Mexico City, Cam raised the subject of a pavilion at the World's Fair, but there was little response to his enthusiasm, and he dropped the subject. There was plenty of work to keep them all busy, and with membership at 1,500 and over, more funds were needed to support each worker and keep the growing number of planes in top shape.

At the biennial conference later that year news was both good and bad. Teams' were now in Ghana and Nigeria. Translation workshops were proving so satisfactory that John Beekman and Ken Pike were predicting that many translators would be able to do two Testaments in a lifetime. Computer experts Drs. Joe Grimes and Ivan Lowe described how computers in Mexico City were greatly reducing the time it took to convert manuscripts into books. Literacy expert Dr. Sarah Gudchinsky felt the literacy workshops she was developing and holding would result in thousands of new readers for published Scriptures.

The bad news was from Vietnam. There had been an attack on Wycliffe personnel. The guerrilla grapevine said the linguists had been mistaken for government people. Gaspar Makil, a Filipino member, his infant daughter, and Elwood Jacobsen were dead. Calling them "Wycliffe's first martyrs," Cam challenged the membership: "The assassins did not know that Gaspar and Elwood were messengers of God's love sent to serve the tribesmen unselfishly, giving them Light and Life. We must forgive; we do forgive. But we cannot forget the two tribes that have been cheated nor the 2,000 more for whom no workers have ever been assigned.

"Bullets cannot thwart God's plan. We believe that a host of new recruits will pick up the task that fell from the hands of our martyred colleagues. . . . Wycliffe needs 200 more recruits this year. . . . By God's grace and with your help we plan to keep on until every tribe has heard the Good News."

Just before the Townsends moved to Colombia in August 1963, a Mrs. Myra Magnuson came to Yarinacocha from New York to see a private hospital near Pucallpa. She asked to stay at the SIL base for a few days. Cam and Elaine welcomed her, and took time to visit with her and tell her about the work.

"Everyone should know about this work," was Mrs. Magnuson's response. "You should have a pavilion at the World's Fair. The world must know what you are doing for the Indians. Listen, I know Bob Moses, the Fair manager. He'll give you a lot free, I'm sure. Then you'd just have to put up a pavilion. Call me next time you're in New York and I'll set up a meeting."

Later as Cam and Elaine talked, he said, "She's the second person who's talked to me about the Fair. Maybe God is trying to tell us something."

After the family had settled into their small apartment on the third floor of the rented group house in Bogotá, Cam took Grace back to school in North Carolina, and then flew on to New York. There he met with Cornell Capa to put the finishing touches on the book *Who Brought the Word*. He also called Myra Magnuson, who set up an appointment for him with the assistant manager of the World's Fair. He was impressed with Cam's idea of imitating a jungle hut and furnishing it with artifacts from primitive tribes.

"There'll be nothing else like it at the Fair," he said. "We'll give you a lot at the corner of the Avenues of America and Europe. It's a great location. But you must have money for the pavilion in three or four weeks and a guarantee that it would be open by next April." Cam was excited at the possibility.

When Cam left the next day for California, Mrs. Magnuson saw him off. "You must have that pavilion," she declared, and pressed a $1,000 check in his hand.

The night after arriving, Cam spoke at a church in Santa Ana and told about the offer of a free lot at the Fair and Mrs. Magnuson's contribution. Afterward, a retired missionary said, "My wife and I will give a thousand dollars."

The next day at lunch two relatives promised five thousand dollars. When the board convened, Cam recited what had happened. "God is calling us to take another step of faith. Think how many people will go through the pavilion during the two summers of the Fair!"

The more conservative board members were worried. "Uncle Cam, we love you," they said "but we've got too many other obligations to consider this."

"But we can sell books, charge an entrance fee. People will give donations," Cam pleaded.

"It's against our policy to go into debt beyond our resources," Pike protested.

"We could sell this building if we had to," Cam said. "The tremendous benefits of a pavilion would be worth it."

Most of the board members still were unconvinced. "All right," Cam declared, "suppose I found individuals who would underwrite a hundred thousand dollars. If we made enough money, they wouldn't be out a cent. I've got seven thousand dollars already."

They debated this proposal awhile, and finally decided Cam could proceed after he had the $100,000 underwritten.

Cam flew back to Charlotte and at noon began calling friends. At ten that evening he reached the mark when a farmer in Illinois said, "Put me down for five."

Lawrence Routh accompanied him to New York the next day to meet with contractor Ralph Howell and the Fair committee. The committee accepted the contractor's guarantee that he would complete the pavilion on schedule, and Cam signed the contract.

Through the fall and winter Cam kept boosting the World's Fair project. He felt that the planned Pavilion of 2,000 Tribes should not only contain rare tribal artifacts, large photographs and charts but should also portray graphically the power of Scripture in the lives of primitive tribesmen. What could be better, he decided, than the story of Chief Tariri painted as a mural. Former President Truman had told him it was the greatest story he had ever heard.

Charlotte restaurateur Frank Sherrill recommended Canadian muralist Doug Riseborough. He went to Peru and first photographed a reenactment of a tribal battle in the jungle. From this and other scenes on film, he painted a dramatic mural one hundred feet long and ten feet high depicting the transformation of Chief Tariri.

Cam also assigned Ethel Wallis to prepare Tariri's autobiography for Harper & Row, to be sold at the Fair. Then having secured $152,000 in cash, gifts, loans, and underwritings, with $18,000 more promised, he left in January 1964 to return to Colombia. There he joined Clarence Church, the new director, and pilot Ralph Borthwick in the search for a base site in eastern Colombia. They located "another Yarinacocha" beside a lake about 150 miles east of Bogotá. When Cam and Church explained their intended use to the Colombian Air Force Officer who owned the land, he donated the 250 acres to the government, which assigned it to SIL for the term of years needed.

Cam left his family again in April 1964 for the dedication of the Mexico Branch's Publication Building in Mexico City. It was named for Moisés Sáenz. President López Mateos himself presided over the inauguration ceremony. The minister of government of Colombia, Camacha Rueda, honored the linguists by attending.

Before leaving Mexico, Cam and Ben Elson talked about the need for an administrator in the California home office. "George Cowan has written that I should move to Santa Ana and be in charge, or else appoint someone," Cam told Elson. "Personally, I feel that my call is to stay pretty close to the firing line, so I'm thinking of asking the board to make you administrative head of all our work. I would just make suggestions and help on special projects."

"I don't know, Uncle Cam. That sounds like quite a job."

"You could do it," Cam said confidently. "Please pray about it. You and Adelle have done a bang-up job leading our oldest and largest branch. And you've worked in a tribe. It may well be, Ben, that you're God's man to lead us."

Shortly after the opening of the World's Fair in 1964, Cam went to New York. As he had predicted, the rustic, aboriginal hut was an interest-getter and stood in sharp contrast to the scientific exhibits, architectural marvels, and other displays of modern progress.

Thousands went through the pavilion, but by the end of the first month it was obvious that gifts and the sale of books would pay only the operating expenses. Cam sent out an appeal calling for 2,000 churches to buy a $100 share each to cover the construction costs. By September the board objectors were really disturbed. They called for an emergency session of the board to determine the future of the project.

Cam had been overoptimistic about the income from the pavilion, but he pointed out that closing it before the second summer would not pay the contractor or the debt to the underwriters. Feeling that it would be best not to attend the board meeting, he flew back to Colombia. A few days later he received a telegram telling him the board had voted to keep the pavilion open.

Relieved, Cam moved his family from Bogotá to the new base at

Loma Linda. They lived by the lake in one of two trailers donated by the Humble Oil Company, while a carpenter added three rooms. The two oldest girls, Grace and Joy, were going to school in Chicago, staying with Elaine's brother. Elainadel was taking her sophomore year by correspondence. Billy, a gangly sixth grader, attended the base school.

Cam was still as romantic as ever. For Elaine's birthday, he penned a jingle:

> She's forty-eight, my precious mate!
>   She's mighty fine, this wife of mine!
> She's young and gay, works every day,
>   To give me joy, she's sweet and coy,
> And smart! She's keen—the best I've seen!
> And overall, she's heard God's call
> To serve the Lord at any cost.
>   We pioneer and never fear.
> We'll e'er have fun till life is done.

Christmas passed and then Cam had his annual New Year's letter to Spanish friends to write. He always tried to include a spiritual message, then would add a personal greeting at the top. The list had grown longer each year.

When Elaine's father died at the end of 1964, Elaine brought her mother back with her to Loma Linda after the funeral. "Grandma" Mielke organized a much needed nursery school for the flock of preschoolers on the base, and her warm, loving smile soon endeared her to all the children.

Meanwhile Cam was out making friends in the adjoining town of Puerto Lleras. He won the friendship of the mayor and the local priest, whom he invited to attend Bible study at the base. The JAARS center in North Carolina was progressing nicely under Goodall's leadership. Lawrence Routh was devoting six months to promote JAARS, the Fair pavilion, and other special projects at banquets.

Ben Elson had been approved for executive director, and he and his wife Adelle were to leave Mexico for Santa Ana on February 1. With the Elsons at the international headquarters, Cam thought that Wycliffe would have good, persuasive leadership.

Despite the internal disagreement over the Fair project, 202 new members had been received in 1964—the highest number to that time. By the spring of 1965 membership was pushing 1,600. It looked as if total donations might exceed three million dollars. This included $100,000 from the International Lutheran Women's Missionary League, the first denominational group to help. They were backing a translation center in Nigeria where both Wycliffe linguists and Lutheran missionaries worked.

The Fair debt was still a worry, even though support was picking up. Lawrence Routh's banquets for "Operation 2000" were arousing interest. And Chief Tariri had been invited to be a special guest of the Fair at the end of July. Don Burns would bring him up from Peru. The Harper & Row biography of Tariri would be out then, and the publisher had some important appearances lined up. July 28, Peru's Independence Day, would be Peru Day at the Fair, with appropriate ceremonies. Dr. Alberto Escobar, one of Peru's top educators, was also coming to show Peru's appreciation of SIL's service.

Cam, Elaine, and the children came up from Colombia ahead of the Peruvian party. In New York they found crowds streaming through the Pavilion of 2,000 Tongues. Attendance was up over the previous year, but receipts from gifts and books still only paid operating expenses.

On July 26 Chief Tariri and Don Burns arrived in New York, with Dr. Escobar representing President Belaunde Terry, and Doris Cox and Lorrie Anderson as interpreters. Tariri was interviewed by reporters, news services, radio stations and programs, including the Today show on the 28th. One interview was given from the gondola of the Goodyear blimp, a story that won a two-page spread in the *Journal-American Sunday Magazine*.

On Peru's Independence Day, July 28, Tariri spent the day at the Fair. At the news conference that morning he told reporters, "My heart used to be bad, but since Jesus came into my heart, I've stopped thinking bad things. Look at all God has given you! Why don't you think of Him?" Later in the day the conference was featured on the Huntley-Brinkley newscast.

In the afternoon there was a ceremony on the rear lawn of the pavilion, with Dr. Escobar, *Señorita* Rosa Corpancho, representing the Peruvian Ministry of Education, and other dignitaries. When Tariri spoke, with Lorrie Anderson interpreting, his regal bearing and forceful speech kept the crowd transfixed.

At 9:15 P.M. a big audience gathered around Dr. Escobar and Tariri at the Fair's Tower of Light. Educator and converted savage

placed their hands on the switch in the center of the pagoda. At
the given moment they pushed the switch. The mighty beacon
pierced the night for a distance of 250 miles.

Cam closed with an eloquent dedication.

*As Chief Tariri's hand, guided by the hand of the personal repre-
sentative of the president of his country, has turned on the most
powerful light in the world, even so the Wycliffe Bible Translators
and the Summer Institute of Linguistics in coordination with the
ministries of education and the various countries where they labor,
as well as the universities and their institutions of learning and research, are bringing the torch of enlightenment to once-forgotten
tribes through bilingual education and giving them, in their own
exotic tongues, the greatest spiritual light in the world—The Bible.*

*We further dedicate this act that has taken place on the 144th
anniversary of the Independence of Peru to the cause of freedom,
reminding ourselves that all men were indeed created free and equal
and that they have an equal right to the Light—the Word and the
Life abundant.*

The Tariri party, including Cam, went on tour the next day,
stopping in Philadelphia, Charlotte, Oklahoma City, and finally
Dallas, where Tariri preached three times at the First Baptist Church
to packed out audiences.

The debt that remained after the Fair closed was a concern to
everyone. Most of the underwriters paid their pledges as donations.
Two who had underwritten five thousand gave twice that much.
Hundreds of Wycliffe members sacrificed from their meager allowances.

Cam felt the results had been worth all the sweat, strain, and
struggle. Over a million visitors had seen the exhibit, with some
632,000 taking time to listen to the narration of Tariri's conversion
while viewing the great mural. Articles had been published in over
100 newspapers and magazines with a circulation of seventy million.
Fifty thousand copies of the Tariri book had been sold. (At Cam's
suggestion a portion of royalties had gone to the chief.) People from
scores of nations had learned for the first time of the over 2,000
Bibleless tribes and many had decided to help the Summer Institute
of Linguistics and Wycliffe do something about it.

"I just wish some of our brethren would wake up to the changes taking place in the Catholic Church."

32. Winds of Change

Colombia was doing well under Director Clarence Church, so Cam felt the family should live in Charlotte during the winter of 1965–66. Here he was near the growing JAARS center and available for public relations work.

As the need arose he traveled—Washington, New York, Philadelphia, California for board meetings, back to Charlotte. Then to Chicago for the funeral of his dear friend Henry Crowell. The loss of such a partner made him feel as he had when Nyman went.

He and Elaine continually marveled at the Lord's provision through friends. They resided again at the riverfront home of Henderson and Ann Belk. Cam wore a broad-brimmed white Texas Stetson, a gift from a friend in Dallas, a topcoat that had been his cousin's, and traveled with second-hand suitcases. When the coat was stolen out of his car, he went to Goodwill Industries and bought another for fifty cents.

December was a busy month with family festivities and Cam's letter to Latin American friends which he sent out at New Year every year. Then there were the plans for Grace's coming marriage in Chicago to a young Christian engineer, Tom Goreth, in February 1966.

Cam could never let an opportunity go by of presenting the need of Bibleless tribes, and at the wedding supper, attended by 250 guests, he gave a rousing challenge for Bible translation. "Remember the story in Luke about the great man's supper?" he asked. "The first people he invited made excuses not to come, so the man sent his servant into the streets to invite the poor, the maimed, the halt and the blind. When they came there was yet room so he told the servant, 'Go out into the highways and hedges, and compel them

to come in, that my house may be filled.' Out there in the jungles
and distant mountains of the world are *two thousand tribes* who
have never heard. Who here will hear the call to take the Word
of God to those who have never heard?"

After the wedding, life settled down to the normal hectic routine
for the Townsends. On one trip to Washington, Cam talked to
Oklahoma's Senator Fred Harris, a friend for several years, about
an idea he had.

"September 30 is St. Jerome's Day. He's the first translator of the
whole Bible. I thought maybe we could get the House and Senate
to pass a resolution calling for the president to proclaim September
30 as Bible Translation Day. The Apache chief Geronimo, who was
probably named for Jerome, must have been born on September 30.
And the American Bible Society just published our Apache New
Testament."

"And you want me to introduce the resolution in the Senate?"
Harris asked.

"I was hoping you would. It would be a natural since you're from
Oklahoma and our main linguistic course is there at the university.
We'd need a Congressman to do the same in the House. Maybe you
could get me an appointment at the White House?"

"All right, Uncle Cam. I'll take your materials for reference in
preparing the resolution, but I don't know about the White House.
I'll try."

Even though Cam was nearing 70, he wasn't slowing down much.
After resting briefly at home, he flew first to Mexico City to help the
Mexican Branch's new director, Dr. Frank Robbins, with some
government contacts, then on to Bogotá for more of the same with
Colombia Director Clarence Church.

While in Bogotá he discussed with Clarence Church a book he
liked. "I wish all our evangelical brethren could read Father Grassi's
A World to Win. It sounds as if someone from Dallas or Fuller
Seminary who had strong indoctrination on Wycliffe methods wrote
it, instead of a professor from a school that trains Catholic missionaries. Father Grassi did take our course at the University of
Oklahoma years ago, you know.

"I just wish some of our brethren would wake up to the changes
taking place in the Catholic Church. One of these days we'll have
a Catholic applicant for membership. That's when our nonsectarian
policy will really be tested."

From Bogotá Cam went on to Lima, where Elaine, Mrs. Mielke, and Mrs. Will Nyman joined him for the twentieth anniversary celebration of SIL in Peru.

Before the celebration got underway President Fernando Belaunde Terry invited Cam to lunch. Belaunde had recently visited Yarinacocha. "Your people are doing a great work for our Indians," he said. "But what really impressed me at the base was hearing your school children sing our national Peruvian anthem."

Cam grinned. "We've tried to teach them to be good citizens of your country."

Next came a ceremony at the University of San Marcos where Cam was awarded an honorary doctorate. Although he had declined three such degrees from schools in the States, he felt this honor from his beloved Peru could not be refused.

There followed a big banquet given by Minister of Education Dr. Cueto Fernandini. The minister introduced dignitaries present, using a long list of impressive titles—Minister, Senator, Ambassador, etc. When he came to Cam, he said, "And—Uncle Cam—as he is to all of us who know and love him."

Then Dr. and Mrs. Cueto Fernandini and a planeload of officials flew with the SIL party to the base for more festivities. Bishop Prevost and the military commander from Pucallpa joined them there to celebrate Cam's seventieth birthday. Bishop Prevost told Cam that his home Bible study groups were going very well.

Cam was pleased with the report of Director Gene Loos: 21 Peruvian tribes with one or more books of the Bible, 211 Indian teachers in government employ from 18 tribes at the last training course, and about 5,000 children enrolled in the government's bilingual schools. "Some of the Amueshas have organized their own churches and have applied for membership in the Peruvian Evangelical Union, and they have their own Bible school. There are several thousand Aguaruña believers. Revenge killing is on the way out. There are new groups of believers in other tribes, too."

The report was the best birthday present Cam received.

After three weeks in Peru, Elaine and her mother returned to the States and Cam went on to Brazil where he helped Director Jim Wilson on some aviation matters. Because of the vastness of the country, the group had five regional bases. Besides Brazilia, Cam visited two others and conferred with translators.

In the state of Matto Grosso he was especially thrilled at the report of Ivan Lowe and Menno Kroeker serving the Nambiquara tribe. "We were the first outsiders ever to spend a night in a Nambiquara village. Now there are new Christians reading Scripture in their own language and writing their own hymns. The Nambiquaras attacked the first missionaries trying to reach them about forty years ago—and killed two of them and a baby."

As Cam listened his memory was stirred and suddenly he felt the hair rise on the back of his neck. The Nambiquaras! Yes, that was the tribe that killed Arthur Tylee! Thirty-six years ago he had heard about the massacre while he and Elvira were checking proofs on the Cakchiquel New Testament in Chicago.

Cam returned to Charlotte for a few days with his family. He played Billy a few games of Ping-Pong at the Belk riverside home. "Either you're getting better or I'm getting older, Son," Cam commented. "I can only beat you two games out of three now."

At seventy he could feel himself slowing down, but only slightly. He napped a half hour or more after lunch now and tried to be in bed by 9:30 or 10. But by 6:30 he was usually up, reading the Bible, praying around the world, planning, figuring.

September came and he was in Washington attending to last-minute details for the September 30th Bible Translation Day celebration. Wycliffe, the Lutheran Bible Translators, and the Catholic Biblical Association were sponsoring the event. The Bible translation resolution had passed the Senate, but not the House, so there was no presidential proclamation as Cam had hoped.

On the 30th Senator Harris welcomed about a hundred guests, representatives of the Bureau of Indian Affairs, church leaders, missionaries, press, and others to the observance. Mrs. Britton Goode, an Apache Indian from Arizona, cut the red ribbon that encircled the Senate proclamation. Morris Watkins, head of the new Lutheran Bible Translation Society, Dr. Louis Hartman, a Bible scholar at Catholic University, and Cam gave short challenges for a speed-up in Bible translation. Britton Goode, in his colorful Apache costume, solemnly presented Apache New Testaments to Senator Harris and Congressman Ben Reifel, a Sioux Indian from South Dakota. Then he thanked translators Faye Edgerton and Faith Hill who had worked twenty-five years to complete the Apache Testament.

A few minutes later the program leaders met in a presidential office and Britton Goode presented a New Testament to President

Johnson's representative, aide Mike Manakos. Cam had hoped to see the president in person, but was pleased with what he felt was one more opportunity to alert the world to the call of the Bibleless tribes. "Next year we'll do it again," he said, "and keep reminding people of the challenge."

When he arrived back in Charlotte, there was a report, not unexpected, that a young Catholic scholar had applied for membership. Scores of priests and nuns had taken SIL training, but until Paul Witte, none had asked to join Wycliffe.

Young Witte seemed to meet the qualifications—educational background, linguistic training, personal character, emotional stability, consent to the Wycliffe doctrinal statement, etc. He gave a strong evangelical testimony that he knew Christ as Savior. He was engaged to a Salvation Army girl who had already been accepted for membership, pending the meeting of certain academic requirements.

Witte said he wanted to be a Bible translator. He did not hold to some traditional Catholic doctrines which are generally objectionable to evangelicals. The hitch was his statement, "I wish to remain a member in good standing of the Catholic Church."

Cam saw no reason why Witte shouldn't be taken in, "if we are true to our stated policy of being nonsectarian. We must not depart from our nonsectarian policy one iota if we are to keep entering countries closed to traditional missionary organizations," he said in a letter to the membership.

Cam was both praised and criticized by Wycliffe members for his stand. Most of the critics said they were not opposed to Witte personally, but feared the reaction of some members and supporters. Some frankly admitted a pragmatic concern: loss of support.

Cam was unbending. He wrote one dissenter:

I object to being forced to take a sectarian attitude that would rob us of many opportunities for Bible translation work. My one goal is that the Word of God be given at long last to 2,000 tribes. Somebody must look ahead and see what is needed to get the Word to the tribes that live in Moslem or Communist lands or behind doors that are closed otherwise. For this type of work the nonsectarian core of SIL and WBT must be preserved. If we are misjudged for this by some, so that support is cut off for some of our workers, God will supply from other sources. He has thus far and He will.

John Beekman expressed the sentiments of many members when he said, "Uncle Cam is probably right. He may be ten years ahe .d of the rest of us, as usual."

The discussion was long and spirited. The issue was, as it had been in the 1949 debate over the admittance of Pentecostals, "compatibility versus incompatibility." The simple question was: Would a Catholic be compatible within the membership? When the vote was finally tallied, the delegates said no by a two to one margin.

Cam confessed his disappointment over this major defeat, but added, "What the majority of you did here will not stop God. Nor will it stop Elaine and me from loving you and from going on in faith."

From Mexico the Townsends flew to Bogotá for the fifth anniversary of work in Colombia. After the big banquet, Cam told Bishop Canyes about Witte's being turned down.

"Our folks were just too narrow," he confessed. "Too afraid to risk offending some supporters. What do you think of Witte working with your Capuchin missionaries? He could go to our jungle camp and later receive technical help from our group here. What matters is that he and his wife give the Bible to a tribe."

Bishop Canyes appreciated Cam's forthrightness. "Yes, I think we could take them," he said. "But we don't have the funds to pay a full salary."

"Elaine and I will help," Cam volunteered. "And Father Louis Hartman might get some money from the Catholic Biblical Association."

"Tell them to come on then," the bishop declared.

Back in the U.S., Cam and Elaine saw Joy and Elainadel enrolled in Columbia Bible College and Billy entered as a high school student at Ben Lippen. Then they went to Memphis to get acquainted with and encourage Paul and Ginny Witte.

"I marvel at your patience, Paul," Cam told his young Catholic friend. "But the Lord is with us. Everything is all set with Bishop Canyes for you to go to Colombia. Besides translating God's Word for a tribe, you'll be a valuable bridge down there between our group and the bishops. However, you should first go to jungle camp. We've let a few nonmembers take the training," Cam assured him. "Go on and apply."

Then it was on to Dallas where Cam met with a civic committee about moving the Wycliffe home office there. The old building in

Santa Ana had been inadequate for years, and additional space was being rented several blocks away. The 1967 conference had decided to move to the Dallas area if certain conditions were met.

The president of the Dallas Chamber of Commerce was at the airport to award Cam the key to the city "in honor of the fiftieth anniversary of your beginning work in Guatemala." Cam blinked in surprise that the Dallas people were aware of the dates.

Cam looked at two sites, then flew to Washington to help Dale Kietzman, now the director of extension for Wycliffe, with the last-minute preparations for the second annual Bible translation ceremony. Elaine continued on with speaking engagements. Senator Carl Curtis presided at the ceremony and Senator Mark Hatfield was one of the speakers. Translator Wayne Snell introduced two Machiguenga Indians as products of Bible translation.

Three days later in Guatemala, educators and officials from four Latin American countries joined in celebrating the fiftieth anniversary of Cam's arrival there.

Cam and Elaine were received by the president of the republic and the archbishop of Guatemala. The mayor of Guatemala City made him an "honorary citizen" of the capital and the minister of foreign affairs awarded him the Order of the Quetzal, by disposition of the president of the republic. The vice president of Ecuador, who had come for the occasion, spoke at a special program in the municipal palace.

After several tributes from visiting dignitaries for SIL's work in their lands, Cam rose to respond, recalling how the Cakchiquel Indian Francisco Diaz had opened his eyes to the need of giving people the Word in their own tongues.

Then accompanied by Elaine and Mrs. Mielke, Cam motored over the green mountains to San Antonio, following the path he had taken by coach and on muleback a half century before. The San Antonio school was still going. Cam was delighted to find that the principal was an alumnus of the school. That night hundreds of Cakchiquels jammed one of the evangelical churches to hear their beloved *don Guillermo* speak in their own language.

From San Antonio the party moved on west, stopping in Indian towns along the way. In one town there had been one congregation when Cam left thirty-five years before. Now there were ten. In another large town the Indians said almost half the population were believers. The Cakchiquel tribe had grown to 250,000 of whom

50,000 or more were believers. At Tecpan they attended a wedding. The bride was the granddaughter of old friends.

At Patzun Cam met more old-timers. Five hundred believers gathered in one of the churches to hear him speak. Some Indians brought fading copies of the Cakchiquel New Testament. "When will some new ones be printed, *don Guillermo?*" they asked. He promised to see about that.

The sentimental journey climaxed in restful Panajachel by the beautiful lake. Pointing to a huge Chinese litchi that spread its umbrellalike shade beside the old mission home near the lakeshore, Cam told Elaine with awe and satisfaction, "I planted that when it was a little sapling forty years ago. Look at its enormous size now!"

Below: Cam preaches to his old congregation in Tetelcingo while Martín Méndez, Aztec preacher and former mayor of the town, listens. *Above:* Méndez preaches while Cam looks on.

Tzeltal Indian chief Marcos Encin
shares a hymnbook with Cam.

Part III
NEW BEGINNINGS

"We will assist in any way we can to promote peace and goodwill between our countries."

33. To the Soviet Union

As Cam looked back on the fifty years since he'd gone to Guatemala and the thirty-five years of SIL and Wycliffe, the old litchi tree at Panajachel seemed somehow symbolic of the tremendous growth of the work God had led him into.

But trees keep growing. And Cam never looked back for long. His eyes were again on the future. "Elaine and I want to invest our next years where they will count the most," he wrote the membership. "We'll have to learn a new language, adjust to a new way of life. . . . Pray for us as we make plans to go to the U.S.S.R."

Russia had beckoned Cam for many years, especially since he had learned of the more than 100 languages spoken in the Caucasus and the successful work of the U.S.S.R. in teaching these many language groups to read not only their own language but Russian. The success was achieved through bilingual education—something Cam had been advocating for almost fifty years.

Being relatively free of family responsibilities—one daughter married, two in college, and Billy in boarding school—Cam and Elaine decided to make Mexico City their base for awhile. In the fall of 1967, after their nostalgic time in Guatemala, they moved into an apartment at the SIL headquarters. Elaine's mother decided to remain for a few months and help with the housework.

They went daily to the home of a Russian woman for classes, and Elaine spent four and five hours a day studying. But Cam kept getting sidetracked with business, although he kept his vocabulary cards with him. At dinner one evening he tried out a sentence he had memorized in Russian on their guests from the Russian embassy. "If I didn't believe God would help me, I'd give up studying this difficult language!" Their guests laughed appreciatively.

251

Cam followed the same approach with the Soviet diplomats he had pursued with Latin Americans for fifty years: personal interest, openness and friendship. His friendship with and esteem for Cárdenas was a natural entrée with many of the Russians who also admired the Mexican reformer. He never disguised his desire to translate the Bible into some of the minority languages of the U.S.S.R., and he stressed the benefits of scientific collaboration and friendship.

At the same time he kept busy with WBT/SIL affairs. He continued to feel a keen responsibility for the expansion of the membership. To over one hundred presidents of Christian colleges, seminaries, and Bible institutes, he wrote letters asking for their interest and help in having workers in "two thousand more languages by 1985."

Cam also urged the board to reconsider their requirement that applicants from non-English-speaking countries learn English. "A linguistic organization like ours should be able to train leaders who speak other languages so they could integrate other nationalities into our program," he insisted. But despite Cam's protests, the board continued to hold speaking English a necessity for "compatibility." However, they did begin accepting non-English speakers with the provision they learn English during orientation.

He also wanted headquarters personnel to do more to recruit black members. At the time the only black member was a widow serving in the Philippines.

Racial discrimination in the United States had long bothered him, although it took the assasination of Martin Luther King to rouse his deepest concern. The day before the civil rights leader's funeral, he wrote a letter to the membership that was part a confession and part a plea for members to become more involved with blacks.

Americans everywhere must be searching their hearts. I am mine. What have I done to help my fellow citizens whose complexion is darker than my own? Oh, when we lived in North Carolina I attended Negro churches eight or nine times, but I didn't visit in their homes or invite them to spend a social evening in mine. I maintained that I loved them, but where was the practical demonstration of that love? I lied. You call on people you love.

Let's put ourselves in other people's shoes—people who differ from us in color, in religion, in social status, educationally or politically. We say that we love them all, but do we? Do we not act toward them in a discriminatory way or at least ignore them? Dear fellow workers, we need to search our souls. Are we living a lie?

As regards the Negroes, we have invited them to special gatherings at our JAARS center in North Carolina. A few have attended but we haven't really shown them love and Christian fellowship as far as I know. Worse, we have gone along with certain prevalent attitudes even though they were obnoxious to us. Another question: Are we doing all we can to get Negro members? Shouldn't we assign someone to visit their colleges with the challenge of Bible translation work and assure them that we would welcome more Negro members? . . .

When will prejudice, discrimination and hatred cease? When Christ takes complete possession of our lives and of the world. For the latter, His Word in every tongue is a vital factor—possibly a prerequisite.

Forward then, in the spirit of Him who died for all men regardless of race, and who wants us all to be brothers and children of God through faith in Him. Yours in memory of Martin Luther King.

Early in the summer of 1968, Cam wrote to the Soviet Academy of Science in Moscow, requesting an invitation to visit the Soviet Union for six months. He noted that several years before, the Soviet Ambassador in Washington had recommended a trip to Moscow for contacts with linguists. "We were too deeply involved in South America then," he told the Academy. "My wife and I can come now."

The first response was, "An invitation will not be extended this year, but maybe next." Cam immediately wrote the Academy, "When you're past seventy, as I am, it is hard to wait another year. We are willing to be responsible for our own expenses if you will invite us now."

At the time they did not have the money for one-way transportation to Russia, and they would need living expenses for six months. But their faith was boosted by an unexpected gift of $1,000 from Elaine's mother.

And then in September the invitation came. Elaine was in the States seeing the children off to school, and Cam phoned her from Mexico City. "Can you be ready to leave in ten days? I've booked seats on a flight leaving New York on Wednesday, October 2. I want to get to the U.S.S.R. on the third, the 51st anniversary of my arrival in Guatemala."

The next day Elaine called eighty-two people to tell them they were going and asked them to pray. One was Pastor Charles Blair at the Calvary Temple in Denver. "We'll pray around the clock," he promised, and then sent $1,000. Smaller gifts came from other friends—enough for the trip. Elaine also wrote a prayer letter and sent it to over 1,000 friends. She was packed and ready to go when Cam arrived from Mexico.

From almost their first day in Moscow, the Mexican and Colombian diplomats were the Townsends' warm friends and boosters. They introduced them to Russians interested in Latin America who joined the Latins in taking them sightseeing, to a ballet and concert, and to favorite restaurants. The best opportunities to explain the work of WBT/SIL came later when Cam and Elaine showed films at institutes and universities. The films provoked questions that made it easy for Cam to tell about Tariri, Manuel Arenas, and other Indians who had been changed through the Bible.

Cam and Elaine had the gift of seeing the best in everything. The banners calling for "Peace" and "International Goodwill" impressed them more than the tanks and missiles which they viewed from their hotel window on the fifty-first anniversary of the Russian Revolution. However, plain-clothes police spotted Elaine holding a microphone out of a window to record the music and speeches and came to investigate.

Rather than being insulted, Cam commented, "In view of what happened from a window in Dallas, we understand your concern."

As he had done in Mexico, Cam wrote articles for the Soviet Press and dispatches on Soviet life for U.S. newspapers which pleased his hosts. For example, he reported for a North Carolina newspaper:

Friendship is the offspring of respect. We found many things in the USSR that merited respect and admiration. Everyone works and there are jobs for all. I am old-fashioned enough to admire hardworking men, but I found it difficult to get accustomed to seeing women driving tractors, running hotels and banks and operating radio stations.

They stayed in the National Hotel overlooking Red Square. Language study and writing took five and six hours of each day. For breaks they took short walks across the great Square, bundled in heavy coats.

As Christmas approached the children seemed even further away. This would be the first time none of the children would be with them for the holidays. Cam wrote a long letter recounting memories of Christmases past, mailing a copy to each. Elaine bought a tiny artificial fir tree and balanced it on a towel-covered suitcase. When the floor supervisor saw the tree, the Christmas cards, the family photographs and Indian weavings scattered around, she smiled and said, "This isn't a hotel room, this is a home."

Ethel Wallis joined them after Christmas for travel into the Caucasus areas where many minority group languages are spoken. Their itinerary was arranged by their official hosts. It was supposed to be warmer in the fabled region between the Black and Caspian Seas, but their plane landed at Baku in a snowstorm. The warm greeting of the head of the foreign language department at the local university, however, more than compensated for the cold.

Every day of the first week they visited an educational institution, conferred with educators, showed films, recorded exotic languages, examined bilingual texts, visited museums (some of which were former mosques), attended the opera, and enjoyed meals in the homes of hospitable linguists and educators.

They followed this pattern for seven weeks, moving from town to town by train or plane, marveling at the unity that had been wrought in the mosaic of cultures in this part of the Caucasus. Educators showed them how illiteracy had practically been erased and proudly displayed bilingual texts. Lenin himself, they said, had insisted that each minority group· be taught to read first in its own language, then in the national Russian language. In some areas this had involved the use of three different alphabets! The linguistic groups had been encouraged to develop their individual cultures and languages with newspapers, magazines, and even radio stations and theaters. Cam, Elaine and Ethel saw ample evidence that all this was so.

An intriguing legend about the origin of the languages in the Caucasus was told them. "The story is that an angel flew over the land distributing languages. He flew too close to a cliff and ripped his bag on a sharp crag. Several dozen of the languages fell out."

At Mahachkala, a "linguist's paradise," they saw bearded oldsters walking firm of foot toward markets. When local hosts boasted that some of the residents had celebrated 100th wedding anniversaries, Cam responded smiling, "If I could be sure I'd be rewarded with a hundred years with my Elaine, I'd surely move here."

At Sochi, the popular resort beside the Black Sea, local scholars took the three Americans to a "Friendship" citrus tree on which 130 grafts had been made. The agronomist in charge handed Cam a tiny knife and a limb. Cam made his graft, remarking, "We need a tree like this in Peru. Someone from each of the jungle tribes could make a graft."

The director of the Armenian Linguistic Institute showed them a petrified Bible. Cam wondered if the archaic translation could be read by the people. "Only priests and scholars can now read the ancient Bible language," he was told. "The ordinary people cannot understand it when they hear it."

Later another Armenian mentioned the infamous religious massacre of 1915, in which a million-and-a-half of his people were killed, as "proof that God couldn't possibly exist."·

"That only proves there is a devil," Cam replied.

In discussions with educators, Cam suggested that SIL linguists could help in the Caucasus by comparing languages and lecturing on linguistic theories. They also would like to translate portions of the Bible. One linguist appeared surprised. "We are atheists. We could never allow that." Then he seemed to have second thoughts. "Well, we do record the ancient legends of the people. The Bible could fall into that category."

Cam and Elaine were tremendously impressed with the educational wonders achieved through bilingual education. Having seen what had also been accomplished in Latin American countries, Cam was anxious to push the benefits of this approach in other countries, including the U.S.

Before returning to Moscow in late February, Cam wrote the president of the Academy of Science about a contractual agreement. The Russian scholar replied that exchanges of linguists could be made on the basis of an existing arrangement with the American Council of Learned Societies.

In Moscow a farewell dinner was given in their honor by the Academy. Afterwards Cam told the director of the Foreign Department of the Academy, "I'm going to talk to an American publisher about the great strides you've made in bilingual education. The world should know about this. We will assist in any way we can to promote peace and goodwill between our countries."

In 1969
at Sochi on the
Black Sea in
the U.S.S.R.,
Cam and Elaine each
put a graft on
the International
Friendship Tree
which bears
several kinds of
citrus fruit.
Above: Cam points
to the signatures in
the guest book being
held by the agronomist
in charge of the
experimental farm
where the tree is.
Left: Cam and
Elaine with
Russian dignitaries
walk to the
International
Friendship Tree.

Cam and Elaine spent the winter of 1969 in the U.S.S.R. Here they stand in front of the Kremlin in Moscow.

*"Instead of two hundred new members a year
. . . we must have four hundred if we're to have
translators in every tribe by 1985."*

34. The Legendary "Uncle Cam"

The trip to the U.S.S.R. was over and Cam and Elaine were home.
Their most immediate need now was a permanent home for the
Townsends. After considering several possibilities, they decided on
a wooded lot in the Waxhaw area, to be near the JAARS center.

The responsibility for planning and building the house fell on
Elaine, and she sketched a rough plan for a multipurpose house.
There would be a lower basement level with a recreation room large
enough for group meetings for the JAARS people, and arranged so
it could be used as an apartment for Wycliffe members needing
temporary housing near the JAARS center. The main level would
have an office for Elaine near the kitchen to save as many steps as
possible. She still had problems stemming from the 1947 plane
accident. A large combination living room-dining room would be
on the same level as well as the bedrooms, bathrooms and laundry
room. Upstairs, Cam's office would have a rear balcony shaded by
a huge beech tree. There would also be an efficiency apartment
with separate entrance for use by JAARS trainees, visiting Wycliffe
members and friends.

While Cam was away in Mexico for the dedication of the branch
headquarters building, Elaine interrupted the house-building to
launch a whirlwind thirty-day coast-to-coast speaking tour about their
trip to the U.S.S.R. After one speech, a long-time financial supporter
lectured her sternly for being "taken in by the communists."

Reduced to tears by the tongue-lashing, she finally managed to
say, "We didn't go to the U.S.S.R. to find fault. We went to see
how we could serve and pave the way for the Bible to be translated
into more languages."

Upon completing the exhausting forty-eight-stop circuit, Elaine

259

returned to Charlotte to oversee the building of the house. She started with about $10,000 from the earmarked donations and the sale of their two South American houses, paying bills as they were received.

Meanwhile, Cam was busy in Mexico City. The latest building at the Mexican headquarters contained administrative and business offices, computer equipment to speed translation work, a museum for tribal artifacts, a library, and an auditorium. It was named for the recently deceased former president, López Mateos, who had helped them get the land. The auditorium in the building was named for long-time friend Aarón Sáenz and the library for long-time benefactor Ramón Beteta, who had also recently died. From the giant sandstone mosaic portraying an Indian carrying a torch on the façade over the entrance to the portraits of distinguished Latin Americans looking down on the corridors, everything was distinctly Mexican. With these facilities the Mexican Branch could host the biennial conference of delegates from the fields that now practically spanned the globe.

Because it was nearing conference time, Cam decided to stay on in Mexico. During the short interim he made a quick trip in early May 1969 to Colombia. Here he talked with various officials about the Colombia Branch's participating in the hoped-for agreement with the Soviet Union.

Returning to Mexico City, he reported to the biennial conference that officials in Colombia would favor an exchange agreement between the Colombian WBT/SIL branch and the Soviet Academy of Science in Moscow. The conference authorized Cam to proceed with the agreement as outlined.

While the delegates marveled at this further extension of Cam's audacious faith, some were not happy with his handling of the Paul Wittes' support. After the 1967 biennial had voted that a Catholic member would be "incompatible," Cam had recommended that the Colombia branch engage Witte as an employee and pay him a small wage. This, when added to the allowance from Bishop Canyes's mission, Cam felt, would be enough to support the Wittes in tribal work. Cam pointed out that Catholic nationals were employed for various duties on bases and in group offices, and that hiring Witte as a "consultant" would be no different.

Hearing that the Colombia branch had taken this action, the

Mexican branch had discussed the matter at their regular conference. The consensus was that their sister branch had violated the 1967 resolution, and they had voted to ask the WBT/SIL board to take action, requesting their Colombia colleagues to end Witte's employment status. The board had done so, though some members disagreed.

At the 1969 biennial of the whole organization, there was some feeling that Cam had violated the will of the 1967 delegates. There were also strong hints that he was getting too old for the job of general director.

But the issue was not brought to the floor. Cam's example in past service overrode any opposition that might have arisen. Many delegates were thinking not just of his achievements, but of acts of menial service they had seen him perform. One recalled in a corridor conversation, "He was at my house when my wife and I were called to attend an important meeting. 'Go on,' he said. 'I'll finish washing the dishes.' He insisted that we—his hosts—allow him—the general director—to do this menial task. Although I find myself disagreeing with some of his ideas, it's hard to speak against him."

So the opposition did not show itself and Cam moved ahead with his challenge for the future. "Instead of two hundred members a year, which is wonderful," he said, "we must have four hundred if we're to have translators in every tribe by 1985."

One evening after a session Dick Pittman cornered Cam about his future travel plans. "I'm going to write a book on bilingual education in the Caucasus," he told the deputy director for Asia. "That requires that we go back to Russia in the fall to do more research. On the way home we thought we might visit the Wycliffe fields in Asia and the Pacific."

"They won't believe it until they see you," Dick said. "We've been trying for years to get you to fields outside this hemisphere."

Cam sighed. "I know, Dick. But I've always been skittish about leaving my area of experience. Besides you've done such a great job leading advances, I felt I wasn't needed."

Pittman grinned. "Your coming will certainly make the branches happy, Uncle Cam. I hope you can do it."

Early in the fall Cam was in Washington, D.C., arranging for visas from the Russian embassy. Ben Elson and Morris Watkins, director of the Lutheran Bible Translators, joined him there for a conference. Watkins reported a half dozen members already serving jointly with his organization and Wycliffe, with forty more ready for training.

"Think what could be done by ten denominational groups like yours, Morrie," Cam sighed. "Add them to Wycliffe and every tribe would really be reached by 1985."

Elson had been visiting Wycliffe fields in the Pacific and Asia. "The Wycliffe members are all looking forward to you and Elaine coming," he told Cam. "You can't disappoint them now."

Cam pulled a paper from his pocket. "Here's our itinerary. We leave for Russia next week, spend a month in the Caucasus getting more information and pictures for the book. Then starting in November we go to India, Nepal, the Philippines, New Guinea, Australia and New Zealand before getting home in January. We've decided to take Bill with us."

"That's a pretty gruelling schedule. Shouldn't you take more time?"

"I wish we could, but Bill has to get back to school and other obligations are pressing."

"You know we'll be praying for you," Ben said looking down at the older man. "And Uncle Cam, I hope you know all of us love you. You've been like a father to me and the other old timers. The Lord has used you to make us what we are and to make Wycliffe what it is today."

Cam took Elson's hand and gripped it tightly. "Thank you, Ben. I appreciate your love and patience. Despite all my complaining about bureaucracy, I know we must have administration and order. I am just concerned about our basic policies that the Lord has used to open doors and keep us in places that otherwise might be closed.

"We've got to reach every tribe. Follow the Lord's command. Wake people up in the homeland to see that souls are dying without a glimmer of light. Read us a chapter, Ben, and then we'll pray."

The next week Cam, Elaine and Billy flew to Moscow. The Academy of Science people recognized the value of the book that Cam would be doing. They helped arrange their trip to the Caucasus and assigned a photographer for the project.

For the next month the Townsends visited schools and interviewed educators in four different republics between the Caspian and the Black Seas. Except for Billy's being detained once for inadvertently taking pictures in an unauthorized area, all ran smoothly.

In November they landed in New Delhi, India, where they were greeted by the Pittmans and called on educators. Then they went on to the high Himalayan kingdom of Nepal where Wycliffe members were studying twelve languages in cooperation with the national university. The Wycliffites hailed from six nations and were expecting to be joined by a Japanese member married to a German. The group had become truly international.

Cam called on the vice chancellor of the university of Nepal, inviting him to participate in a brief dedication of a new "goodwill" plane for service in his country. Several other important university people and government officials were present.

Moving on across Asia, the Townsends spent twelve days in the Philippines where 156 members were serving 42 language groups.

In Manila, Director Tom Lyman took Cam to see General Carlos Romulo, the minister of foreign affairs, whom Cam knew and admired greatly. Romulo expressed his appreciation for SIL work, and offered help in getting a government land grant for a group headquarters in the capital.

Next came two weeks in New Guinea where over three hundred members were involved in eighty-seven tribes. The big base with its JAARS planes and other facilities reminded them of Yarinacocha. But they were most impressed by the progress that had been made in training New Guinea tribesmen to run such technical operations as the sawmill and print shop.

When Director Al Pence remarked that the branch had over 500 more languages to reach, Cam did some quick mathematical calculations. "You should pray for at least fifty new workers for New Guinea this year and larger numbers each year in the future, if you intend to enter them all by 1985."

He saw needs all over the base and kept Pence busy writing them down. Perhaps it was because Billy was along that he showed special concern that the base teens have manual arts training. He dipped into his general director's fund and gave money to start a building for this project.

In an assembly he presented to the New Guinea members his impressions of needs in the U.S.S.R., India, and Nepal. "The group has only one pilot in Nepal." he said. "Would you give one of your pilots to help them out?" They would and Cam paid for the move from his general director's fund.

In New Guinea a radio report on the house caught up with them.

The construction account was $5,000 in the red. Although concerned, they kept on with the trip trusting that the Lord would supply. Their next stop was Brisbane, Australia, where they were interviewed and photographed by the local press as they arrived. With over a hundred and fifty members serving in Wycliffe, Australia was second only to the United States in Wycliffe membership.

Businessman Alfred Coombe, the chairman of the Australian home council, and his wife Sabina were their hosts. The day after their arrival, Coombe flew with the Townsends eighteen hundred miles to the base in Darwin where the Wycliffe members were gathered. The vast distances over which the translators were spread staggered Cam. Some had come over 1,000 miles across the hot dusty outback to the meeting and to see the general director and his wife. As at the other stations, everyone wanted to hear from the legendary "Uncle Cam." Then Director David Glasgow took Cam and Coombe by plane to four aboriginal tribes and to visit government educators.

Although it was after midnight when they returned to Brisbane from Darwin, Cam spoke the next afternoon at a big rally. During the next three days he challenged students at the Australian SIL. Then on Christmas Eve they enplaned for Melbourne, a thousand miles to the south for a planned ten days of rest. But when they arrived, they learned that a Bible conference was in session with over two thousand people present. The leaders insisted that the "distinguished Dr. Townsend must speak."

By this time, even Billy, soon to be seventeen, was beginning to run down. Elaine could tell Cam needed rest. A month's constant travel through changing time zones had sapped much of his energy. When he began experiencing shortness of breath between Christmas and New Year's she wanted him to see a doctor. "No," he insisted. "I'll try to take it easier from here on and get a checkup when we get home. It won't be much longer. I'll make it, Honey. You go on and get Bill back in school. Don't worry about me."

Shortly before Elaine left, a cable came from California saying they would receive an inheritance of over $3,000. With that good news, Billy and Elaine left for California, and Cam and Coombe flew to Canberra, the capital of Australia. Here they called on the minister of aboriginal affairs, who took them to see the minister of the interior.

Coombe listened in admiration as Cam established quick rapport.

"It's wonderful that your country wants to have all its languages analyzed, Mr. Minister. Our linguists are here to help you accomplish that purpose. We're ready to serve in any capacity."

"We're very happy about the language study your people are doing," the minister responded sincerely. "Is there any way my office can help, Dr. Townsend?"

"Well, yes, we are short of housing. Some mobile living quarters for our linguists out in the field would make their work more efficient and life more pleasant."

"I'm sorry, but we can only provide six," was the apologetic response. But Cam was jubilant; he knew how his colleagues had been living without proper housing.

By mid-January, when Cam landed in Auckland, New Zealand, he was feeling better. The Wycliffe council there gave him a royal welcome and the round of speeches, interviews and dinners started all over again. Then notification came of the death of his sister, Oney. "We'll see you when you get to California," sister Ethel telegraphed. "Don't try to come for the funeral."

About the same time a letter came from Elaine. The inheritance was from the Woodsun estate—the Woodsuns had helped Cam in Guatemala, a half-century before—and it was five thousand dollars instead of three. "Just what we owe on the house. It is manna from heaven!"

Now he had only a plane change in Hawaii before touchdown in California. But even in Honolulu there were friends and admirers to greet him. One young member of the Vietnam branch was on leave to complete his doctorate.

"I've always wanted to meet you, Uncle Cam," he said almost in awe. "When I heard you would be changing planes here, I had to come even if I could be with you only five minutes."

"I believe God is going to help us reach them all."

35. "Faith, Mighty Faith"

It seemed fitting somehow that the new decade of the 70s should begin on a double note of the new and the old. The new year had found Cam half-way around the world on his first visit outside the Western hemisphere, seeing the farflung results of what he had started in such a small way and presenting graphically the opportunities that lay ahead.

The old was very much in his mind as he visited his sisters Lulu and Ethel, who were eighty-two and eighty-four respectively. Oney was eighty when she died. His brother Paul had returned to Oklahoma where he was living in semiretirement and pastoring a small Presbyterian church. Cam recalled his family heritage and the help and loyalty of his sisters and Paul that enabled him first to go to school and then to leave for Guatemala at such a seemingly inauspicious time.

While he was in Santa Ana, Cam saw in the paper that literacy pioneer Dr. Frank Laubach was to be honored at a church in nearby Anaheim. He and Ben Elson drove over for the affair, and Laubach recognized Cam from the platform. He plugged Wycliffe's work and asked Elson to dismiss in prayer. Then the two old soldiers of the faith greeted one another. "I've had my eightieth birthday," the white-haired apostle of literacy said. "I don't have many more years left. But I predict that within five years you'll be in mainland China."

Back in North Carolina, Elaine reminded Cam of the checkup he had promised to get. "Oh, I'm feeling fine now," he assured her. "I'm going to Chicago in a few days to see about getting help for a second plane for Nepal. And I'm invited to speak afterwards at the

University of North Dakota. And then I must get to writing the book on bilingual education in the Caucasus."

"Honey, I love you," she sighed, "but you must slow down."

"I will when I get back," he promised.

Soon after Cam returned, they moved into their house. Their first overnight guest was Father Boni Wittenbrink, a dynamic priest who had helped Cam set up past Bible Translation Day programs. Wittenbrink asked how the Wittes were doing.

"We keep in touch," Cam said. "They're in Colombia, but aren't getting enough financial help. You should start a Catholic translation society, Boni. Since our round-the-world trip, I've been doing a lot of thinking and praying. At the rate Wycliffe is growing we're not going to reach every tribe by 1985. Perhaps we could get together a council or a board of leaders that would help other groups start their own translation societies. There could be a Catholic, a Baptist, a Presbyterian society and so on. Just as the Lutherans have done."

Wittenbrink laughed. "Uncle Cam, I wish I had your faith."

There was still a lot of fixing to do around the house. Cam enjoyed working in the yard in spare moments. Elaine was commuting every day to Queens College in Charlotte for Russian study. She redeemed the time behind the wheel by listening to Russian tapes.

When Cam's shortness of breath recurred and he started having chest pains, Elaine insisted he get an appointment with a heart specialist. An electrocardiogram showed an irregular heartbeat. "I'm going to put you on digitalis," the doctor said. "And you must slow down or you'll never make it back to Russia. Stay home awhile."

After so many years of constant on-the-go, Cam found it hard to obey doctor's orders. But there was his book on Soviet bilingual education in the Caucasus to write. And lately he had been thinking about the racial situation in the area.

They had been driving into Charlotte to attend church, but one Sunday morning Cam suggested they visit one of the black churches nearby. When they walked in the Methodist pastor was already into his sermon. He stopped and looked at them incredulously while the congregation stared. "You're the first white folks ever to enter this church!" the pastor exclaimed.

The next Sunday they visited the tiny black Shiloh Presbyterian Church located in back of the railroad track in Waxhaw. Cam and Elaine enjoyed the services. Elaine was asked to play the piano, and both were given an opportunity to share the work of JAARS. They kept attending this church and finally decided to join as associate members. The congregation welcomed its first white members joyfully.

Their first black dinner guests were ill at ease when they arrived. But Cam and Elaine quickly made them feel at home. Others followed. Billy became close friends with a black athlete at the consolidated high school both attended, and brought him home for meals and to spend the night. When racial trouble erupted at the school, Billy climbed on the bus and rode home with the black kids, though most of the white students took other transportation.

Cam was gently prodding the JAARS folks to develop friendships with blacks. "Let's have them in our homes for social occasions," he suggested. "Let's visit their churches and not just ask them to come to ours. Why if every white Christian in North Carolina would visit a black church only once a month, wonderful changes would occur."

He wasn't making much progress with the book these days, though, because of interruptions at the house. People were constantly coming and going. The phone rang incessantly. "I've got to get away," he told Elaine. When Arthur and Irene Morris invited him to use their Florida beachside apartment for a while, he gladly accepted. He got more work done there and rested up for the upcoming board meeting he planned to attend in Santa Ana.

The big item on the agenda was new buildings. The board voted to build the new administrative headquarters on a site near Santa Ana, and a linguistic training center and museum in the Dallas area.

Returning home Cam was just in time to see Joy and her fiancé David Tuggy, son of missionaries to Venezuela, graduate from Columbia Bible College. Their wedding followed on June 6 at the Calvary Presbyterian Church in Charlotte. At the reception Cam delivered his challenge for the tribes as he had after Grace's wedding. He was delighted to add the news that the newlyweds planned to attend SIL, then go to Mexico to finish the translation of the Aztec New Testament which he had started in Tetelcingo.

Meanwhile, Bible translation enthusiasts in Washington were promoting a Congressional resolution calling for the president to declare 1971 as the "Year of Minority Language Groups." Cam flew up and talked to Senator Curtis. "We think this will get through both the Senate and House," Curtis said.

The Nebraska legislator also wrote a letter to President Nixon, asking for an interview. Cam's nephew, Lorin Griset, now mayor of Santa Ana, knew Robert Finch, the presidential counselor. Ed Boyer, a high official in Health, Education and Welfare, talked to his contacts. Several other Congressional leaders, in addition to Curtis, pushed the resolution as well as a presidential meeting.

This time the resolution passed both the House and Senate. The president signed the proclamation and aides looked for a spot in his appointment schedule.

In October a tremendous jolt came when Cam's old friend Cárdenas died in Mexico. Cam left the same day he received the telegram to extend his sympathy to the family and attend the funeral of the man who had done so much for the group's linguistic research and service to long-forgotten tribes.

On December 2, 1970, President Nixon welcomed Cam, Senator Curtis, Ben Elson, Dan Piatt and James Hefley into the Oval Office.

After introductions, Cam showed the president a picture of the plane he had dedicated in California for Peru when he was vice president. Nixon recalled the ceremony which had taken place shortly after his father's death.

"How is your work going now?" the president asked.

"Mr. President, we've just entered our 500th language," Cam replied.

"What an achievement! You're doing two things. Giving them the Bible and teaching them to read. What can I do to help?"

"Mr. President, there are still over two thousand language groups without Scripture, or even an alphabet. We need eighty-five hundred new recruits, both translators and support personnel such as pilots and printers. Would you write a letter that we can use in challenging young people to volunteer?"

The president promised he would and handed Cam an autographed Bible.

During the spring of 1971, Cam and Elaine's twenty-fifth wedding anniversary neared, they became aware of secretive whisperings and sly glances. When the Henderson Belks invited them to dinner, they decided that a dinner party had been planned.

Arriving at the Belks' home, they went to the back door, as had always been their custom, but the maid refused to let them in. They looked at each other and grinned. "Well, it looks like we're to be treated like 'company' tonight," Cam said, as they entered the mansion through the front door. They suspected something, but were totally unprepared for the crowd waiting to call out "surprise." Grace and Tom were there from Chicago, as well as over a hundred others, some of whom had also come great distances. Joy and David were in jungle camp and couldn't make it, but had sent a message of love and best wishes. Elainadel had come from Columbia Bible College with her fiancé, Robert Garippa. They too were planning on missionary service. Billy and Mrs. Mielke arrived from the JAARS Center in "Don Lázaro," the vintage blue Chevrolet Cárdenas had given Cam in 1938.

There was a basketful of telegrams, cards and letters, as well as many silver pieces for their silver anniversary, and a luscious buffet dinner. All the love and good wishes were a little overwhelming, but what thrilled them most was that their "kids," especially Grace, had gotten together with Juanita Goodall and Ann Belk and planned the whole celebration.

The next "anniversary" was the fortieth year since the publication of Cam's Cakchiquel New Testament. Friends Jack and Pat Morris of Charlotte and Scripture Unlimited financed a new edition of 2,700 copies to mark the occasion.

Cam mailed complimentary copies to mayors and other key leaders in Cakchiquel towns, then sent Fr. Boni Wittenbrink and evangelical missionary Larry Jordan to Guatemala to sell the rest. With the blessing of the local Roman Catholic bishops, the interfaith team sold every Testament in eight days.

The Caucasus book was almost completed in rough draft when time came for the 1971 May biennial in Mexico City. It would be a climactic milestone for Cam, for he had decided to resign as general director.

Perhaps it was that decision that made the statistics reported by Executive Director Ben Elson seem so dramatic to him. Membership had grown to 2,504. Annual income had leaped to $7.9 million. Wycliffe was now serving in 510 language groups in 23 countries. It had been a long uphill climb—and there was much yet to do.

Elson continued his report:

The world has changed since WBT was formed. Conditions today are not the same as they were in 1935 or in 1942. Uncle Cam set forth in those days revolutionary ideas about missionary service, about specialization, about internal organization, about relations with governments and those who oppose us. *People could not quite make us out. We did not fit into neat categories. But those ideas were right and a lot of them have become standard practice with many other groups. We don't receive the same criticisms we received in the 50s since many of our brethren quietly acknowledge that Uncle Cam's ideas and methods were right after all, but were far ahead of their time.*

. . . Are we ready for the new challenges that we will face in this revolutionary decade? Does God have more for us to do? I believe He does.

Then in a dramatic moment, Cam asked that he be relieved of the office of general director:

God has been good to us. He led us into our unusual policies. Let's be true to them. Let's forge ahead till every tribe has heard in its own tongue the Word of God. This involves a close adherence to our basic five points: The linguistic approach; the Bible first, last and all the time on a nonsectarian basis; pioneering; service to all; and a faith that takes God at His Word and forges ahead wherever there are Bibleless tribes regardless of barriers.

Leaving the conference, Cam returned to North Carolina as a Wycliffe board member, but no longer the roving "chief" of the organization he had founded. His future would be devoted to the Caucasus. He was polishing the book on bilingual education * when his seventy-fifth birthday rolled around.

On July 9, 1971, about a hundred friends gathered in a wooded grove across from the JAARS hangars—members of the Wycliffe family, friends from Charlotte and Shiloh Church, and Cam's family. The children and Elaine recited poems Cam had written years before. Harold Goodall presented Cam a bound, freshly typed copy of *A Thousand Trails,* Cam's own account of early adventures in Central America. Then before cutting the cake, everyone's "Uncle Cam" was asked if he had a word to say.

He stood erect on the portable platform. Typically, he thanked everybody effusively. Then waving his arms in a half circle, he cried, "Out there are two thousand tribes who still don't have the Bible! I believe God is going to help us reach them all. Don't you?"

---

* *They Found a Common Language: Community Through Bilingual Education* (New York: Harper & Row, 1972).

Suddenly he shouted, "I'm happy about what He's going to do. Aren't you? If you are, and if you believe, let's sing Legters's chorus that we've marched to all these years."

And so they sang with Cam's confident voice leading out:

Faith, mighty faith the promise sees,
And looks to God alone.
Laughs at impossibilities
And shouts, "It shall be done!"

Epilogue
by
Karen Lewis

Anyone who ever met Uncle Cam holds a special feeling for him. Those who were fortunate to know him for years have a wealth of memories. I only have two, but they are dear.

I was brand-new to Wycliffe Bible Translators when Uncle Cam and Elaine attended chapel at our center in Huntington Beach, California in the fall of 1981. I couldn't keep my eyes off them. I was drawn like the proverbial magnet to this godly couple. How different they were from each other, yet how complementary.

As I watched, Wycliffe artist Mary Kathleen Greene greeted Elaine and suddenly turned my direction and beckoned. Joining them, I heard Mary Kathleen say, "This is my friend Karen, the writer I was telling you about." Almost without hesitation, Elaine turned to Uncle Cam—who was involved in another conversation—and said, "Cam, here are two girls to help us with the Alphabet Museum." His smile seemed to say, "That's nice, Elaine. Make the arrangements."

Three months later I found myself on a short-term loan to the gradually evolving Alphabet Museum at the JAARS center in Waxhaw, North Carolina. The museum was one of Uncle Cam's dreams for "connecting" people from around the world. He wanted it to showcase the history of written languages and challenge people to reach minority language groups with Scriptures in their own tongue.

The museum was in its early stages of creation. The staff had just begun to put in place the exhibits researched and planned for months by Wycliffe members Richard Pittman and Katherine Voigtlander.

Uncle Cam was eager to watch the progress, but his health declined through the winter. Elaine called the museum often for progress reports. She optimistically said, "The first day Cam is able, we'll bring him over. He's so anxious to see all you're doing."

That day did arrive. Uncle Cam was so weak he had to be driven the 500 yards from his home to the museum and then "toured around" in a wheelchair. Though physically feeble, Uncle Cam was mentally alert. He carefully listened to Katherine's explanations of exhibits already in place and her plans for others. He asked penetrating questions, added illustrative stories of his own and praised the Lord for the progress that had been made.

After the staff posed for pictures with "the boss," we asked him to pray. I think most of us sensed this would be Uncle Cam's last visit to the museum. We wanted his benediction on our efforts. We gathered in a circle, holding hands. Uncle Cam prayed his way around the world, always praising God for his goodness. It was a moving moment for all of us.

As he was leaving the building, Uncle Cam took both my hands in his and looked at me a long moment. I felt he focused on my very soul. Then almost inaudibly, he said, "Thank you."

I'll never know exactly what he was thanking me for. Holding the door open? I doubt it. The tour? Maybe. But in my heart of hearts, I think he was thanking me for being there. For being part of the team. For doing my tiny part to give the Scriptures to the 200 million people who have never heard God's precious message in their own tongue. I think Uncle Cam was feeling thankful for all of God's goodness. I certainly felt God's presence in a very special way in that moment.

God is so good. That was the constant theme of Uncle Cam's life. Of the many things that are remembered about him, one of the most outstanding has to be his thankful heart.

Believing wholeheartedly in God's goodness allowed Uncle Cam to dream impossible dreams and see them come into being. Believing in God's goodness allowed Uncle Cam to pioneer, exploring new ways to see his vision fulfilled, involving increasing numbers of people in the Bible translation task. Believing in God's goodness allowed Uncle Cam to see countless lives changed through reading God's Word in their own language. Believing in

God's goodness allowed Uncle Cam to "laugh at impossibilities and shout, 'It shall be done!'"

Uncle Cam, and the mission he founded, reached many milestones in the years between the birth of this book and his death in 1982. He completed his book, *They Found a Common Language: Community Through Bilingual Education*, and made several trips to the Soviet Union. In 1973 he was invited by the president of Pakistan to lecture on bilingual education and in 1974 he was invited to India by Indira Ghandi. He received a number of awards and honors, including a presidential citation from the Philippines in 1978; the Order of the Aztec Eagle from Mexico in 1978; El Orden del Sol, Peru's highest honor given to foreigners, in 1981; and an honorary doctorate from Biola University in 1981.

Uncle Cam was especially pleased in 1979, when the Summer Institute of Linguistics received the UNESCO literacy award for outstanding work done in Papua New Guinea. It represented both service and excellence, basic principles of the organization.

Also in 1981 a crowd of 6,000 people gathered in the Convention Center in Anaheim, California, to celebrate the fiftieth anniversary of the publication of Uncle Cam's Cakchiquel New Testament translation. Billy Graham was the main speaker. Wycliffe colleagues and friends from around the world participated in the program.

During these years, some of Uncle Cam's dreams for support facilities in the United States came into being. The JAARS center in Waxhaw, North Carolina continued to grow. Several additions were made, including the Mexico-Cárdenas Museum. In Dallas, Texas a permanent facility was built for the Summer Institute of Linguistics' year-round academic program. Although linguistic training had been offered by SIL every summer since 1934, it was not until a group of Christian business people joined forces to purchase the 110-acre site in Dallas that year-round classes could be offered. The international administrative offices of Wycliffe Bible Translators and the Summer Institute of Linguistics also were housed at the facility. And in 1981 the International Museum of Cultures opened at the Dallas center. Focusing on contemporary minority cultures, the museum became a valuable resource for local communities as well as out-of-state and international visitors.

Between 1971 and 1982 the membership of Wycliffe grew steadily. There were over 3,000 members in 1973, 4,000 in 1979 and nearly 5,000 at the time of Uncle Cam's death—nearly 5,000 men and women following in Uncle Cam's footsteps, answering God's call to take His Word to the forgotten peoples of the world.

During that time the Summer Institute of Linguistics began new work in the Solomon Islands, Sudan, Malaysia, Vanuatu and Costa Rica. Every new work involves a series of God's miracles, but Uncle Cam was especially excited about the unusual way God provided for launching the work in Vanuatu (formerly known as New Hebrides).

A couple in California contacted Wycliffe officials and said, "We'd like to underwrite the expenses for you to start a new work somewhere. We've been interested in the Pacific area for a long time. Are you planning to start something there?" This extraordinary offer came just as God was opening the door in Vanuatu.

Vanuatu is a chain of some 80 islands in the South Pacific with a population of 112,000, including more than 100 indigenous language groups. About half of these languages need linguistic work and Bible translation.

The generous couple was delighted to underwrite the start-up costs—$20,000 for a careful and extensive language survey and a computer in which to enter and codify data. The computer also would speed language analysis and Bible translation for years to come.

The announcement of the completion of each New Testament in a language previously without the Scriptures brought the greatest joy to Uncle Cam. In 1979 he rejoiced with all of Wycliffe and SIL in the dedication of the one-hundredth New Testament: the Amuesha of Peru, translated by Martha Duff and Mary Ruth Wise.

Although every milestone over the years caused Uncle Cam to thank God for His faithful goodness, several events during the last year of his life were particularly significant.

The first one involved a young recruit of the seventies: Chet Bitterman, Jr. Chet's parents feel that God had His hand on Chet even as a child and that He directed him into Bible translation. Chet was completely committed to serving God in that way. In a letter he sent to Wycliffe before he joined the team, he wrote, "I cannot see any more direct or any more essential ministry toward fulfilling the Great Commission than Bible translation ... I come with a mind and heart open to God's best for me. Perhaps He'll lead me to bury my life with Wycliffe in Bible translation."

As it turned out, that is exactly what happened. Chet Bitterman was kidnapped and murdered at the hands of M-19 guerrillas of Colombia in 1981. But Chet had been prepared. When contemplating the situation in Latin America sometime earlier, he had written in his diary, "The situation is getting worse .... I think of Mordecai's statement to Esther. Maybe this is just some kind of self-inflicted martyr complex, but I find this recurring thought, that perhaps God will call me to be martyred for Him in His service in Colombia. I am willing."

Chet used his captivity as an opportunity to witness. As a colleague said, he had become "a living translation of God's Word." In one of the letters Chet was allowed to write to his wife Brenda he told her, "I continue to find much to make me happy, especially from the Scriptures."

Major Colombian newspapers printed Chet's letters, which always mentioned Scripture references without quoting the verses. At the U.S. embassy one day, one of the SIL men met someone who said he was going out to buy Bibles because they wanted to know what Chet's letters in the newspapers meant. Even the Marxists were interested in the Scripture references and their newspapers printed out the verses for everyone to read.

Worldwide, lives were turned upside down, first by Chet's captivity and then by his martyrdom. People everywhere—Christians and non-Christians alike—reevaluated their priorities and commitments and values. Direct results of Chet's life and death abound. It is reported that at least one member of the M-19 group has turned his life over to Christ. Hundreds of God's people have volunteered for missionary service, some expressing the desire to continue Chet and Brenda's work among the Carijona people of Colombia.

The end of this story is not yet known, but one remarkable chapter was added in 1982. Uncle Cam, quoting I John 4:7 to Chet's parents—Beloved, let us love one another for love is of God—suggested that memorial money be raised to give an ambulance to Colombia.

In April 1982, just days before Uncle Cam died, the Bittermans

Above: Cam and Nobel Peace Prize nominee Kenneth Pike shared their commitment to Bible translation for 47 years. *Right:* Martha Duff and Mary Ruth Wise were translators of the Amuesha New Testament in Peru, the one-hundredth completed by Wycliffe Bible Translators.

Left: Chet Bitterman enjoys a light moment with two Ica men in Colombia. He was killed just as he was beginning work among another group, the Carijonas.

Below: Tumi Chucua Center, home of SIL's Bolivia team for 27 years, was turned over to the Bolivian government in 1982.

delivered that ambulance to the country where their son had served and died. A college student from there admitted later, "My friends were members of the terrorist group that killed Chet. There were two things we never could understand about that situation. First, we were sure SIL would leave the country in exchange for Chet's life. We gave them a month to get out, but they never budged. Second, we could never understand how his parents could bring down an ambulance for the people of Colombia in memory of their son. We expected revenge and retaliation, not love."

Perhaps that young man's questions were best answered by one of his own countrymen, an editor of *El Tiempo*, one of Colombia's most widely circulated and respected periodicals. He said, "They have not come to ask drastic measures of punishment because of the assassination of their son, Chester Allen. They have not come to cry arrogantly for justice against the climate of insecurity that exists in Colombia. No, they have come to pardon; they have come to say they are Christians and that, as such, they want to apply balm on the wounds and pardon those who inflicted them."

Uncle Cam was deeply touched by Chet's martyrdom. But even as he comforted the Wycliffe team, he called on everyone in the organization to remember the remaining task. Characteristically, he reminded the worldwide membership that 3,000 language groups still wait for the Scriptures in their own language.

One of the delights of Uncle Cam's last year was the announcement that SIL linguist Dr. Kenneth Pike had been nominated along with the Summer Institute of Linguistics for the Nobel Peace Prize.

Even in the earliest days of the Bible translation thrust, Uncle Cam had known that his little group of budding translators must strive towards academic excellence in their efforts. At the second Camp Wycliffe, in 1935, he and the other staff members prayed for a "genius" who could carry the linguistic leadership as the Bible translation effort expanded. As they observed the six students, the most likely candidate for the genius slot was Kenneth Pike. But he was so fragile. Brainy, indeed. But he was thin and nervous and tended to let his mind wander. Yet Uncle Cam sensed that this was God's man for the job. He began to encourage him to develop his linguistic potential.

Pike went to Mexico in 1935 to translate the New Testament into the Mixtec language. Shortly after he began this project, at Uncle Cam's insistence, he made his first significant contribution to the science of linguistics—a book on phonetics.

Over the years, Pike balanced linguistics and translation, receiving his PhD in linguistics at the University of Michigan in 1942 and completing the Mixtec translation in 1951. He has been further recognized for his contributions in the areas of sound systems and grammar (tagmemics) by honorary doctorates from the Sorbonne, the University of Chicago, Wheaton, Gordon, Houghton and Huntington Colleges. He has served as example and mentor to countless young linguist/translators. The Nobel Peace Prize nomination came in recognition of the significant contributions of Pike and SIL to the indigenous ethnic groups of the world.

Another very satisfying event occured just 20 days before Uncle Cam's death. The event was the result of years of hard work and of faithfully believing in God's goodness.

Conscious of people's tendency to settle down, Uncle Cam had always warned his teammates to keep the goal of giving the Bible to every language group clearly in mind. "There still are over 3,000 language groups to go," he constantly reminded them. "We have to keep on pioneering, moving on to other groups who need our help."

Thus, it was a dream come true when on April 3, 1982, the Summer Institute of Linguistics turned its Tumi Chucua center in Bolivia over to the Bolivian government. That event meant SIL's work was measurable and the job was getting done.

The Tumi Chucua facility was transferred to government officials "in deep appreciation to the Bolivian people for their strong support and cooperation over the past 27 years." The Minister of Education and Culture, Lieutenant Colonel Juan Vera Antezna, accepted the gift on behalf of the Bolivian people. Ambassadors from five countries—Germany, Switzerland, Great Britain, Peru and the United States—and civil and military authorities from Bolivia witnessed the event.

Originally Tumi Chucua had been a piece of jungle. The Institute had developed 78 buildings on the 200-acre property, as well as a 3,300-foot airstrip.

"We've nearly finished the linguistic and educational goals we

Above: Cam received El Orden del Sol from Peru's President Belaunde Terry in 1981. *Below:* Cam was a family man. His four children remember "Daddy" fondly. At the time of his death, he had 13 grandchildren. He was able to dedicate two of them to the Lord in his last six weeks.

Above: The handsome Mexico-Cárdenas Museum at the JAARS center in North Carolina honors both Mexico's late President Lázaro Cárdenas and his country. *Below:* Cam was buried between the Mexico-Cárdenas Museum and the Alphabet Museum. His grave and the museums are constant reminders of the language groups yet without the Scriptures.

agreed on with the Bolivian government in 1954," said Dave Farah, SIL's director of government relations at the time. "In a few years, we'll be leaving the country. After we've gone, we want the property to continue to be used to serve the Bolivian people, especially ethnic minorities." The transfer of the Tumi Chucua center was a fitting event to occur at the conclusion of Uncle Cam's life, a life devoted to the indigenous people of the world.

On April 23, 1982, the man who had dreamed of God's Word for every "tongue, tribe and nation" joined thousands of representatives of different language groups around the throne of God. What a celebration there must have been as they greeted one another and praised God for His loving faithfulness and goodness.

Thousands of expressions of appreciation and loss were sent to Elaine Townsend and others in Wycliffe and SIL. Fernando Belaunde Terry, president of Peru, was one of 40 heads of state who knew Uncle Cam personally. He telegrammed, "Profoundly moved by the irreparable loss of our dear friend Cameron .... In this sad hour, the Peruvian government recognizes once more the outstanding services which he made available to the communities in the jungle and the great work he did in spreading the Good News, culture and brotherhood for which he worked so intensely and fruitfully exalting spiritual values in the quality of life of isolated minority language groups."

A Mexican friend, Professor Onesimo Rios, wrote, "Mexico has lost one of its greatest friends." And evangelist Billy Graham wrote, "No man in this century has given a greater vision for being used of God to advance the cause of Christian missions as Cameron Townsend. He was a great personal friend and inspiration to me during most of my ministry. I'm sure the organization he founded will continue with great effectiveness because of the legacy of dedication he left."

Billy Graham was right. It is a testimony to Uncle Cam's leadership and God's faithfulness that Wycliffe Bible Translators and the Summer Institute of Linguistics not only did not die with him, but did not even stumble. In the days following his death, the work went forward around the world. Hundreds of translators worked at desks with their language assistants, moving toward the completion of more New Testaments. Hundreds of pilots, school teachers, office workers, mechanics, computer scientists and government relations specialists all went about their daily jobs supporting the task of Bible translation. Thousands of faithful supporters at home continued their prayers and gifts.

Fellow students in Uncle Cam's 1914 graduating high school class had predicted that he would become a U.S. senator within 10 years. Instead he became one of the most outstanding missionary statesmen ever known. He often is grouped with such greats as William Carey and Hudson Taylor.

Kenneth Pike has said, "Not since the third century has there been a man like Cameron Townsend who attempted so much and saw so many dreams realized in his own lifetime."

Uncle Cam's foremost dream was expressed in the words placed on his gravestone: "Dear Ones: By love serve one another. Finish the task. Translate the Scriptures into every language."

Finish the task. Translate the Scriptures into every language. God is so good. The themes of Cameron Townsend's life. It wouldn't be hard to imagine that Uncle Cam, when the commotion of his arrival in heaven began to settle down, said to his friends, "God is so good. Let me teach you a little chorus." And with hundreds of languages joined together in profound praise, the streets of heaven rang with:

> God is so good.
> God is so good.
> God is so good;
> He's so good to me.

Karen Lewis is a journalist with Wycliffe Bible Translators.